Carolyn B. Attneave

✒ Designing
Evaluations
of Educational
and Social
✒ Programs

Lee J. Cronbach

with the assistance of
Karen Shapiro

Designing Evaluations of Educational and Social Programs

Jossey-Bass Publishers

San Francisco • Washington • London • 1982

DESIGNING EVALUATIONS OF EDUCATIONAL AND SOCIAL PROGRAMS
by Lee J. Cronbach, with the assistance of Karen Shapiro

Copyright © 1982 by: Jossey-Bass Inc., Publishers
433 California Street
San Francisco, California 94104

&

Jossey-Bass Limited
28 Banner Street
London EC1Y 8QE

Library of Congress Cataloging in Publication Data

Cronbach, Lee Joseph
  Designing evaluations of educational and social
programs.

  Bibliography: p. 340
  Includes indexes.
  1. Educational accountability.   2. Evaluation
research (Social action programs)   I. Shapiro, Karen.
II. Title.
LB2806.C75   379.1'54   81-48664
ISBN 0-87589-525-5   AACR2

Manufactured in the United States of America

The paper in this book meets the guidelines for permanence and durability of the Committee on Production Guidelines for Book Longevity of the Council on Library Resources.

JACKET DESIGN BY WILLI BAUM

FIRST EDITION

Code 8216

A joint publication in
The Jossey-Bass Series
in Social and Behavioral Science
& in Higher Education

Special Adviser
Methodology of Social
and Behavioral Research
DONALD W. FISKE
University of Chicago

To the memory of the

STANFORD EVALUATION CONSORTIUM

⚡ *Preface*

This volume is intended to help students of evaluation, professional evaluators, and those who commission evaluations to plan more effective studies and to appreciate the limitations of any plan. I seek to sensitize the prospective evaluator and the critic of evaluations to the innumerable decisions that should lie behind what the evaluator does. In particular, I take the position that evaluations are to be judged by the extent to which they help the political community achieve its ends. The logic of science must come to terms with the logic of politics.

"Design of experiments" has been a standard element in training for social scientists. This training has concentrated on formal tests of hypotheses—confirmatory studies—despite the fact that R. A. Fisher, the prime theorist of experimental design, demonstrated over and over in his agricultural investigations that effective inquiry works back and forth between the heuristic and the confirmatory. But since he could offer a formal theory only for confirmatory studies, that part came to be taken for the whole.

Those who become investigators quickly learn that the formal, preplanned design is no more than a framework within which imaginative, catch-as-catch-can improvisation does the productive work. Even in basic research, nature does not stick to the script. Planned treatments go awry, and surprises lead the investigator down new paths. Questions posed to get the inquiry under way prove to be far less interesting than the questions that emerge as observations are made and puzzled over. Not infrequently, questions arising out of the observations prove to be more important in the long run than the facts that the study was designed to pin down.

Although my argument will be abstract at times, design of evaluations cannot be reduced to a formal scheme comparable to Fisher's. To help the reader appreciate the realities facing evaluators, I shall rely heavily on examples. The graduate student in any social science or in a policy field should be able to follow all the argument. The statistical concepts employed, with a few exceptions, are commonplaces taught in the first course in statistics. The reader should be familiar with such concepts as random sampling and the use of control groups, but no technical knowledge of Fisherian design is required. A few parts of the argument are technical or philosophical; the reader who does not care to pursue that kind of argument will, I trust, still find the conclusions accessible and important.

Chapter One provides two kinds of background. First, it summarizes a theory of evaluation as a political institution; my conception of design derives from this theory. Second, the chapter reviews disputes about design that I intend to clarify and reconcile. Enthusiasts have championed two competing styles of inquiry: one requires pointed questions and strong controls, while the other is naturalistic, broad, and exploratory. These two styles are not mutually exclusive and should be combined in various proportions for various purposes.

Chapter Two describes three evaluations: of a nutritional program to aid children's development in a poor country, of a curriculum in high school physics, and of a plan for helping high schools reduce violence and fear of violence. These richly textured evaluations illustrate various choices in design and the reasoning behind them.

Chapter Three introduces a formal scheme. An evaluator asks about treatment plans as they impinge on units (persons, institutions, or communities) in a particular setting. These three (plans, units, and setting), together with specified variables (observing operations), constitute the domain chosen for direct investigation. The evaluator's sampling plan ultimately produces data from which to make an inference back to the domain; that is an internal inference and has greater or less internal validity. Questions about activities, conditions, or events not directly represented in the study constitute one or more other domains. These inevitable questions lead the evaluator to a concern with external validity.

Chapter Three having developed the view that evaluations are used mostly for external inferences, Chapter Four therefore considers just why others have given primacy to internal validity.

Chapter Five explains how the validity of an external inference—an extrapolation—is to be defended and what the pitfalls are. Chapter Six continues in a more technical vein. In particular, it summarizes recent literature on difficulties in statistical extrapolation.

Chapter Seven discusses how to choose questions for investigation. The evaluator of the program first identifies the widest possible range of potentially important questions, after which resources are allocated among these possible lines of inquiry. The criteria for making the allocation are prior uncertainty, information yield, cost of inquiry, and leverage.

Chapter Eight describes the controls available for strengthening internal validity—that is, for making it more likely that a direct replication would produce a similar answer to a focal question. The strongest message is that assignment of subjects to treatments (which has been featured in most writings on design) is just one of a great number of pertinent controls. Chapter Nine takes the opposite tack, suggesting how to generate data that will help in extrapolating beyond the conditions directly studied.

Chapter Ten draws the moral. The evaluator should almost never sacrifice breadth of information for the sake of giving a definite answer to one narrow question. Which controls will be profitable is a judgment specific to each study. To arrange to collect the most helpful information requires a high degree of imagination, coupled with the flexibility to change plans in midstudy.

My ideas on evaluation developed over many years, under many influences.

My training under Ralph W. Tyler from 1938 onward introduced me to a then-unorthodox view of evaluation; nearly two decades of close association with J. Thomas Hastings at the University of Illinois, another Tyler alumnus, reinforced those ideas. Although I wrote directly on program evaluation only once during that period, the paper (Cronbach, 1963) precipitated debate by encouraging the heresy now called formative evaluation. Outside the Tyler group, social scientists and policy makers had seen the central task of program evaluation to be the summing up of treatment effects. That view dominated the studies of instruction in science and mathematics that the National Science Foundation was sponsoring in the 1960s. Following Tyler, I argued that assessing the impact of a fixed plan is not the best use of evaluation; improving plans and operations is a higher goal, and one to which formal quantitative comparisons usually contribute little. The 1963 paper, stimulated by my conversations as consultant to the foundation and some of its projects, was an attempt to balance out the prevailing emphasis on summative evaluation.

A full and balanced statement is much needed today. Writings and actions promoting expansion of evaluation were excessively rationalistic throughout the 1970s. I was in enthusiastic accord with the call for policy research that came from Campbell (1969b, 1975d) and Rivlin (1971). As a participant in the Social Science Research Council, I was on the fringe of the effort that produced *Social Experimentation* (Riecken and Boruch, 1974), and I had the opportunity to make friendly criticisms as the book was drafted. I became convinced, however, that this and other pronouncements fostering summative evaluations, preferably in the form of randomized experiments, created an unacceptable imbalance. Other writers have voiced the reservations this book will express; for example, Campbell (1974) and Rivlin (1974) cautioned against unrealistic expectations from "scientific" method. But these scattered and parenthetical cautions did not lay out a positive rationale for flexible and relevant evaluative inquiry. I seek to do that in this book.

Discussions in the 1950s about research on clinical practices in psychology—a kind of evaluation research— foreshadowed the issues now salient. Perplexing, multifaceted aspects of behavior were the object of those inquiries, and only open-ended exploration could serve; yet discipline was required for an investigator's inquiries to be respected by others and used in their thinking. If the effort to be rigorous forced explorations into an inappropriate mold, that would clearly have a bad effect. The profession was struggling then with puzzles similar to those now being encountered in research on community problems. I commented on these puzzles at the time (see Edwards and Cronbach, 1952; Cronbach and Gleser, 1957; Cronbach and Meehl, 1955). The present book has obvious affinities with our thinking of that period, although the philosophy of evaluation has moved onward and there are new things to be said.

In 1974 colleagues at Stanford joined me in forming the short-lived Stanford Evaluation Consortium. We were uneasy about what was being written on evaluation policy and about evaluations that government agencies were sponsoring. Intent upon developing a fresh charter for evaluation, the consortium worked from 1975 to 1979 under support from the Russell Sage Foundation. The fruit was two monographs; this is the second to be published, though in conception it is the elder.

Toward Reform of Program Evaluation (Cronbach and

others, 1980), prepared by a team of eight writers—Sueann Ambron, Sanford Dornbusch, Robert Hess, Robert Hornik, Denis Phillips, Decker Walker, Stephen Weiner, and me— from almost as many disciplines, presents a theory of evaluation as a political process. The functions of evaluation identified by that theory provide the base for the theory of design offered here. (The influence also went in the other direction: ideas on design influenced the team's sense of what evaluators should be asked to do.) But the two works are distinct. *Toward Reform* is a committee statement; selectivity and compromise were appropriate. I have written the present volume independently, with much advice but with no pressure to express group opinion. I believe that my former colleagues agree with my argument in the main.

Donald Campbell's ideas are central topics. I first encountered him when we were participants in the conversations of the 1950s on research related to personality and personality change. It was in 1957 that he introduced the concepts of internal and external validity, which he later extended to educational and social research. As best I can judge, Campbell, his recent collaborator Thomas D. Cook, and I are in almost complete accord on the current issues. An evaluation plan that Cook and his associates (1977) worked out for the Peace Corps exemplifies, as well as any evaluation I know, the strategy I shall advocate here. Yet my argument also pushes *against* the writings of Campbell and his teammates. Let me explain. The Campbell-Stanley monograph (1963) had a profound influence on evaluators. It said that research should strive for both internal and external validity, but internal validity was its main theme. I reverse the emphasis that a generation of social scientists, students of education, and commissioners of evaluations took from Campbell and Stanley and the later monographs of Cook and Campbell (1976, 1979).

Lectures for my advanced course in evaluation at Stanford University were the first step toward this book. In the early 1970s, students had overdosed on Campbell and Stanley, and I found it important to argue against some ill-bal-

anced advice given there and (later) in *Social Experimentation*
(to which Campbell contributed). My monograph was in
rough draft when, in 1976, Cook and Campbell published a
more moderate statement. I revised my paper to acknowledge that progress, while still resisting the primacy given to
internal validity. At the end of 1977, I sent my material to
Campbell's group at Northwestern University. When I visited
there soon after, Campbell insisted to my surprise that he was
in nearly complete agreement with me. That interchange was
reflected in my revised draft, distributed informally as "Designing Educational Evaluations" (Cronbach, 1978).

Soon afterward, Cook and Campbell had *Quasi-Experimentation,* a revision of their 1976 statement, ready for the
press. Their changes met some of my criticisms and reacted
against others. Now it is my turn. I do not wish to discredit
what they say but, rather, to place our common ideas in another perspective. As Cook and Campbell (1979, pp. 2, 343)
acknowledge, they neglect the designing of studies that do
not have comparison of treatments as their main purpose,
and much that they leave out *would* be discussed in a treatise
on planning evaluations. Cook (1981) has said outright that
the intent of evaluation should not be primarily summative.
Whether a particular evaluation should be summative and
comparative is, I believe, a major question to resolve during
the planning. Where comparison is intended, decisions about
randomization and the like are to be made in the light of the
intended function of the research. So design in the large is
my subject.

Perhaps emphasis is all we differ on. Campbell's
writings on method have been chiefly concerned with basic
science and the long-term evolution of scientific explanations.
Approaching evaluation from the standpoint of an applied
psychologist, I am concerned with knowledge for short-term
use. If our roles were interchanged, perhaps each of us
would make the other's arguments. Throughout his career,
Campbell has advocated hardheaded research, but that advocacy is tempered by his desire to see inquiry into social concerns, including those about which definite answers cannot be

expected. I have advocated investigating what is important, whether or not the questions fit conventional paradigms. That advocacy has in turn been tempered by a desire to reduce overconfident interpretation and misinterpretation. Our conceptions of excellence in evaluation make Campbell and me near-neighbors.

I make a similar claim regarding Carol Weiss. For many years I used her valuable, succinct *Evaluation Research* (1972) as a textbook, and her view of evaluation as a means to illuminate the complex working of institutions surely influenced me. She stresses—as I shall—that realizations of a plan for intervention vary, that process is as important to study as outcome, and that information from a field test is most likely to be used in shaping new plans, not in a stop-or-go decision regarding the intervention studied. I mention alongside Weiss's book the highly original textbook on research method of Runkel and McGrath (1972). It covers many of my topics, all in the context of field research. We are in harmony, but a primary concern with basic research places their advice close to Campbell's.

Many colleagues have helped me. The title page acknowledges Karen Shapiro's contribution. She did much to shape my thinking but is not responsible for what is said. When the ideas for this work were taking form, she was active in the pertinent seminars and kept track of the arguments and counterarguments. More important, she engaged me in countless profitable hours of one-on-one argument and made penetrating comments on the various drafts. But I wrote most of the first draft when one or both of us was away from Stanford, she collecting data in New York for a dissertation, I enjoying the hospitality of the Jerusalem–van Leer Foundation or the social psychology department of the London School of Economics. Along with thanks to the Russell Sage Foundation go thanks to those organizations. At present, Karen Shapiro is employed in systems research with the Bank of America in San Francisco, having received her Ph.D. degree in communication research from Stanford in 1982.

Although all the conversations and team activities of

the consortium contributed to the forward movement of my views, four colleagues require special mention. Since 1965 I have worked closely with Richard E. Snow, and many points I emphasize are themes of his writings on design. Robert Hornik, Merrill Carlsmith, and Lincoln Moses were particularly active in working groups where some of the issues were thrashed out. I do not suggest that any of them agrees with what I shall say here.

Many others provided valuable criticisms and suggestions. I thank them all, especially Robert Stake, Donald Fiske, David Krathwohl, and Herbert Walberg. It was my good fortune that colleagues at other institutions were willing to use "Designing Educational Evaluations" in advanced seminars. Extensive and valuable written comments came in from students of Eric Gardner and Krathwohl at Syracuse and from students of Mary Corcoran and Jack Merwin at the University of Minnesota. In addition, I had a chance to meet with these groups and with a seminar organized by Jay Millman at Cornell. They, like the Stanford students, challenged my thinking productively and showed me where my statements were unclear. This book, then, owes far more than most books to junior and senior colleagues. I am truly appreciative.

Stanford, California Lee J. Cronbach
April 1982

✍ Contents

Contents

⚡ *Tables and Figures*

Tables

Figures

🖎 The Author

Lee J. Cronbach is Vida Jacks Professor of Education, *Emeritus,* of Stanford University. He received his B.A. degree (1934) from Fresno State College in mathematics, his M.A. degree (1937) from the University of California at Berkeley in education, and his Ph.D degree (1940) from the University of Chicago in education. He holds honorary degrees from Yeshiva University, the University of Gothenburg, the University of Chicago, and the University of Illinois.

Cronbach's main research activities have been in educational and psychological measurement and the related theory of psychometrics and individual differences. His experience with evaluation includes participation in Evaluation in the Eight-Year Study, the National Assessment of Educational Progress, the research of the School Mathematics Study Group, and other projects. In 1979, he received the Gunnar and Alva Myrdal award for scientific contributions to evaluation from the Evaluation Research Society. Cronbach's books include *Essentials of Psychological Testing* (1970), *The Dependability of Behavioral Measurements* (1972, with others), and *Aptitudes and Instructional Methods* (1977, with R. E. Snow).

Cronbach was Director of the Stanford Evaluation Consortium from 1974 to 1978, and headed its subgroup that prepared *Toward Reform of Program Evaluation* (1980).

Designing Evaluations of Educational and Social Programs

1

✍ Issues in Planning Evaluations

Designing an evaluative investigation is an art. The design must be chosen afresh in each new undertaking, and the choices to be made are almost innumerable. Each feature of a design offers particular advantages and entails particular sacrifices. Further merits and limitations come from the way various features combine. A broad theory of validity and utility is thus required to provide a base both for judging research plans and for generating more satisfactory ones.

A design is a plan for allocating investigative resources (Finney, 1956). In evaluation—as in basic science—the designer's task is to produce maximally useful evidence within a specified budget of dollars, a specified number of person-years from the evaluation staff and of person-hours from informants, and other such constraints. "Maximally useful" is a key phrase. Most writings on design suggest that an investiga-

tion is to be judged by its form, and certain forms are held up
as universal ideals. In contrast, I would argue that investigations have functions and that a form highly suitable for one
investigation would not be appropriate for the next. This is to
be, then, *a functional theory of design.*

The central purpose of evaluation differs from that of
basic social research, and evaluations fit into a different institutional and political context. The strategy of evaluative research therefore requires special consideration. Logic is necessarily the same in all disciplined inquiry, but the translation
of logic into procedure should depend on context, purpose,
and expected payoff. Many recommendations appropriate
for long-term programs of scientific research are ill suited to
evaluation. Hence, general writings on design and scientific
method are inadequate to guide the evaluator. General recommendations on evaluation can also mislead; evaluations
should not be cast in a single mold. For any evaluation many
good designs can be proposed, but no perfect ones.

Many kinds of inquiry and pseudoinquiry are called
evaluations. I restrict attention to inquiries that represent serious attempts to improve a program or a kind of service by
developing a clear picture of its operations and the fate of its
clients. The investigation may be a pilot study of an early version of the program; or it may be a review of a long-established operation, made with an eye to possible change or even
termination. In a fully professional, public evaluation, the
evaluator tries to plan so that his work will serve voters, managers, operating personnel, and policy makers.* Nothing else
justifies the effort. Occasionally, an evaluation is commissioned with the thought that the commissioning itself will
score points in a contest for power. When he can afford to
choose, the social scientist ought to undertake an evaluation
only if it appears that the political system will give a serious
hearing to all findings, welcome and unwelcome.

Evaluations of programs are the concern here. A program—a treatment method—is an operational plan or direc-

---

* To avoid the clumsy gesture of "he or she" and to reduce ambiguity of pronouns, I speak of the investigator as "he" and of a significant
other person (such as a decision maker or a client) as "she."

tive (not necessarily detailed) for rendering some service. Such a plan is evaluated empirically after it has been realized in one or more sites. The fact that the plan could be realized elsewhere—that it, or at least its central hypothesis, could be propagated—motivates more formal evaluations than an everyday manager requires.

Programs go through stages of development. *Toward Reform* (p. 107ff.; see also Berryman and Glennan, 1980) speaks of a breadboard (developmental) stage, a stage at which one or more pilot tests are made under ideal conditions, and a prototype stage (preferably a realistic field test). Out of this process there finally emerges an established operating program. This book is chiefly concerned with prototype trials. At the breadboard stage, a program is in such flux that the evaluation must be reoriented frequently and can scarcely be "designed." I shall not ignore ideal conditions ("superrealizations"), but they are too rare to be the main concern here. Established programs are comparatively immune to serious evaluation, save as proposed modifications lead to a new study of prototypes.

Since I focus on studies of programs, my remarks will have no more than incidental relevance to personnel evaluation or routine monitoring of local service. The evaluation of a local arrangement, carried out for local purposes—a self-study by a medical school, say—has special characteristics that I shall not go into. I do not deal directly with private evaluations of an agency, in which the evaluator is consultant to a staff and his comments are for internal consumption. These evaluations can scarcely be "planned," and the interpersonal relations of the evaluator with the staff influence his usefulness as much as does the quality of the data. Even so, private evaluations can have much in common with the kind of public evaluation I shall recommend; for an example, see Tharp and Gallimore (1979).

The fact that my experience is mostly with evaluations of education and training influences the argument presented here. Responsibility for educational decisions is widely diffused, and those who participate in making them have discordant interests. The same directive or curriculum or administrative policy will turn into a different activity in different planes (McLaughlin, 1980). These characteristics call for a kind of inquiry that would be less appropriate in evaluating a standardized arrangement for traffic control, vaccination, or disbursement of welfare funds. Even so, the orientation toward education is not highly restrictive. Educational programs range from a nationwide plan for providing daycare, to a system for instructing adults by means of telecasts, to a course of study being pilot-tested in one university, to an effort to improve the economic judgments made by prospective retirees. An analysis of evaluation that stretches over this range will apply to evaluations of many noneducational programs.

I shall discuss planning as if a lone evaluator has already been given a broad commission and an allotment of funds and has accepted a target date for completing the evaluation. This is a rhetorical device. In the first place, no one individual is qualified to make all the judgments that go into design and interpretation; almost always, responsibility is shared within a team. Moreover, it is often advisable to ask several groups to inquire into the same program. Splitting up the work has logistical advantages. It brings in multiple perspectives and promotes healthy professional debate. In the second place, the commission given the evaluator ought to be tentative. Then the study can be extended, restricted, or redirected as fieldwork identifies critical uncertainties. Although my rhetorical device bypasses the decision to evaluate, all that will be said has implications for the timing, scale, and appropriateness of any proposed evaluation. Even the possibility of abandoning the evaluation remains open.

What Evaluations Are of Most Worth?

As noted in *Toward Reform,* two images of decision making may be contrasted:

The Platonic image of concentrated power and responsibility is one of two long-standing ideals of governance. The second image—of pluralist ac-

commodation—is truer to most governance of social programs and most shaping of policy. It is convenient to speak of a context of command and a
context of accommodation. Both images are realistic and each has its philosophical base. At any given
time, some elements of public affairs are under the
authority of an official or body that has full command, while active roles in governing other public
affairs are scattered among the various ranks of society. . . .

The theory of evaluation, however, has been
developed almost wholly around the image of command. It is supposed that information flows to a
manager or policy official who has a firm grasp on
the controls. She can reach a "correct" decision and
act on it. Once her decision is made, subordinates
follow orders; the action that she wants, she gets.
Hence, she bears full responsibility.

Actually, however, most action is determined
by a pluralistic community, not by a lone decision
maker. Parties having divergent perceptions and
aims bear down on lawmakers and administrators.
Information can change perceptions but is unlikely
to bring all parties to agree on which facts are relevant or even on what the facts are. If the term *decision* is understood to mean a formal choice at a particular time between discrete alternatives, decision
making is rarely to be observed. When there are
multiple participants with multiple views, it is
meaningless to speak of one action as the rational
or correct action. The active parties jockey toward a
politically acceptable accommodation [pp. 83–
84]. . . .

It is this volatile, fragmented community that
today exercises power on any issue it chooses for attention. And it is for this reason that evaluation
must learn to serve in the context of accommodation
and not dream idly of serving a Platonic guardian
[p. 100].

Nearly all the literature on evaluation speaks of it as an
attempt to serve a decision maker. That language may be ap-

propriate for technical studies commissioned by an official in a mature, stable organization. In such an agency, a consensus about goals and basic policies has been achieved, and responsibility for the program operation has been delegated. The officers know what information is needed to adjust the operation. They specify what the evaluator is to look into and are attuned to use what he reports. When a firm considering whether to add a new product to its line commissions market research, the study does directly serve a defined decision maker. So does measurement for quality control in a factory.

In a politically lively situation, however, a program becomes the province of a policy-shaping community, not of a lone decision maker or tight-knit group. Persons who play roles in approving the program or in advocating alternatives, as well as most of those who carry out program operations, are part of this community. Perhaps, nominally, the decision sits on one person's desk, but that person will need concurrence from other administrators, from legislators, and from interested publics. She becomes more an arbitrator, more an architect of compromise, than an independent weigher of evidence.

Evaluation Design. Decisions about whether a program will be evaluated and on what scale are often made before any thought is given to design. Large evaluations are typically undertaken at the request of an administrator or a central agency. The commissioning agent may reduce the evaluator to a technician by setting forth the questions to be answered and asking him simply to apply his skills of sampling, measurement, and statistical analysis. But no one can judge whether an evaluation will be profitable without an impression of the kind and credibility of information likely to result from it. Administrators should ask evaluators to think through the design possibilities before agreeing to support a study (Wholey, 1979). The evaluator should not substitute his judgment for that of the sponsoring agency, but suggesting what and what not to investigate is a proper professional task.

Traditional writings on design tell an investigator who has already picked an aiming-point how to bring his weapons to bear. They tell him how to answer a fixed and limited question. Another question is for another day, that study to be designed when the time comes. Fixed and limited questions are suitable for basic research, since the available theory specifies a particularly timely question for any one study. The evaluator, in contrast, is not allowed to ask questions in endless series, mounting the thousand-and-first study of the problem after digesting the first thousand. He is not allowed the pure scientist's luxury of setting subquestions aside for investigation in a future year. Therefore, he ought to spread his shots.

The evaluator's ultimate product is more than a summary of what occurred in certain sites where a certain program was in operation. The community will want to know what can be expected in new sites and what can be expected of a modified program. The evaluator, then, is called on to illuminate the whole problem area in a comparatively short period of time. In doing so, he may come to recognize a large number of politically relevant questions about the program. But he cannot hope to answer them all and should not investigate each of them with equal intensity. To put extra effort into answering one question is to limit what will be learned about another. Identifying relevant questions and determining the emphasis each should have are central tasks in design. The selection among questions is guided by practical and political considerations, as well as by substantive ones.

Designing an evaluation is a continuing process. What variables deserve close attention will be discovered as the fieldwork proceeds. A decision to look intensively at one variable implies scanting investigation of some other variable. It may be reasonable to "hold constant" some aspect of delivery, to draw a representative sample, or to administer a pretest. But the designer cannot make those kinds of judgments purely in terms of the logic of the proposed control. He must recognize the opportunities that will be forgone if a particular design feature is adopted, and he must determine whether, on balance, the credibility of the study will be increased or decreased by the choice. The cost of answering one question well must be weighed against the cost of leaving other questions unanswered.

The Evaluator as Teacher. It is not the evaluator's task to determine on his own whether a program is worthwhile or what action should be taken. The evaluator cannot judge for others, any more than a counselor can decide what career a student should prepare for. Still, the evaluator-teacher should feel free to take a stance. If he concludes that a policy has predominantly good consequences, attempting to persuade others to adopt it is entirely proper—as long as he does not suppress evidence inconsistent with his conclusion. Social institutions learn from experience; so do program clients and political constituencies. The proper function of evaluation is to speed up the learning process by communicating what might otherwise be overlooked or wrongly perceived. The evaluator, then, is an educator. His success is to be judged by his success in communication; that is, by what he leads others to understand and believe. Payoff comes from the insight that the evaluator's work generates in others.

A study that is technically admirable falls short if what the evaluator learns does not enter the thinking of the relevant political community. That community may include clients, program staffs, taxpayer leagues, environmentalist lobbies, legislators, bureaucrats, and interested citizens. An evaluation fulfills its function to the extent that it assists participants in the political process to resolve conflicts intelligently.

The evaluation can rarely play its proper role by letting a single decision maker or a single center of power set the questions for its attention. This statement runs counter to the recommendation of several astute commentators, notably Boruch and Cordray (1980) and a committee of the National Research Council (Raizen and Rossi, 1981). The committee would have the legislature or some other sponsor specify just what questions are relevant: "Responding to the myriad, often conflicting expectations of all the audiences is likely to diminish the integrity of an evaluation and limit its usefulness to any one audience. . . . The design of the evaluation should anticipate the primary audience(s), and the procedures, methods, analysis, and language of its reports should correspond to the needs and expectations of the primary audiences. . . . Defining the audience and targeting the message will reduce the frustration that often accompanies the more eclectic attempts to speak simultaneously with many tongues in many groups" (Raizen and Rossi, 1981, p. 39). The thinking of the Stanford Evaluation Consortium is reflected in the working title that *Toward Reform* once bore: "Evaluation for a Free Society." I quote Coleman and associates (1979, p. 6) to show that our view is not idiosyncratic: "The policy researcher is not the servant of the government official. He, like the official, is the agent of the people—the people not as a mass, but through their various roles, activities, and interests. In this conception, policy is the outcome of a clash of interests, not the product of a governmental policy maker. The proper function of social policy research is to inform those interests—not a particular subset of those interests, not government, but the interests themselves—so that they may be better informed about their interests and thus press more rationally for them."

Evaluation ordinarily speaks to diverse audiences through various channels, supplying each with political ammunition, and with food for thought. Participants in political action use messages for many purposes. Some challenges to the report will be politically motivated; catch-as-catch-can counterarguments are to be expected. It should surprise no one that the process by which evaluation contributes to community opinion is less disciplined than is the generation of scientific consensus.

A decade ago technical excellence was the accepted criterion for evaluation. In those terms the summative evaluation for Harvard Project Physics (see Chapter Two) was exceptionally good, and it undoubtedly advanced the craft of evaluation. But if—as seems to be the case—the study had little influence on decisions and on thought about the teaching of science, it did not make the hoped-for contribution.

Teaching begins when the evaluator first sits down with members of the policy-shaping community to elicit their questions. It continues during every contact the evaluator has with program participants or with others in his audience. The end report is only one means for enabling audiences to understand the program and how it impinges on their interests. Teaching does more than transmit *answers*. The teacher's responsibility is not merely to know his subject matter and convey relevant facts, conclusions, and techniques. Educating is as much a matter of raising questions as of providing answers. Especially where the topic is value-laden, the educator's responsibility is to help others ask better questions and determine what actions are appropriate to their aims. Ideally, the client comes to see the nature of the world more clearly and arrives at a better understanding of what she wants and of the political moves suitable for her purposes. Intellectual analysis is no substitute for that kind of negotiation.

Citizens do not serve their political interests if they operate on false assumptions. Instances abound of actions taken without sufficient understanding. Thus, unfortunate side effects sometimes appear after a program has been accepted and put into use. Statements such as "We never thought to check on that possibility" or "We were misled by the developer's assurances" strongly suggest that the process of decision making was inadequate. Other commonly heard remarks point to the same problem: "If those facts had come to my attention, I'd have voted the other way." "I see now that we gave too much weight to the initial costs of the alternative programs and not enough to the problems of maintaining each one." "We failed to realize how much our community differs from the tryout communities where the program worked well."

An evaluation ought to reduce uncertainties, but it should also challenge simplistic views (Cohen and Weiss, 1977). Insofar as the evaluation activity and its reports enable everyone to appreciate the range of consequences that may follow a social action, the evaluation enables each participant to throw weight behind a truly preferred course of action. The foresight and open-mindedness of publics are limited, as are the resources for evaluation, and consequences are to some degree unforeseeable. The evaluator cannot hope to extinguish all doubts, nor can he hope to persuade all segments of the political community to make full use of his findings. Still, his target lies in that direction.

Since communication is a vital part of policy-oriented research, it ought to be considered at the planning stage. As Wilensky (1967, p. ix) has said, excellent policy research is *"clear* because it is understandable to those who must use it; *timely* because it gets to them when they need it; *reliable* because diverse observers using the same procedure see it in the same way; *valid* because it is cast in the form of concepts and measures that capture reality (the tests include logical consistency, successful prediction, congruence with established knowledge from other sources); *adequate* beause the account is full (the context of the act, event, or life of the person or group is described); and *wide ranging* because the major policy alternatives promising a high probability of attaining organizational goals are posed or new goals are suggested."

If the communications from the evaluation are the products that count, these questions should be asked of the completed evaluation:

- Did each fraction of the audience attend to the message?
- Did each understand it?
- Did each find it credible?
- Were the significant questions answered as well as possible?
- Did the answers alter the preconceptions of the audience?
- Was the dialogue leading to decisions enriched and elevated as a consequence of the evaluation?

The same questions phrased prospectively ("Will each fraction . . . attend to the message?") are to be raised when an evaluation plan is sketched out.

All the persons whose voices may be raised during the political discussion and all those who will shape the program as it operates are part of the evaluator's target audience. Ideally, he will reach even further, to normally silent citizens whose voices *should* be raised. Even when a single manager or board appears to be in full control, an evaluator can alert a wider audience to its stake in the decisions. The influence of Ralph Nader and his team on decisions made by General Motors is a case in point. When an evaluator is commissioned by an official, his contract may restrict him from addressing outsiders directly, but he can still serve all parties by bringing the concerns of outsiders into the inquiry and its interpretation. The sponsor may not be cordial to an inquiry that recognizes the perspectives of clients and political adversaries. But, as Coleman (1972) pointed out, a narrow evaluation serves the sponsor badly. If an evaluation does not collect data capable of dispelling (or validating) an objection voiced by critics of the program, the evaluation may do nothing to change attitudes.

Formative Use of Findings. A single definite question is often the starting point of an evaluation. The question is usually cast in one of three forms: (1) "Is the program achieving its goals?" (2) "Does the program have an effect?" (3) "How much larger, on the average, is the outcome under Plan A than under Plan B?" These questions assume that the form of the program has been fixed and that the aim of evaluation is to assess its merit. Scriven (1967) christened such evaluations *summative,* to contrast them with the *formative* study that regards the program as fluid and seeks ways to better it. Scriven's terms are convenient, but they suggest a false division of studies into two classes.

Evaluation that focuses on outcomes can and should be used formatively. When a trial fails, the social planner wants to know why it failed and how to do better next time. When the trial succeeds and the proposal is considered for use under changed conditions, the intelligent planner does not conclude that its effectiveness has been proved. She now asks about the reasons and essential conditions for the success. Even when the trial of a plan has satisfactory outcomes, the policy maker should be prepared to consider any alternative that has a chance of working appreciably better.

In principle, evidence of disappointing outcomes could lead administrators to cut off funds for a program. But this almost never happens to established social programs; once installed, such programs generate their own political support. Moreover, to cut off a program without substituting an alternative is to abandon the commitment to alleviate the social problem in question. To develop an alternative is a formative activity. (This paragraph echoes a book written before the 1980 election and is supported by considerable evidence, notably that of Kaufman, 1976. It is too early to say whether any social program has been mortally wounded by the 1981 cuts in the federal budget, but it is evident that program evaluations did not determine where cuts were made.)

Purely summative studies have been useful in the testing of drugs and vaccines. These can fairly be regarded as fixed treatments. A successful trial leads to acceptance of the substance as a treatment. If delivery during the trial was adequate and the treatment nevertheless fails, the investigator goes back to the test tube and the animal lab; no data from the field are likely to suggest what change in molecules would produce better results. The average summative result is convincing because the effect of the substance is almost surely independent of social circumstances and institutional arrangements. The substance may affect some types of individuals more than others, but soundly designed research will detect those interactions and will qualify accordingly the statement about average results. While educational and welfare systems do not have the fixed character and the independence of circumstances of the drug or vaccine, Gene Glass (personal communication, 1977) has pressed upon me the view that pure summaries of outcome can be profitable in social research. I shall comment on two examples that represent his thinking. Both have to do with treatments that were ill conceived and on which the evaluation properly had a destructive effect.

First, consider a system for helping retarded readers that was promoted as a proprietary service by its inventors. The system had no roots in psychology, and the rationale offered for it seemed arbitrary. Research on the program indicates that children treated in this manner were not demonstrably benefited, and a professional who knows of this finding will not refer children to the service. But evaluation makes only a limited contribution here, since it cannot guide improvement of the system. No plausible rationale links the prescribed exercises to performance in reading, so it is pointless to ask where the chain of intervening effects broke down. Yet that would be the first step toward worthwhile modifications.

The second example is the common practice of placing retarded pupils in separate classes; in principle, these special classes could adopt procedures suited to the children. Large-scale studies have reported, however, that children in special classes did no better on average than comparable children whose schools kept them in regular classes. Possibly some localities had effective special classes, but it became evident that the policy—as applied in schools generally—was not working. This average finding provided potent ammunition for reformers who favored "mainstreaming" of the retarded; partly as a response to these summative evaluations, policy has shifted toward mainstreaming. Still, I think formative research would have been a better investment. There is a chance that it might have shown how to benefit the slow learner.

Most educational programs are loosely defined, allowing room for adaptation at the state, community, and classroom levels. An estimate of average or global benefit is only moderately helpful to national planners (Light and Smith, 1970), and it is much less helpful to local decision makers. No group concerned with a particular site wants to know how a program has operated in some mythical "average" site. "How will it work for us?" is the question. A national planner must consider whether changes in the social context in the course of a decade—a higher unemployment rate or more unionization of teachers, for example—are likely to affect outcomes. Similar variation over levels of government, over localities, and over time is found in many noneducational services.

When the program is new, the image of a fixed program is especially unrealisic. The pilot study of a new program, installed in Year 1, may be scheduled to end in Year 5.

The planners often speak as if in Year 5 a "go/no-go" decision is to be made about the program set up in Year 1. In actuality the decision is likely to be spread out in time and to be multiply branched. The program will necessarily be modified by operational decisions during Years 2, 3, and 4. Even if assessment in Year 5 is encouraging, variants of the treatment or its delivery will be suggested. As insight into the limitations of the original plan emerges, fundamentally different programs will be invented. Indeed, political developments or a changed perception of the social problem may have altered the whole direction of social action (Rivlin, 1974). The decision process profits little from a report that simply compares the end results of a now-obsolete Plan A and a now-obsolete Plan B.

Breadth and Flexibility. Evaluation studies should be thoughtful, not mechanically objective. Modest studies buy more thought per person-year of effort than million-dollar ones, or so it has been in the past. To be sure, some questions can be addressed only on a large scale, and I am not defending penny pinching, whatever the size of the study.

The following recommendations of Berryman and Glennan (1980, p. 31) speak to this point:

> *Large education programs should have a multiyear plan of evaluation studies.* Large programs such as Title I, Vocational Education, and the Education for All Handicapped Children programs have multiple objectives, complex delivery chains, and many sites. They consequently have complex information needs, and call for a *plan* of studies to be undertaken over the next several years. The governance and intent of the program should determine the questions that these studies should address. Their schedule will depend on the expected life cycle of the program.
>
> *The plan of studies should consist of studies with limited objectives, instead of ones with multiple purposes.* We recommend against multipurpose or omnibus studies for three reasons. First, because they are complex, they take a long time to plan and to com-

plete. Any evaluation study, limited or not, incorpo-
rates a vision of the policy problem. The longer the
study takes, the more likely it is that the policy community will reconceive the problem during the
study. Omnibus studies thus often become out-
dated, and their results irrelevant.

Second, if a multipurpose study fails for any
reason, the consequent information gaps are large
and consequently less remediable.

Finally, a multipurpose study often has conflicting design and management requirements. Re-
solving the conflicts tends to compromise the quality of the study.

(Berryman and Glennan may seem to dispute my earlier argument that an evaluation sheds light on a great variety of
uncertainties and that it should be planned for such "wide-
band" use. But my statement applies to the comparatively
limited study, while their comment bears on the multimillion-
dollar contract that tries to cover all the current questions
about a program on the basis of a single cohort of installations.)

Experienced and judicious members of the evaluation
staff should be free to think deeply about events and data,
and the senior investigators ought to dirty their hands by direct contact with events in the field. In large studies, however,
the senior investigators are almost inevitably chairbound,
free only to send the signals that guide a swarm of data collec-
tors and data processors. For logistical and bureaucratic reasons, the design tends to become rigid; questions that emerge
as the study progresses receive too little attention. As staff
roles within the large team become differentiated, members
become less able to see the program whole and in living color.
The data reach the chief investigators as colorless aggregates.
Hence, the final conclusions are likely to rest more on near-
mindless data processing than on appreciation of the events
themselves.

As illustration, consider a large evaluation of bilingual
education that *was* thoughtfully interpreted (American Insti-

tutes for Research, 1977). The contractor was to assess outcomes of a federally supported program of bilingual instruction intended primarily for children of Hispanic origin who had limited command of English. The program was based on the idea that children who speak Spanish better than English would profit more if they were taught first to read in Spanish and were then shifted over to English. The investigators discovered, however, that the program was not being applied to the intended population. Many schools were shunting into the bilingual program all the Hispanic children who made a poor start in reading, even though, according to the teachers, a large fraction of them spoke English better than Spanish. Moreover, the planned transition to instruction entirely in English was not made; once the child could read in Spanish, the typical school did not return her to the mainstream of instruction. The summative evaluation had to be discounted. It would have been sensible to call off the effort, but Congress had ordered an evaluation and the wheels could not be stopped. Elaborate testing was not needed to establish that it is counterproductive to teach in Spanish when a child understands Spanish poorly or not at all. The merits of transitional bilingual education for the Spanish-dominant child could not be observed if instruction was directed wholly toward maintenance of Spanish. The point of the example is that this evaluative study was exceptionally perceptive. Many a large-scale study, failing to check how a program was actually carried out, has "appraised" an innovation that was never tried.

In diverse and changing circumstances, an evaluation is a better guide to action when the outcome information is supplemented by information on situational variables and intermediate processes that condition the results. Resources should therefore be allocated to describing the sites where the intervention was implanted, as well as the events that interacted with and modified treatment events and the client's response. These kinds of narratives tell what went on and so give some basis for inferring what is likely to occur under changed conditions. The evaluation is then as much a historical inquiry as a scientific one.

Berk and Rossi (1976, pp. 340–341) have criticized conventional evaluation for its lack of this very kind of perspective:

> Our standard evaluation tools tend to neglect historical and social processes. Elaborate factorial experimental designs can only handle a relatively small number of causal factors, and, perhaps more important, independent variables are purged (through randomization) of correlations with other phenomena in the world to which they are inevitably linked. A desire to maximize . . . "internal validity" . . . has spawned research methodologies which in effect make social programs orthogonal to other social forces that might cause differential outcomes between experimental and control groups. . . .
>
> The New Jersey–Pennsylvania Income Maintenance Experiment, for example, was superimposed upon an existing welfare structure and food stamp program, plus a wide range of ethnic, geographical, and class variations. Yet such factors were ignored in a research design which focused almost exclusively on work effort of households. The implicit model of society was clear: social structure is composed of modules relatively independent of one another and therefore subject to alteration without producing any important ripples throughout the system. In principle, most social scientists subscribe to a very different notion of society, but this classroom posture has simply not been translated into evaluation research practice.

Beyond the Stand-Alone Study. Enthusiasts for "hard" evaluation have offered the dubious suggestion that a single firmly designed study, standing alone, can provide the signal to continue a program or abandon it. But Baker (1967, p. 211), writing when large evaluations were just beginning to appear, saw that the requirements of complex fieldwork cannot be captured within the Fisherian model of narrowly targeted stand-alone studies: "The current situation presents an opportunity for a new conceptualization of experimental design which is as great as that which existed during the 1920s" (when Fisher did his seminal work). Planning an evaluative inquiry is more like planning a campaign of investigation than like planning a single experiment, as was noted by Berryman and Glennan (1980). The designer has to prevision the work as a whole, but he should not harden the plans. The *Viking* investigations of Mars (Lee, 1976) provide an analogy to the evaluator's work. Each day, the automated lander gathered data on a dozen kinds of questions and sent them to earth, where scientists examined them. A few hours later, the command team transmitted back to Mars the lander's instructions for the next day's work. The messages reflected priorities emerging from the interpretation of the latest printouts. Evaluation at its best has the same fluid responsiveness to incoming observations and to the changing concerns of the political community.

Sophisticated writers are aware that conclusions about programs are based on the cumulation of findings and not on one study, and they favor an evolving pattern of diversified studies rather than a single focused trial (Raizen and Rossi, 1981). The literature on design, however, does not adequately reflect this view. The present volume will therefore attempt to discuss in detail the rationale for planning multi-strand investigations.

Understanding comes out of accumulated knowledge, not from the stand-alone trial. Finney (1956, p. 15), a successor of Fisher, has written: "In agricultural research today, advance rarely comes from a single dramatic experiment. More commonly, improvements in agricultural practice can be based only on the critical appreciation of evidence from a large number of experiments which are not necessarily all of the same type or even all from the same organized program." Finney calls for a synthesis of information from all past research on the subject, including studies with weak designs. Although he finds value in experimental control, Finney sees no one comparative trial as pivotal. Cook and Campbell

(1976, p. 227) think similarly: "We would delude ourselves if we believed that a single experiment, or even a research program of several years' duration, would definitely answer the major questions associated with confidently inferring a causal relationship, naming its parts, and specifying its generalizability."

Rivlin (1974), who, like Cook and Campbell, is a strong advocate of tightly designed social research, goes further in circumscribing the use of formal experiments. To develop proper program designs and measures for studying complex instructional treatments takes several years, she says; and by the time the plans are set, policy makers may no longer be interested in such programs. As for programs such as tuition vouchers and performance contracting, which would alter whole institutions, "it may never be possible to do 'experiments' on which firm statistical inferences can be based" (p. 353). Why? Because the policy leads to different local responses. It becomes far more important to trace the effects of the unplanned variations than to average the outcomes over the heterogeneous trials (Berryman and Glennan, 1980; Cook, 1981).

Experiments are most clearly worth their cost, Rivlin (1974) argues, when the treatment is easily specified and controlled and can be delivered to individuals or households. Prime examples would be cash payment plans, as in the well-known New Jersey income maintenance experiment (Rossi, 1978, p. 588). The controlled study can give information on significant variables affecting individual response even if the conditions of delivery during the trial are quite unlike those of an operational program. An educational counterpart would be the laboratory studies with very small groups of children that were used in developing lessons for "Sesame Street" and "Electric Company" (Boruch, 1975, p. 39).

Some who find merit in large, strongly controlled tests of government programs would reserve such tests for exceptional political decisions. Some of the social scientists at the helm of the New Jersey income maintenance experiment came to believe that the government should support such experiments only when they provided information relevant to *major* policy questions and when such information could not be attained without a controlled experiment (Timpane, 1970).

Conceptual Uses of Results. Evaluations have typically been seen as ways of reaching better decisions about the program being evaluated. In truth, evaluative findings frequently have no direct effect on the program studied, whereas large consequences follow from indirect, "conceptual" uses of the information (Rein, 1976; Weiss, 1977; Lindblom and Cohen, 1979). Beliefs about the central problem—about the causes of poverty and unemployment, for example—are altered. So are social goals and priorities, and beliefs about the probity and efficacy of schools or other institutions and of public servants generally. The direction that new program proposals take is influenced by perceptions that grew out of experience with earlier programs; evaluation is only one means of capturing and dramatizing that experience. Again I quote from *Toward Reform:*

> The perceptions of individuals and subgroups, shared through communication, blend into a prevailing view of a program or institution. Many times such impressions command a near-consensus [p. 118].
>
> Remarkably sweeping changes in social views occur even within a single generation, and social institutions change accordingly. The process is one of slow extension of a new interpretation from a few believers to a wider segment of the community and ultimately, perhaps, to nearly everyone [p. 122].
>
> An evaluation concentrates on a particular present program, but . . . studies of prototypes and established programs have their greatest implications for programs that differ—perhaps radically—from the one actually surveyed [pp. 122–123].
>
> When a new perception commands attention, it is relayed to a wider, less specialized circle of com-

munication. Here again, it may reverberate or die
out.

   But if its audience does widen, the message
becomes generalized. Even among officials, Weiss
and Bucuvalas (1977, p. 228) found that discussion
proceeds at an abstract level, with little or no reference to the specific program from which the original observation came. Almost never is a specific
evaluative study either the main support of an
emerging proposal or the main source of doubts
about an established one. Accounts of personal experience, journalistic analyses, recollections of history, and possibly echoes of scholarly theory or-
chestrate the new themes [p. 125].

A program manager may have highly specific questions; but inquiries of many kinds, not all of them evaluations
and not all of them on the same specific topic, feed into conversations of the policy-shaping community. The studies of
Piaget, as transmitted by Hunt (1961) and others, had as
much influence on thinking about compensatory education
in the late 1960s as did the Westinghouse evaluation of Head
Start. Intensive tryouts of particular forms of training (along
Piagetian lines, for example) affected thinking as much as did
the large-scale assessments. The evaluator does not have the
responsibility to deliver—indeed, should not deliver—a firm
answer to a specified policy question. The evaluator's responsibility is that of any other social agent who seeks to help in
selecting action alternatives: to illuminate the corner of the
world where the problem resides. In this, evaluation research
does not differ from basic research on child development or
income or delinquency.

Conflicting Ideals for Evaluation

   The typical essay on how to conduct or judge evaluations rests on a preconception of proper form. Sometimes the
essay makes the preconception explicit and argues for it;
sometimes not. Radically though some of these preconcep-

tions differ, direct confrontation of one with another has been rare. Typically, a writer ignores ideals other than his own, dismisses them as "not really evaluation," or acknowledges that they are appropriate in studies he regards as comparatively unimportant. I hope instead to offer a synthesis of views.

I overdramatize only slightly when I contrast a scientistic school of evaluators with a humanistic one (as Campbell, 1975a, has done before me). Writers at one pole prize experiments; those at the opposite extreme find evaluative experiments misinformative.

I shall not treat the scientistic and humanistic positions symmetrically. I shall comment particularly on literature advocating or criticizing strong designs, since quantitative studies have been reviewed with a sharp eye and balanced assessment of them seems to be possible. Qualitative evaluation has become more prominent recently, and much has been said in favor of the approach. Enthusiasts vary widely in their practice and concept of qualitative evaluation, but they have felt it necessary to present a united front to gain a hearing for unorthodox practices. When their spokespersons feel secure enough to criticize naturalistic evaluations that illustrate one or another of the particular heresies, issues will be defined and clarified as they have been during debates over experiments and quasi-experiments. Advice on integrating qualitative methods into plans for program evaluation can then become more pointed than the advice that I can offer here.

My predilections color what I say. In forty years of evaluative work and methodological studies, I have specialized in quantitative and statistical methods and have been a technical consultant for large surveys, experiments, and near-experiments. I have supervised a number of pure-experiment dissertations, but a design with controlled assignment has never seemed appropriate for a study of my own. I have switched back and forth between measurements and less formal methods. In evaluating a Stanford program of courses in Values, Technology, and Society during the 1970s (with a report restricted to internal use of the program staff),

I relied almost entirely on interview, observation, questionnaire, and judgment. But during the same time period, my students and I piled up mountains of computer printout in an effort to devise a statistical framework for certain parts of a nationwide study of school violence.

⎩ *The Scientistic Ideal.* A true experiment, as described in the literature on evaluation, concentrates on outcome or impact and embodies three procedures: (1) Two or more conditions are in place, at least one of them being the consequence of deliberate intervention. (2) Persons or institutions are assigned to conditions in a way that creates equivalent groups. (3) All participants are assessed on the same outcome measure(s). Fairweather (1980) insists that an adequate effort toward social change must be scientific, and he equates the term *scientific* with *experimental*. Although surveys, correlational studies, and quasi-experiments have a place, he says, "finally, for an accurate evaluation . . . it is *absolutely essential* that an experiment be carried out with random assignments of participants" (p. 248). Writers whose language is less absolute quite commonly equate high quality in evaluation with this particular design, seeing all other qualities as secondary. According to Gilbert, Mosteller, and Tukey (1976, p. 296), "Ethical justification for failing to make a randomized trial [comparison of new and old, or new and null, treatments] is never easy and often impossible. Inadequately evaluated programs can usually be regarded as 'fooling around' with the people involved."

Significantly, a new report commissioned to advise Congress regarding evaluation policy (Boruch and Cordray, 1980) identifies evaluation with estimating the comparative effects of programs having similar aims, calls emphatically for quality of design, and equates quality with the randomized experiment. Similar language appears in the companion volume of recommendations to Congress from a committee of the National Research Council (Raizen and Rossi, 1981).

Although Boruch and Cordray admit that the randomized trial is not always to the point, the alternatives they mention are limited inquiries into strictly political questions: Is the program politically feasible? How much service does a program deliver to whom? Hence, Congress is being given the message that, if the aim is to study the consequences of installing a program, only the randomized experiment rises above the level of "ambiguous," "misleading," "inadequate," and "inept" (sec. 5, p. 20). Nonexperimental approaches to the study of consequences are considered reluctantly, and only because of the political infeasibility, costs, and practical difficulties of random assignment.

The Humanistic Ideal. Writers at the humanistic extreme find experiments unacceptable. For them, naturalistic case studies are the panacea. A humanist would study a program already in place, not one imposed by the evaluator. If persons are assigned to a treatment, that is because the policy under study calls for assignment; assignments are not made for the sake of research. The program is to be seen through the eyes of its developers and clients. Naturalistic investigators would ask different questions of different programs. Benefits are to be described, not reduced to a quantity. Observations are to be opportunistic and responsive to the local scene, not pre-structured. Some of the humanists abjure objectivity; their ideal is the sensitive, appreciative observer. Several members of this school are conveniently represented in a work provocatively titled *Beyond the Numbers Game* (Hamilton and others, 1978). The following remarks, even out of context, adequately illustrate the book's drift:

> The researcher . . . makes no attempt to manipulate, control, or eliminate situational variables, but takes as given the complex scene he encounters. His chief task is to unravel it [Parlett and Hamilton, 1978, p. 14].
> Educational criticism aims not only at revealing . . . meaning and conventions made and broken . . . in a classroom but also aims at using language . . . so vivid that it enables the reader to participate vicariously. . . . Educational connoisseurship and criticism have not been encouraged. An ounce of data, it seems, has been worth a pound of insight [Eisner, 1978, pp. 97, 98].
> The first duty of the evaluator should be to

offer the client a comprehensive portrayal of the
program. . . . We need to portray complexity. We
need to convey holistic impression, the mood, even
the mystery of the experience. . . . Such styles are
not likely to be those of the specialist in measurement or theoretically minded social scientist [Stake,
1978, pp. 162, 164; sentences reordered here].

The Emerging Reconciliation

Extreme statements imply greater conflict between the
two schools than exists. The strong recommendations on either side are intended to apply in limited circumstances
(though it is the rare writer who tells us what circumstance he
has in mind). Most advocates of strong designs in evaluation
see them as serving central decision makers who are looking
for a standard policy to be applied over a large region. Naturalistic evaluators are usually interested either in improving
services in the site(s) studied or in leading those on the front
line elsewhere (principals and teachers, for example) to perceive their own circumstances and activities differently.

It is good to see a recent article with the title "Beyond
Qualitative Versus Quantitative Methods" (Reichardt and
Cook, 1979) and to come across a work on "multiple-method
approaches" (Saxe and Fine, 1979), in which it is argued that
the more an evaluative effort is spread over multiple studies,
the greater the place for a mixture of styles. Saxe and Fine,
seeing the worth of large, less controlled studies and small
rigorous experiments that give strong answers to pointed
questions, urge that the approaches be made deliberately
complementary: "The data developed from the macro and
micro studies should not be viewed as orthogonal. They interact to identify those aspects of the program worthy of investigation by the alternative form of analysis. . . . Data
from the two levels feed into each other in a cyclical fashion
in order to identify those program elements requiring revision or special attention" (p. 64).

While these tolerant writings are welcome, eclectic tolerance is not enough to guide the designer. The evaluator has to decide how to distribute investigative effort month by month. Broadly speaking, the scientific method consists in imposing controls on what would otherwise be casual and perhaps untrustworthy observations. This is true of naturalistic as well as quantitative inquiries. Both kinds of science must be concerned with, for example, the sampling of sites and informants and with the framing of questions; and each has developed devices to improve the quality of observations. Each control has a particular purpose, and a control that strengthens a study in one respect is almost certain to restrict it in another or to increase its cost. These trade-offs should be brought to the forefront of consciousness.

On several matters members of both schools seem to agree. To begin, they agree that society should innovate. Social institutions and services are by no means as good as they could be, and arrangements that once worked well may collapse when social conditions change. They also agree that a well-intentioned change—even one supported by a strong rationale—may do little good and may do harm. Whenever the character of an innovation and the political tempo permit, the change should be tentative and reversible (Campbell, 1969b).

Evaluation should be empirical, examining events in sites where the program is tried and scrutinizing the reactions and subsequent performance of the persons served. The "objective" scientist gives a stronger meaning to empiricism than the humanist does. The humanist would judge a human creation in its own terms; if the audience at a play fails to respond, for example, the fault may lie in the audience and not in the work of art. The study of *Hamlet* in school is defended by Stenhouse (1978) simply on the grounds that *Hamlet* is worth studying; and, in his opinion, no one can say what effect on particular students the instructor should want Shakespeare's play to have, and very little of the effect is measurable.

Although Stenhouse and other writers contributing to *Beyond the Numbers Game* (Hamilton and others, 1978) trust

sensitive observers much more than they trust measurements, the hard-nosed test of a hypothesis can be worth its
cost when the hypothesis is properly mature and important
to verify. Cook and Campbell (1979, p. 345) put it this way:
"It is rarely desirable to conduct an experiment until [one is
sure] that the manipulations are exactly the ones of interest."
This is true for both the experimental and the control or contrast conditions. But while a program is evolving, Cook and
Campbell add, less formal methods of study are appropriate.
Indeed, all evaluators favor pilot work, and few would call for
a high degree of "control" at that stage. If there is a difference of opinion, it is about the duration of the exploratory
phase. Advocates of experimentation usually speak of less
controlled trials as "preexperimental," implying that in time a
hard test will follow.

The statisticians Gilbert, Mosteller, and Tukey (1976,
p. 297) speak of the rigorous confirmatory test as the cap-
stone of a development effort that starts with "insights"
derived in part from "anecdotal evidence—that is, careful
case studies." What language could be more congenial to the
humanists? In principle, exploratory work can lead ultimately to a well-defined scientific proposition. To confirm
that proposition for the record, the scientist designs a formal
experiment with experimental and control treatments. It can
be run off with little likelihood of surprise; the comparison is
expected to document what has already been learned. Textbooks on "design of experiments" discuss the study-for-the-
record, not the pilot work. In contrast, humanistic evaluators
tend to oppose freezing a policy in a form that can be tested
and made permanent if it passes the test. They prefer to keep
plans and operations in flux. They presumably would never
get around to a hard-nosed appraisal.

Writers of all persuasions accept the importance of the
"threats to validity" that Campbell and Stanley (1963) made
the litany of a generation of graduate students. However the
investigator proceeds, awareness of these threats brings a
caution to his interpretation that was frequently lacking in
quantitative fieldwork prior to 1963. The critical logic of

Campbell and Stanley (restated in Cook and Campbell, 1976, 1979) plays a large part in commentary on evaluations (though caution in the planning and interpretation of evaluations is less than universal).

The quantitative-minded are now inclined to agree with the humanists that compressing evaluative data into a single index of benefit or into a significance test cannot do justice to the reality being evaluated. Some evaluators try to sum up costs and benefits, but translations of multiple outcomes into simple indexes are in truth no more than heuristic devices. Utility analysis cannot displace political negotiation, according to the experts (Keeney and Raiffa, 1976). Even the goals set for the program are subject to reconsideration. What compression gains in succinct communication is offset by loss of information and by the concealing of value judgments. Some time back, many professional evaluators were content to try to answer a yes-or-no question: Did the program achieve its goals? Today everyone would want to be informed about side effects and would want to see a fuller description of the levels of the several outcomes.

Randomized experiments were once regarded as quite distinct from trials where comparison groups are not strictly equivalent. Now the quantitative options are all seen as approximations to experiments (Boruch, 1975). The term *quasi-experiment* was introduced by Campbell and Stanley (1963) to encompass studies that examine data collected under contrasting conditions, without random assignment of subjects. Those who press for rigor have always been ambivalent about quasi-experiments because the category includes both close and distant approximations. In fact, Campbell and Stanley overshot their mark. Aiming to show that careful interpretation could make *good* use of quasi-experiments, they inadvertently led some less sophisticated readers to believe that quasi-experiments are suspect. Some readers were even persuaded that a design that classifies subjects into types before assigning them to treatment at random is inferior to a fully random assignment. Readers were also led to think of experiments as impeccable, but the ideal experiment can rarely be achieved. A randomized design in a field study is likely to produce no more than an approximation to a true experiment, because of attrition and other departures from the plan.

In emphasizing degrees of approximation to the true experiment, I shall refer to "strong" and "weak" designs, the former including controlled-assignment and repeated-measures designs. The strong designs (ideally executed) are unbiased. That is to say, if the design is used to compare two treatments whose effects on a certain population and in a certain setting are identical, the difference found in comparisons of samples, averaged over many samples, will be zero.

Whether a design is strong or weak, all conclusions from it are inferences. They reach beyond the data with the aid of assumptions or presuppositions, and each one has a degree of credibility. Some advocates of strong designs suggest that conclusions from them can be "certain," but that is not the case. An interpretation rests not on data alone but also on a large body of understandings, many of them potentially open to challenge (Lakatos and Musgrave, 1970, especially pp. 76–79, 99–103, 131). Even a determined operationist will fail to make explicit the presuppositions that separate him from other theorists in his field; that is, his operational definitions will ignore those aspects of the experimental setting that, in his mind, make little difference anyway (MacKenzie, 1977, pp. 132–133). Campbell has written much about the inevitable need to rely on plausible inference and commonsense knowing in interpreting even true experiments (see especially Campbell, 1974). Gilbert, Mosteller, and Tukey (1976, pp. 369–370) have this to say on the same point: "Even if we are able to follow the best guidance we now have—when we must evaluate either a natural experiment or an unrandomized trial—namely, to seek out alternative methods of error-prone inference, to use a few or even several that appear likely to be prone to separate sources of error, and then to discuss their results together, recognizing their fallibility—even if we do all this, we cannot be sure of our results, only somewhat less uncertain. But we have an obligation to do as well as we may with the data we have."

Basic Questions

Four main questions run through many of the discussions and disagreements between and within schools of evaluation:

- Are causal conclusions required in evaluation?
- Should evaluation have a conservative influence?
- Should inquiry be targeted?
- Should treatment conditions be standardized?

Although these questions are interconnected, I shall try to consider each in turn.

Are Causal Conclusions Required in Evaluation? The following statement is representative of the scientistic point of view: "Evaluation research . . . attempts to show causal relationships—for example, that A, the program Head Start, causes B, the desired outcome, equalization of cognitive skills among all preschool children. To be useful, the investigator must be able to rule out alternative explanations for changes noted" (Bernstein and Freeman, 1975, p. 88). Approximations to experiments are accepted by Boruch and other writers of this school only in reluctant acknowledgment that controlled assignment may be practically or politically unfeasible. Investigations with weak designs are likely to be dismissed as inadequate. Outright rejection of certain designs is a tradition going back to the Campbell-Stanley monograph of 1963. In the 1970s, however, Campbell (1974, 1975c) came to see case studies as playing a legitimate role and retracted as a "caricature" his earlier remarks that they were "of almost no scientific value" and "unethical" as dissertation research.

Those who see a causal statement as the intended fruit of an evaluation envision a conservative, hard-to-convince decision maker who will accept an innovation only when its worth has been proved. The Rossi-Freeman-Wright text (1979) illustrates how stern was the scientistic ideal of just a few years back: "Impact evaluation needs to be undertaken as systematically and rigorously as possible in order to document the causal linkages between intervention inputs and program outcomes. Such a task requires, to the best of our abilities, ruling out other explanations for the results (or lack of results) of social interventions (p. 161). The problem of discerning the effectiveness of a program is identical with the problem of establishing causality (p. 162). The basic aim of impact evaluation is to estimate the *net effects* or *net outcomes* of an intervention . . . free and clear of the effects of other elements present in the situation under evaluation" (p. 163). Whether it is meaningful to speak of treatment effects as existing independently of other elements will be a key topic in later chapters of this work. Here it can be said that a treatment effect results from the interaction of population, treatment, and setting; therefore, the quest for an effect "free and clear" of other effects is unrealistic. (Rossi himself has since endorsed this position; see Raizen and Rossi, 1981.)

There is also reason to doubt that decision makers are crucially interested in causal inference; they need "a rough, but constantly refined, set of understandings as to what is associated with what," says Moynihan (1969, p. 194). Simon (1960) describes most decision making as "satisficing." The executive, like the person in the street, notes the state of affairs subsequent to an action. If that is within a satisfactory range, she continues with the same course of action—unless an alternative that might yield even better outcomes attracts her attention. She needs information on consequences, but a satisfactory state of affairs is a gift horse that she is unlikely to anatomize.

Should Evaluation Have a Conservative Influence? The stress on causal testing in evaluation seems to arise from a skeptical, if not a conservative, political position. Riecken (1976, p. 43) criticizes those who act without providing for assessment of results: "The history of social reform and amelioration is littered with examples of large-scale and costly catastrophes . . . as well as more modest mistakes . . . and simply ineffective treatments that appear to have done neither good nor harm, but only expended public funds. None of these programs was undertaken in the spirit of playing

with people's lives, yet they affected the lives of a larger number of people at a considerably greater cost than experimental programs would have done." Experimentation is prescribed as an antidote to overselling by those who cater to
putative beneficiaries of a program. Moreover, it puts a check
on administrators who cover up the defects of weak programs. Thus, Stanley (1972, p. 69) advocates strong designs
because "powerful methods can yield results from which the
administrator may have no place to hide."

Although some support for evaluations comes from
conservatives who oppose public spending and new services,
those who favor strong designs generally advocate vigorous
attack on social problems. The conservatism of these evaluators is best articulated by Campbell (1975b): Existing institutional arrangements have emerged from centuries of societal
evolution and have passed pragmatic tests in the process.
Further evolution requires ceaseless innovation, but mutants
are many whereas improvements are few. Constant culling is
required, and early evaluation increases the likelihood that
only genuine improvements will come into regular use. Berk
and Rossi (1976), however, fear that evaluation is undermin-
ing the impulse to seek improvements. The accumulation of
evidence that weak interventions have weak effects or no de-
tectable effects contributes to "a growing sense of social problem intractability" (p. 338).

The methodological conservatism of the experimenta-
lists has a political slant, as is seen in the formulation of impact assessments as tests of null hypotheses. Size of effect is to
be considered only *after* the data show a dependable "treatment effect" (Cook and Campbell, 1979, p. 41; Rossi, Freeman, and Wright, 1979, p. 161). When "no significant difference" is interpreted as a program failure, the burden of
proof is placed on the innovation.

The methodology used in evaluation ought to be hard
boiled, according to Fairweather and Tornatzky (1977):

[It] is most important that a stringent level of
significance be adopted because inferences made

from such an experiment might be used by the
agents of society to instigate social changes. . . .
Since the usual social practice with which the experimental models are compared has been assidu-
ously developed by society's agents over many
years, it would be foolhardy to recommend a
change in the manner society has developed to handle its problem unless a better solution has been
manifestly demonstrated. This suggests that in statistical terms a probability level of at least .05 should
be established as the acceptable level for recom-
mending changes.* . . . It should be adopted because social changes are distasteful to many individuals and should not be recommended unless they
are clearly warranted. The selection of a .05 level of
statistical significance is, however, perfectly arbitrary. The acceptance of any level of significance as
representing the point at which the hypothesis will
be rejected is determined by the weight of many
factors [p. 347].

As Robert Stake points out (personal communication,
1978), the arguments about method are to a significant degree an outcropping of divergent opinions about the complexity of the world. Some social scientists and social planners
believe or hope that straightforward general conclusions can
describe the main features of social processes. They believe
that some treatments or policies are better than others and
that these should become standard practice. For them, standardization is a feature of rational management, not just of
investigation. Other social observers believe that probabilistic
generalizations are almost worthless, since much of what happens is determined by the specifics of a situation and the perceptions of participants. Those who perceive this complexity

---

* The context, calling for one-tailed tests, indicates that Fairweather and Tornatzky advise acting as if the null hypothesis were true
unless the tabled probability for a t or an F falls below .025. An earlier version of these same sentences (Fairweather, 1967, p. 201) had demanded the
.001 level of significance.

fear that authorities who trust a generalization are likely to take Procrustean action.

The evaluator serves one or more political forces. As was pointed out in *Toward Reform,* evaluators help political figures remain in power if they supply them with information that other participants in the political process do not possess, and this may contribute to centralization of power. It should be possible, however, for the evaluator to cast himself as adviser to the entire polity if his information is disseminated and speaks to the concerns of the many constituencies with interests at stake. MacDonald (1976, p. 133) suggests that an evaluator places himself in one of three groups—"autocratic," "democratic," or "bureaucratic"—by the commissions he accepts. (The third category matches a context of command, where a manager has been charged with executing defined plans and needs the evaluator purely as a technician. As *Toward Reform* argues, programs rarely operate in that context, and I neglect it in this book.)

Those pressing for strong designs want the evaluator's role in governance to be large. In MacDonald's phrase, the role they seek is one of "policy validation" or, one might say, policy legitimation. The evaluator offers to certify that a policy, if adopted, will live up to its advertising (or will not). For his report to be strongly persuasive, he must have adopted strong techniques. Also, he must be perceived as impartial, free from political interference and censorship. If a policy question can be defined as empirical, rationalists say hopefully, answers can be certain and decisions can be removed from politics (from the people?). This aspiration, for MacDonald, is "autocratic" (but it seems fairer to say that the intent is to be "authoritative"). If the question the design addresses directly is *the* pivotal question, if the design is powerful enough, and if there is no prospect that the relationship will change from year to year, evaluation might resolve the question. But even if the evaluation achieved that end, to remove a topic from politics by narrowing the issue has a disenfranchising effect because the concerns of some parties are left out of the account.

MacDonald, in discouraging the evaluator from taking an autocratic stance, is typical of the humanistic school. Studying the political function of evaluation, my colleagues and I in the Stanford Evaluation Consortium reached a similar judgment. In a pluralistic system, different participants will weigh facts differently, and too many questions arise for definitive evidence to be collected. Facts affect the participants' negotiations, but the fate of the program is never removed from politics. The democratic evaluator therefore should help each participant to judge the legitimacy of the policy; focusing on a predefined question may push into the background what would be most pertinent to some of the parties.

Humanistic evaluators see a large payoff in what the community learns firsthand during the evaluation; some see this as more important than the learning that comes from the evaluator's reports. Robert Stake (personal communication, 1978) suggests this contrast: The scientist sees the rank and file as suppliers of data and as an audience awaiting what he distills from the data; the humanist is a teacher who turns the rank and file into investigators. They are to refine their perceptions without the aid of an intermediary or authority. Evaluation and use of evaluation thus become a communal process. This approach minimizes the role of power and expertise.

Should Inquiry Be Targeted? On the one hand, a communication system can send out many bits of information in a fixed time, accepting the risk that a comparatively large fraction of the message will be lost in transmission or garbled. To communicate with minimum loss and distortion, on the other hand, the communicator has to make his message simple and the transmission redundant. Neither represents the ideal; a balance between bandwidth and fidelity is wanted (Shannon and Weaver, 1949). In research the term *fidelity* refers to the dependability of an answer to a particular question. The term *bandwidth* refers to the number of questions for which an answer is offered, whether dependable or not. Focusing all resources on one limited message improves fidelity. That is the reason for making the SOS message highly redundant: nothing but the cry for help and the all-important map coordinates of the ship, over and over.

Distributing resources over possible questions, an evaluator strikes a balance between focus and diffusion. A narrow investigation provides a peak amount of information on one question. On other questions it provides tangential information that reduces uncertainty slightly. About the remaining matters, it does not reduce uncertainty at all. The report therefore has high fidelity on some point. A wide-band inquiry spreads attention more uniformly, yielding information of medium fidelity on most matters. As bandwidth increases, fidelity drops. At some threshold the evaluation planner becomes unwilling to reduce further the fidelity of evidence on major questions for the sake of learning a small amount about some minor ones.

In later chapters I use the term *reproducibility* in place of the metaphoric *fidelity*. When the design is so structured and the sample so large that two persons carrying out the same study would reach the same conclusion, the conclusion on the operationally specified question can be taken as definitive. When a study speaks to several questions, each answer has its own degree of reproducibility. A premium on reproducibility is warranted when certain well-defined questions are of overriding importance, but ordinarily it makes sense to reduce uncertainty about a larger number of issues, many of which are loosely defined. Strong tests of hypotheses are intended to ensure reproducibility. By standardizing treatment and by reporting only "significant" relations, the designs limit bandwidth. Few resources go into the recording of variables and events that do not enter into the hypothesis. Moreover, some descriptions of the ideal experiment suggest specifying plans so exhaustively that the study could be executed by aides who scrupulously followed the detailed guidelines; no place is left for exploring what is not anticipated.

Naturalistic investigators spread resources widely over treatment, process, and outcome variables, and they sift subsets of data for patterns. They report and interpret relations that are not statistically significant. That is, they opt for band-width and sometimes accept dubious reproducibility. Though a scientistic evaluator prefers to narrow an inquiry for the sake of reproducibility, a formal experiment can be broad. Testing multiple hypotheses, as in a factorial design, increases bandwidth. A person concerned with many outcomes of several treatment variants on many demographic subgroups or types of community could in principle build each comparison into a randomized design.

The choice between bandwidth and fidelity arises in reporting as well as in data collection. At one extreme, what the study learned can be compressed to fit into a headline. At the opposite extreme, a narrative report (or a film) tries to give the reader a vicarious experience that will allow her to arrive at a personal interpretation of the observations. Insofar as the evaluation plan has reduced the bandwidth of the data, the report is sure to be focused. The converse does not hold. A wide-band inquiry can be brought to as pointed a conclusion as a narrow inquiry.

In traditional writings on psychological research methods, the investigator is advised to design a study with high fidelity to settle a sharp question. These ideas have strongly influenced writings on evaluation. I came to a contrary view thirty years ago, as I considered the multiscore tests then coming into use for measuring aptitude profiles and for appraising personality. When a test devotes an hour to checking on a dozen aspects of an individual, no one of its findings can have the precision of a test that concentrates an equal effort on measuring one aspect. In applied measurement it is often appropriate to sacrifice some fidelity to increase bandwidth; the balance depends on the specifics of the problem. I take the same position here (for earlier statements see Cronbach, 1954, or Cronbach and Gleser, 1957).

In 1952 Allen Edwards and I carried the discussion over to the design of experiments for one kind of evaluation. We had been invited to speak to clinical psychologists on testing the effectiveness of psychotherapeutic procedures. Edwards, author of a text on experimental design in psychology, stressed controls and parsimony. I argued that formal testing of null hypotheses failed to make the most of the data. Testing a prespecified hypothesis is an appropriate way to hold enthusiasm for a therapeutic method in check, but open-ended study of successes and failures brings out more provocative hints. What kinds of patients a method serves well, and where the treatment goes awry, should be examined. The point of the story, however, is not that Edwards and I disagreed when preparing our talks independently but that we could agree in the end. E. Lowell Kelly, the chairman of the symposium, persuaded us to join our papers under a single title and joint authorship, toning down contentious sentences without discarding content. Each of us could in good conscience sign the final version because each of us appreciated what the other advocated. (See Edwards and Cronbach, 1952.)

The usual emphasis on strict and precise inferences found in advice to social scientists is tempered in a statement for evaluators by the statistician Walter Deming, who foreshadows my argument in Chapter Four. Writing on "the logic of evaluation," Deming (1975) emphasizes causal interpretation and finds virtue in strong designs—and then turns to their pitfalls: "The most important lesson we can learn about statistical methods in evaluation is that circumstances where one may depend wholly on statistical inference are rare (p. 55). Statistical inference in an analytic [causally oriented] problem is most effective when it is presented as conclusions valid for the frame studied and for the range of environmental conditions specified for the tests. . . . Other conditions may well be encountered (p. 62). Extreme accuracy in an analytic study is wasted effort" (p. 65).

Deming goes on to say that an overwhelming outcome difference in an experiment may justify a decision in favor of the winner but that a modest difference cannot provide a firm basis for decision because an experiment almost invariably leaves important variables out of account. Similarly, Gilbert and Mosteller (1972, p. 376), even as they campaign for strong designs, recognize that interactions can undercut conclusions about the main effect of a treatment contrast: "When the same treatment under controlled conditions produces good results in many places and circumstances, then we become confident that we have found a general rule. When the payoff is finicky—gains in one place, losses in another—we are wary because we can't count on the effect."

Social action, Deming says, always relates to situations, treatments, measures, and/or populations other than those of the direct investigation. Two questions lead one away from direct reliance on the experimental result. Is the treatment truly fixed? If not, it can possibly be adapted on the basis of an understanding of its effects. Second, is it possible that the treatment interacts with characteristics of clients, the institutional setting, or other conditions? As Deming says, only an expert in the subject matter can deny that a change in one of these respects will make little difference in the outcome. Once these questions are raised, the evaluator finds it important to look within the treatment and within the population to identify differentiated effects. When contentious rhetoric is put aside, it appears that everyone wants to make predictions that reach beyond the fixed experimental situation and wants both bandwidth and fidelity to some degree.

Should Treatment Conditions Be Standardized? In field research one uses whatever sites and participants come conveniently to hand, draws a representative or deliberately diverse sample, or selects a near-uniform set. The researcher lets treatments take their natural course or specifies exactly what service is to be delivered. Standardization appeals to the experimentalist, outcome-oriented investigator. For him, tampering with a treatment in midtrial—even to make it work— spoils the experiment. Natural variation in events from unit to unit makes interpretation equivocal; the treatment should be fixed. Freeman (1964, p. 194) would have the evaluator "remain within the environment, like a snarling watchdog ready to oppose alterations in program and procedures that would render his evaluation efforts useless." The humanist is skeptical of standardization of social interventions and services, and doubly skeptical of attempts to make them standard for the sake of investigation. To do so is to lose the natural variety of human response that he finds most instructive.

The Fisherian model of experimentation identifies a limited number of factors believed to be causally significant and crosses them to define cells (for example, seed 3 and fertilizer level b). All plots of land assigned to that cell are treated the same way with respect to the control variables. Factors not specified for control, such as slope and orientation of terrain, are allowed to vary. Fisherian designs are not much seen in evaluation, but Fisherian control is often held up as an ideal. Thus, in *Social Experimentation* (Riecken and Boruch, 1974) we read that "the most important variables will be treated factorially if possible, and . . . *they must be* if causal inferences about their effects are sought" (p. 68; italics added). Cook and Campbell (1979, p. 43) value strict control for another reason: "Lack of standardization both within and between persons [delivering services] will inflate error variance and decrease the chance of obtaining true differences. The threat . . . can be most obviously controlled by [making] the treatment . . . as standard as possible across occasions of implementation."

But doubts about standardization arise even among the experimentally minded. I shall later quote Fisher himself in favor of *not* standardizing any variable save the main ones. Cook and Campbell (1979, p. 65) favor controlled diversity: "There is really no substitute for deliberately varying two or three exemplars of a treatment, *where possible*." Their example is a study of the effect of a communication delivered by prestigious communicators. Only the use of several prestigious figures, each with a different subgroup, gives confidence that a result is attributable to the general variable of prestige and not to the unique characteristics of a lone communicator. Although the tradition is to standardize measuring operations, they too may be chosen with an eye to representativeness and diversity. Cook and Campbell (1979, pp. 66–80, 366) call for observing diverse treatment realizations, subjects, and indicators of outcome for the same reason that Gilbert and Mosteller (1972) wanted to check out a program in many localities.

To get diversity one may reach out for maximally dissimilar instances or draw a representative and, hence, mixed, sample. Brunswik (1956) introduced "representative design" as an alternative to laboratory controls. Research on perception, Brunswik thought, could well ask the subject to judge targets sampled from her everyday environment—instead of asking her to judge squares of standard size and uniform color, presented at a standard distance under standard illumination. In the natural environment, some variables tend to be associated. The Fisherian design "unties" the variables to form unnatural situations. This can be good science, but it can also lead to false interpretations.

An unsophisticated evaluator assessing grouping of grade school students by ability would standardize by requiring fast, slow, and mixed class sections to study the same arithmetic lessons, thus holding constant all variables but one. The evaluator who accepts the Fisherian ideal would create at least two standard treatments, one easy and one difficult. If naive, he would form unnatural cells—for example, he would require some of the slow sections to struggle with difficult lessons. The Brunswikian would avoid such constraints and would instead look at naturally occurring events (Snow, 1974). He would like to know what happens when teachers' decisions about content and pace of lessons produce a correlation between the treatment and student ability—"confounding them," a Fisherian would say. Accepting a rationale similar to that of Brunswikians, sociologists such as Kish (1975) value the realism and representativeness of survey research. The sociologist would find it reasonable to correlate the school-by-school averages of fourth graders on a statewide achievement test with principals' descriptions of the grouping practices in their respective schools.

Even experimenters concerned with a fixed national policy (with guidelines regulating bilingual instruction, for example) may consider it useful to observe what happens when the fixed directive is implemented by staff members in typical sites. The experimenter could not hope to ensure that every site will follow the directive in every particular; and if he could cause that to happen, the situation would be unnatural. Does it really make sense for the applied scientist to investigate a standard treatment that is unlikely to operate once the investigator's pressure for compliance is removed? Or should he permit, and collect data on, the heterogeneous interpretations that schools place on the directive under normal operating conditions?

The evaluator can choose a plan anywhere in the range from the fully reproducible, fully controlled artificial study to the essentially opportunistic naturalistic study. In the Violence study to be described in Chapter Two, the sponsor envisioned using an ecologically representative sample of the schools wanting to act at that time to reduce violence and fear. The treatment was not controlled; the team in each school was to act as it thought appropriate in *its* school under the prevailing circumstances. The set of teams thus provided a cross section of what could be expected if violence-plagued schools in general were encouraged, nondirectively, to take action. Another planner, seeking tighter control, might have tried to persuade every experimental team to adopt the same highly specified plan for dealing with violence and fear, or he might have tried to sell distinct plans to equivalent groups of schools. Whether the controlled treatment could later be put in place as an operating program would depend on its appeal to program operators and clients and on the extent to which a policy officer would be able to command obedience.

Standardization of data collection fosters objectivity, but humanists prize subjective information. Typically, they want the observer to pick out events he considers significant and to filter what he observes through his conceptual system. Great value is placed on the observations and interpretations of participants. The approach that ethnographers take to distant cultures has recently commanded the enthusiasm of humanistic evaluators. The ethnographer sets out to comprehend how the native observer apprehends events; he tries to set aside his preconceptions and categories in order to register the mental world of the informant. This approach to evaluation reflects several themes of the humanists. First, no outsider can specify in advance what is important to observe. Second, only the person affected by the program knows what is important to her, and each person's values should be treated respectfully. Finally, even though the intervention may have a fixed plan, it is interpretations by program staff and clients that determine the outcomes. What is important, then, cannot be manipulated, standardized, objectified, or quantified.

Toward a Sophisticated Differentiation

The contrast with which this discussion began is now seen to refer to views on a number of aspects of research planning and reporting. A person with a scientistic viewpoint will prefer preplanning, focusing, standardization, quantification, and controls; a humanistically oriented evaluator will lean toward greater openness. But few individuals would adopt either style for every aspect of an investigation, and none would insist on applying a uniform style to all studies.

Speaking of experiments and naturalistic case studies as polar opposites is a rhetorical device; evaluation planning is not a matter of choosing between irreconcilables. It almost always makes sense to impose control on some aspects of data collection when treatments are naturalistic and to do some naturalistic observation when the treatment plan is elaborately controlled. The balance between the styles will vary from one subquestion to the next and may well shift (in either direction) after early evaluation activities change the evaluator's sense of the job to be done. Experimental control is not incompatible with attention to qualitative information or subjective interpretation, nor is open-minded exploration incompatible with objectification of evidence.

Campbell (1975a, p. 10) makes a positive recommendation: Evaluations with strong designs should also "attempt to systematically tap all the qualitative commonsense program critiques and evaluations that have been generated among the program staff, program clients and their families, and community observers. . . . Where such evaluations are contrary to the quantitative results, the quantitative results should be regarded as suspect until the reasons for the discrepancy are well understood. Neither is infallible, of course. But for many of us, what needs to be emphasized is that the quantitative results may be as mistaken as the qualitative." Campbell goes on to lament the polarization he sees in American evaluation practice, where sponsors have sometimes opted for an anthropological study of an innovation and sometimes for a formal quantitative assessment, but not for the evaluation in which the two kinds of activities support each other.

Evaluators need not—in fact, they should not—decide which school of thought they "belong to." Something is gained when an evaluation becomes more objective, more reproducible, more concentrated. Something else is gained when the evaluation becomes more phenomenological, more flexible, broader in its coverage. The choices should differ from evaluation to evaluation. The considerations that should enter into such choices are the subject of this book. The next chapter illustrates some concrete choices that were made, or could have been made, in three evaluations. These examples illustrate how the superficial question of effect size becomes elaborated into a nearly endless array of questions, and how qualitative information enriches even highly structured experimental comparisons.

2

❧ Three Illustrative Studies

This chapter describes three studies. The design of each will be placed within a full context; specific design decisions described here will be used later to illustrate general arguments.

The first study—which I shall call the Nutrition study —was directed by Robert Klein at the Institute for Nutrition of Central America and Panama (INCAP). It sought to test whether providing a protein supplement to expectant mothers and young children would improve the children's intellectual performance as they grew. The second example—to be referred to as the Physics study—evaluated the curriculum prepared by Harvard Project Physics for use in high schools. The final example—the Violence study—is hypothetical. Though suggested by an actual program of investigation, it is a free interpretation of a possible design, not an account of events. The research is being carried out in stages, and at each stage the design is reconsidered. To bring out certain issues, I have constructed a fictionalized single stage of investigation.

Various considerations led me to select these examples. The studies are reasonably compact in their agendas, and their topics are dissimilar. All three assigned units randomly between two treatment groups, yet the questions that were of interest ranged far beyond the experimental contrast. In each example we have what Boruch (1975) calls "quasi-experiments-within-experiments." Each example, moreover, points up the function of case studies of sites. The Violence study exemplifies the messy contemporary projects that defy conventional analysis, and it shows the difficulty in drawing conclusions from free-form events.

I had good opportunities to learn about these inquiries. For the INCAP study, I was one of many consultants on design and analysis. My responsibility was slight, but I did gain much understanding of the thinking behind the choices that the staff made. I had no role in Harvard Project Physics, but over many years I had correspondence and discussions with Wayne Welch, Herbert Walberg, and Robert Bridgham of the project staff, and I have also been able to use the unpublished report of the study. I was formerly a consultant to the Social Action Research Center, the contractor conducting the actual Violence study, and have had an excellent opportunity to see the problems through the eyes of Joan and Douglas Grant of that agency. (I thank Klein, Walberg, and the Grants for comments on a draft of this chapter.)

I shall criticize the design choices that were made in these three studies, but I intend the criticism as fair comment, not complaint. Judgment enters, and to judge differently is not to suggest that the original judgment was indefensible. Since there are few or no rules of design, a design can rarely be called "right" or "wrong." The two studies to be described veridically were carried out by qualified persons, and some decisions that I question were supported at the time by first-rank consultants.

INCAP Nutrition Study

The INCAP study is closer to a basic research project than to an evaluation of a prototype for an operational program. The field activities that were set up to permit an intensive longitudinal study would not be cost-effective as a large-scale, lasting intervention (Klein and others, 1976, p. 315). In retrospect, the procedure was said to be "not very successful as an effort to treat populations" (Yarbrough and others, 1978, pp. 204–205). Most children in the experimental sites received only a modest fraction of the supplementary calories (100 or more each day) that would have provided a good level of nutrition. Nonetheless, the study is significant for practice. The parametric information it offers would be of value in designing a practical intervention (and in designing *its* evaluation). The aspects of design and analysis to be discussed here would be relevant also in evaluating an operational program of nutritional supplementation. My general overview is closely in line with that of Klein (1979); I rely also on personal communication and several research papers from INCAP.

Social Experimentation (Riecken and Boruch, 1974, p. 16) held up the Nutrition study as a shining illustration of the use of randomization to test a sharp causal hypothesis: "that protein supplements in the diets of pregnant women and preschool children can reduce or eliminate retardation in cognitive ability at school age. . . . The experiment seeks to disentangle the effects of the nutritional and health variables per se from the sociocultural."

The investigators (for example, Freeman and others, 1977, p. 234) speak of the design as a moderately well-controlled quasi-experiment. However, the controlled assignment of units that was carried out plays little part in the arguments these authors used to reach their conclusions. The inquiry is perhaps not best described as a quasi-experiment. I see it as a set of four parallel case studies with controlled collection of data and largely quantitative analysis. The design changed as the study progressed, and the questions under

study were reshaped as the analysis went forward. The variables at the center of attention in the published papers are
not those the experimenter controlled, the analysis is essentially correlational, and many of the statistical comparisons
rely on post hoc matching. The fact that the study is hard to
label is not a sign of inadequacy; rather, it underscores the
inadvisability of judging investigations by their labels. The
data collection and analysis of the INCAP study were intri-
cate, and the legitimacy of any inference has to be judged by
tracing *its* logic, not by examining whether the underlying design of the study approached some ideal.

Treatments Contrasted. In the mid-1960s, a number of
studies in less developed countries had shown that children's
performance on mental tests was correlated with the apparent adequacy or inadequacy of their diets. The evidence
was equivocal because test scores and diet both correlated
with socioeconomic status. Although the INCAP study
sought to assess whether a food supplement would improve
ability, the intent was never to give a yes-or-no answer. The
concern was to understand as much as possible of the interplay among nutrition, age, health, social stimulation, physical
growth, and performance on diverse tests.

Experts had come to think that protein deficiency impairs intellectual development. To test the idea, an experiment was mounted under the auspices of the Pan-American
Health Organization with assistance from the U.S. National
Institutes of Health. A sizable experimental group in Guatemala was to be supplied protein-rich *atole* (a Pablum-like
gruel). Roughly three years of preliminary discussion, pilot
testing, site selection, and instrument development went on
prior to intervention in the main sites in 1969.

To supply the food under conditions that would permit an exact record of who took what amount of it, a public
health station was staffed in each of four *aldeas*—small, isolated villages. The researchers were aware that the medical
services provided by the stations might influence learning
ability; also, the social stimulation of a village meeting place
was seen as possibly affecting a child's development. It was

therefore thought necessary to set up stations in control villages. To encourage control mothers and children to visit
these stations regularly, the investigators decided to offer
them a food supplement—but one low in protein. Two *aldeas*
received this control treatment, and two received the experimental treatment. A medical-care-only control was once projected for two additional *aldeas,* but this was judged not to be
the best use of funds.

The decision to provide social stimulation rather than
"no treatment" was the first of several steps in defining the
treatment contrast. One design proposed was along the classic lines of "holding all variables constant save one." The control stations were to make available a gruel physically similar
to the experimental *atole* but lacking in protein. This plan was
dropped, one factor in the decision being the difficulty of devising a low-protein substitute that closely resembled the *atole.*
The next plan was to provide control villagers with a calorie-
free soft drink sweetened with cyclamates. The social stimulation that the children received at the station would thus not
be confounded with a change in nutrition. Just at this time,
however, cyclamates were exposed as a possible hazard to
health; the investigators therefore switched to sugar. The actual control treatment was a drink called *fresco*—a sweet, col-
ored, low-calorie drink with no protein. Available nutritional
theory was the basis for the seemingly illogical decision to
confound presence of protein with richness in calories. Caloric content of the *fresco* had to be held down because, according to this theory, persons given plentiful carbohydrates
could utilize, as protein, substances in the normal diet that
would otherwise have been converted to energy; in that
event, the protein-free supplement would have had an effect
similar to that of increased protein supply. Impoverished
though it was in nutrients, *fresco* was an ethically acceptable
treatment because it provided the control subjects with calories that they otherwise would not have had. (Both the *atole*
and the *fresco* were enriched with vitamins and minerals. In
view of what I said in Chapter One about fixed treatments, it
is worth noting that in the third year of the study both for-

mulas were changed by addition of, for example, fluoride. This was taken into account in analyses.)

The food was available twice a day to any resident who came to a center, but data were collected only on mothers and young children. A person could have as many cups of *atole* or *fresco* as he or she wished. Mothers were encouraged to drop into the centers to take a cup of *atole* or *fresco,* to chat, and to supply data. The center was the site for regular assessment of the children's physical and intellectual development. A mother who made little use of the center was requested to come in when a test or physical examination for her child's birth cohort was due.

Active intervention made the study more valuable than a study of variation within prevailing diets would have been. Extending the range of nutritional intake within the community, the intervention brought out more clearly how developmental variables depended on food intake. If anything justifies referring to this project as an experiment rather than as an intervention, it is that, of the four similar villages, two were assigned at random to receive *atole* and two to receive *fresco.* Activities of program personnel—nurses, doctors, psychological testers—and the physical facilities of the stations were equated across *aldeas.* Therefore, on the assumption that experimental and control subjects would come to the centers with equal frequency on average, the design equalized the amount and character of social stimulation, including contact with cosmopolitan visitors and testers.

Sample Selection and Data Collection. The *aldeas* represented a narrowly specified type of community. More than a dozen rules were set up to define the population of eligible *aldeas.* (For example, at least 80 percent of the homes had to be within a radius of 1,000 meters of the center; at least 80 percent of the residents had to have been born in the vicinity; and there had to be less than 2 percent annual migration.) Screening on a few variables reduced the census list of all communities to a roster of 179 villages to be visited. In the 45 villages passing that screen, a census was made. The 10 villages that met all criteria were then studied further to identify a nearly matched set of four well-separated villages. (Even this sifting did not produce true homogeneity. Psychological tests given to rather small samples of five- and six-year-olds showed significant village-to-village differences, but different villages came out ahead on different tests. The investigators were aware of differences in gene pool, diet, and culture.)

Quality control of the data was exceptional. The supplements were analyzed chemically from time to time to ensure stability. The care with which station personnel recorded attendance and food intake was checked each week, and a monthly refresher course reviewed the procedures to be followed. Similarly, staff members collecting anthropometric data carried out exercises each month to make sure that all were adhering to the same standards. Moreover, 10 percent of the anthropometric data were checked by remeasurement. A similar degree of control was applied to other data sources.

Lengthy home interviews covered practices and history related to health, eating, childrearing, work, income, and so on. An anthropologist observed the communities and their reception of the center's services. Several intellectual processes were measured, most by more than one procedure. This proved to be worthwhile. The original hunch was that a physiological intervention would have its greatest effect on simple processes. But the tests showing the largest association with the nutritional variable (at ages three and four) turned out to be the tests of vocabulary and inference. No one had thought that a complex process such as the drawing of inferences would be particularly responsive to biological development, but fortunately it had been measured.

According to the literature of the 1960s, the preschool years are the critical period of intellectual growth, and the original plans stressed tests at ages four to six. Just one battery, largely psychomotor, was scheduled at six, fifteen, and twenty-four months. While the study was in progress, however, some new psychological research drew the attention of investigators to developmentally important intellectual processes of infants. Klein and his associates decided to test cognitive processes during the second six months of life and also to test behavior just after birth.

Analysis and Interpretation. The experimental treatment consisted of setting up the center, offering *atole* or *fresco,* and giving tests. The treatment delivered was an amount of food, which depended on the mother's (or child's) interest. To compare six-year-olds in *atole* villages with those in *fresco* villages would be the logical end point of the random-assignment design. That would be a fair summative comparison of the two interventions, but it would not be a sound comparison of the benefits *from extra food.* Food intake was subject to self-selection.

That kind of simple comparison would be even less a test of the protein hypothesis. The *atole/fresco* contrast of villages confounded protein/no-protein with high/low caloric intake and with village characteristics. If the original experimental contrast had dominated the analysis, however, it seems certain that a positive overall result would have led readers to conclude that added *protein* makes a difference.

The treatment operated at the community level. The supplement was fed to individuals, but intellectual growth was presumably affected by the degree of stimulation that the child's village provided. Even though 1,550 children were observed as they developed, the study was limited to two realizations of each treatment. That is, the number per treatment was two units. (To conduct the intensive study with additional villages would have been prohibitively costly.) Over the years, uncontrolled aspects of the realization were noted. For example:

- The staff members who greeted mothers at the centers differed in their ability to establish rapport. Attendance varied correspondingly.
- In the neighborhood of one station, political disaffection developed, with some antigovernment guerrilla activity. This might have affected mothers' participation in the government-approved study.
- One *aldea* experienced a very poor harvest. With greater

hunger during the next winter, attendance at its center
rose.
- During the summer the *fresco* was attractive. Boys frequently came to the station for it without their mothers.
Girls were less venturesome.

The first two of these could be considered accidents of
sampling; whatever influence they had *could* have happened
with either treatment. In a random experiment with forty
aldeas rather than only four, such influences would have
nearly averaged out over treatments. In the actual Nutrition
study, however, the last two interacted with treatment to generate or limit attendance: The *fresco* had power to draw
overheated boys, and the *atole* to draw hungry mothers. Randomization did not protect against this threat to valid interpretation.

The earliest analysis of data came after a considerable
number of women in the study had given birth. It was found
that average birth weights of the children of *atole* and *fresco*
mothers did not differ when mothers with similar caloric intake were compared. This observation led to an analysis of
the home diets and to belated recognition that diets in the region were far more seriously deficient in calories than in protein. In consequence, caloric supplementation became the
major "independent" variable. It was decided to control statistically on supplementary calories received (whether in the
form of *atole* or *fresco*). To control on total food intake would
have made better theoretical sense, but mothers' reports of
food consumed at home were inaccurate and could not be relied on in this way. Supplementary intake was accurately recorded. The controlled variable protein/no-protein dropped
into the background. The observation that regressions of
outcome variables on level of supplementation were much
the same in all four villages seemed to justify minimizing the
status of *atole/fresco* as "treatment variable."

The assessments of infant performance introduced in
midstudy may in the end prove to be highly important for interpretation of the study, since the early analyses (Klein,

1979) indicate that only supplements to the mother, given prenatally, affect the child's intellectual performance; the child's own intake has little or no such effect. This conclusion rests on contrasts among temporal patterns of attendance and food intake that were not under experimental control. Recognition of the interaction of treatment with age represents a radical reorientation of the study. There was also an interaction of supplement with socioeconomic status. Neither the theoretical nor the practical implications of such findings are like those of a main effect for food intake.

Although the design of this research is integrated, its analyses are multiple and diverse in style. Subsets of cases and measures are sliced out of the data and entered into whatever sort of cross-tabulation, regression analysis, or correlation will bear on a specific hypothesis or counterinterpretation. This is almost in line with the somewhat propagandistic remark of Cook and Campbell (1979, p. 56): "With quasi-experimental groups, . . . instead of relying on randomization to rule out most internal validity threats, the investigator has to make all the threats explicit and then rule them out one by one. His task is, therefore, more laborious. It is also less enviable since his final causal inference will not be as strong as if he had conducted a randomized experiment." A randomized experiment *was* conducted here; but supplementary hypotheses came to the forefront of attention, as they do in most experiments with alert observers. Only the process of reasoning from many angles permitted a persuasive interpretation.

The papers from INCAP lump all cases together, ignoring village boundaries and treatment boundaries. For example, on one main hypothesis, the analysis of the composite ability score is summarized as in Table 1. This comparison is correlational. The logic is the same as in the study correlating economic success at age thirty with completion/noncompletion of high school—a study that Campbell and Stanley (1963, p. 240) condemned as inadequately controlled. In the Nutrition study, to attribute higher test scores to more food, it is necessary to argue that Group 0 was equivalent to Groups

Table 1. Mean Ability of Four-Year-Olds in Relation to Level of Food Supplementation

Group	Intake of Food Supplement	Number of Children	Mean on Ability Scale ("Cognitive Composite")
0	Low	215	−17.53
1	Intermediate	241	56.52
2	High	31	67.87

Pooled SD: 291.50
$F = 4.08$; significance level 0.025

Source: Klein and others, 1977, p. 106.

1 and 2 in all respects except food intake. Attendance at the center had its own causes, and these could also have influenced development. Foreseeing this complaint, the investigators carried out tighter analyses, matching groups on socioeconomic status as well as on food intake. (Elaborate regression analyses were also made; these too embody a matching logic.) The trend held up because, as it happened, there was a slight tendency for supplementary food intake to be negatively associated with social class in the sample (and with food intake in the home). Children in Groups 1 and 2 evidently did not come from more nurturing and educative homes. The experimental-manipulation feature of the study did nothing to protect it from this counterhypothesis. Had the well-to-do chosen to visit the centers frequently, the causal explanation would have been little clearer than similar explanations in the uncontrolled correlational studies of the 1960s.

   A reader who does not believe that food supplementation improved ability is still at liberty to question the comparability of the groups. In most studies of this kind, a challenge to the reliability of the socioeconomic classification would weaken the inference; but the exceptional care taken in assessing background in the Nutrition study makes it unlikely that such a challenge to these data would stick. The rich data will enable the investigators to check out almost any alternative explanation that a critic may later think of. It might be suggested, for example, that social stimulation from attendance at the center was the significant factor. But food intake and attendance did not correlate perfectly, so the investigators can use regression analysis to counter that criticism. From the standpoint of program evaluation, the ambiguity in identifying the cause might not be highly important anyway. If setting up such centers in most *aldeas* were a practical social option, finding that benefits are associated with participation would be enough to tilt the scale. Action would not await a conclusion as to whether the "cause" is food or stimulation.

One further substudy—a within-family comparison—requires mention because Klein and his colleagues (1977, p. 116) call it "the strongest evidence ever gathered for a direct and causal link between malnutrition and deficient mental development." Mothers who received supplementation during each of two pregnancies were singled out. A contrast was made between the child whose birth was preceded by the greater intake of supplement and the other child (who might have been born earlier or later). This was a purely "correlational" analysis, which Cook and Campbell (1979, pp. 99, 128) class as "one of the least interpretable" designs. The design, however, might be classed as an interrupted time-series with some counterbalance of order. This design, we are told, stands up well against the threats usual in time-series designs (Cook and Campbell, 1976, p. 274; 1979, p. 207). It is worth noting that experimental intervention was not needed to produce this "strongest evidence." The same comparison could in principle be made by recording mothers' diets in a village where there was no supplementary feeding. Convincing reasoning about causation, then, may be possible in almost any kind of design. Once more we see the limitations of a classification system that leads to appraisal, in the abstract, of some types of design as excellent and others as defective. The INCAP papers refer to many cross-checks and chains of reasoning similar to those I have summarized. It is this painstaking, creative mixture that will win acceptance for the investigators' interpretations or expose their data to counterinterpretation.

Villages as Units. Recognizing a collective unit is necessary in many evaluations. In this study the research team originally thought of individuals as the units treated, and the published analyses have followed that lead. However, if village characteristics differ, we must say that the forty-eight-month data came from four cases, not 487; the F test cited in Table 1 then becomes pointless. Village-by-village case studies were planned; these would use qualitative observations to make sense of differences across villages. (But costs of publication may keep these anthropological reports forever buried in files.)

Where village factors make a difference, significance levels based on the pooled data are false. I would favor a separate regression analysis in each *aldea*. Suppose that the *atole/fresco* distinction is set aside. Then the null hypothesis takes this form: "In the hypothetical population of treated *aldeas* of which these four are considered to be a random sample, the median of the regression coefficients is zero." Imagine that a test score is regressed on food intake, and coefficients for all four villages are found to be positive. Under the null hypothesis, this result (four heads in four tosses) is expected to occur with probability .125; hence, the sample finding cannot reach significance. Even with a more powerful statistical technique, it is unreasonable to hope that a study of four villages could establish formal statistical significance for the generalization. A test of significance within a village would count children as degrees of freedom, but it would have little meaning because the children in that fixed village were not sampled from a larger population and did not respond independently to the treatment. The verdict on the study derives from the persuasiveness of the total body of data, not from the significance tests.

Descriptive analyses might change considerably if distinctions were made between (1) analysis within each village, (2) a between-village analysis, and (3) the pooled analysis that the papers now report. Some important conclusions drawn by Freeman and colleagues (1977, p. 238; 1980) rest on small differences among correlations in the pooled analysis. My experience with multilevel analysis suggests that correlations computed at level 1 would very likely tell a different story.

Although the papers on the Nutrition study seem to generalize not only over villages in Guatemala but over developing countries as a whole, the investigators are aware that this is hazardous. Having reported the seeming unimportance of protein intake for certain developmental variables, they note: "In other populations with other diets, however, the situation might be entirely different. The best supplement for one population might not necessarily be the best for another; indeed, it might even be harmful rather than beneficial" (Klein and others, 1976, p. 304).

Physics Study

High school physics was withering on the vine in 1957; texts and curricula were stale, and few students elected the course. In the wake of *Sputnik,* the Physical Science Study Committee (PSSC) developed a course of study that emphasized up-to-date theories and the supporting research. According to some observers, however, the PSSC course was so difficult that its adoption was contributing to a further decline in physics enrollments. Thus, in 1963 Gerald Holton and Fletcher Watson obtained funds to attempt to develop a more popular alternative, one with a humanistic emphasis. Harvard Project Physics (HPP) was an attempt to reach able students who did not see themselves as prospective scientists and to present science as a way of knowing, of living, and of social progress. HPP stressed the history of science more than other courses in physics did, and it stressed theory and calculations less.

HPP was planned to be realized in a variety of ways. The teacher was offered key materials—a text, plans for laboratory activities, supplementary readings, and so on. Although text chapters were to be taught in a fixed order, the teacher was encouraged to use the materials selectively and creatively, emphasizing the aspects of the course content—humanistic or experimental—that she considered appropriate to the class. A unit for evaluation and research was installed in HPP. (The evaluation is described by Welch, 1971, and by Welch, Walberg, and Watson, 1970; a limited but more accessible account appears in Welch and Walberg, 1972.) The work got under way when national funding agencies were just beginning to ask for formal evaluations of innovative efforts, and the design was developed by the staff with little or no dictation by the sponsors.

The investigators took seriously the frontier statements on design in curriculum evaluation. At that time formative and summative evaluations were seen as separate enterprises. Accordingly, the HPP evaluation had two phases. A formative study during the pilot run of the course collected detailed information of various types and supplied it to the writing team. This information was also used in planning the experimental trial. A formal experiment was conducted in the academic year 1967–68, the final year of the project budget, to appraise the effectiveness of HPP. The HPP formative evaluation was in line with recommendations I had made (Cronbach, 1963). I say little about that evaluation here because, in a limited space, it would be difficult to draw implications for other projects from the fluid, project-specific experience of evaluating HPP. The summative evaluation did its best to realize the ideals of Scriven (1967) and Campbell and Stanley (1963), within a budget of less than $50,000 (apart from program operations). Because of that effort, the study attracted considerable attention among evaluators and has been held up as a model. Gilbert, Light, and Mosteller (1975, p. 84) and the authors of *Social Experimentation* (Riecken and Boruch, 1974, p. 305) were enamored of the experimental plan; their accounts of the study are not entirely in line with my differently motivated description.

The summative findings were disseminated only to a limited extent. The main posttest data were collected in 1968. Brief articles appeared in journals during the next year or so, but the documented reports from the main study were complex research analyses, not evaluative statements for consumers. (The belated 1972 article by Welch and Walberg is an exception.) The publisher's advertisements for the finished course have included succinct statements about positive findings. The investigators intended a book-length presentation of the evaluation; and, by 1969, although the project had ended and the investigators had scattered to new jobs, a reasonably complete monograph had been assembled. Efforts to find a publisher failed. A lengthy report made to the sponsor was withheld from circulation, perhaps because hope of finding a publisher persisted; I am indebted to Wayne Welch for a copy of the manuscript.

The summative experiment, then, seems not to have had much influence on science education. In retrospect, it is hard to believe that experimental findings—whatever they might have been—could have halted or delayed publication of the HPP materials. Disastrously bad test results would perhaps have discouraged publication of the materials in the version tried out; but pilot work prior to the experiment, including extensive testing in classes of forty-one volunteer teachers, had already indicated the course to be reasonably effective. The experimental comparison of average outcomes of HPP with average outcomes in a contrast group could offer nothing except a more precise statement about level of effectiveness. Further positive evidence would have little value other than for promotional purposes. The findings might have influenced consumers; but, in fact, the HPP course found its place in the market long before the evaluators reported to outsiders (unless a sentence or two in an advertising leaflet is counted as a "report").

Sample Selection and Assignment. The design was systematic, a "representative" sample being randomly divided into experimental and control fractions. First, a sample was drawn from a national roster of physics teachers. Each randomly chosen teacher was asked whether she would be willing to teach in the experiment and administer the several tests called for by the design. The teacher agreed that, if assigned to the experimental group, she would attend a summer training workshop and teach the HPP course the next year. If assigned to the control group, she would continue with whatever course of study she had been using. To reduce possible Hawthorne effects, the control teachers were invited to Cambridge for a short morale-building conference at which prominent scientists talked about contemporary physics. Of 124 teachers approached, not all were willing (or free) to participate. The 72 who accepted the invitation were divided: 46 to the experimental group, 26 to the control group.

About 25 percent of the teachers were lost from the final sample. The final data came from thirty-four experimental and nineteen control teachers. Some teachers dropped out because of personal circumstances having nothing to do with the experiment; such losses should not disturb the equivalence that random assignment promised. But another possibility raises serious questions. Perhaps some teachers dropped out as a consequence of the assignments they received, and this might have removed the less motivated teachers from one or the other group, unbalancing the design. One can imagine a teacher volunteering in the hope of receiving the materials and guidance the project offered the experimental group, and losing interest after drawing a control assignment that would impose some inconvenience and offer little reward. One can also imagine that a teacher marginally willing to participate might decide not to give up several weeks of vacation to attend the summer workshop for the experimental group.

An anecdote illustrates how assignment to treatment can fail. The question "What textbook is your class using?" appeared in a general questionnaire given to students midway in the year. (The investigators were curious as to whether students are conscious of their texts.) Members of one class whose teacher had been placed in the experimental group named a prominent traditional text as the book they used. Data from that class were discarded.

The control teachers had been using various texts, the most prominent ones being the PSSC course and the traditional book by C. E. Dull and H. C. Metcalfe (*Modern Physics*, first published in 1922 and kept alive by various third authors in later editions). The investigators apparently did not ask teachers in the experimental group which text they were accustomed to use. And, though the text in use was recorded for control teachers, the project staff decided that the report should describe a single control group, with no separation of PSSC and traditional classes. At least two considerations entered this decision. First, the Harvard directors wished to avoid any appearance of direct rivalry with PSSC, which had been developed across town at M.I.T. Second, those planning the summative study had committed themselves to a "true experiment" in a true sample. The design could not make the PSSC subset of the control group equivalent to the HPP teachers or to an identifiable subset of them, so comparisons of subgroups could not satisfy the formal ideal of the team. As PSSC adherents very likely had rejected the Dull-Metcalfe text and Dull-Metcalfe adherents the PSSC materials, to compare HPP results with those for a composite of PSSC and Dull-Metcalfe classes answered no consumer's question.

Since the consumer will want to know how HPP compares with her favorite approach, a tighter comparison could have been achieved. When the national sample was first drawn, the teacher could have been asked which text she was teaching from. Minor texts could have been discarded from the sample, leaving one or more prominent competitors to HPP. Those competitors would have defined strata within which assignment to the experimental or control condition could have been made. This would have created comparable experimental/control groups within "PSSC users" and within "Dull-Metcalfe users." Admittedly, the modified design would lose sight of many texts. The control data would not have been "representative" of the market HPP wished to enter. Why should they have been?

Analysis. The early reports compared an HPP mean with the mean of the composite control group. The control group was subdivided in some later HPP reports, the six PSSC and thirteen traditional classes being averaged separately (Ahlgren and Walberg, 1973). On certain posttests HPP fell between the PSSC and traditional means, which makes it obvious that the original experimental/control contrast did not do justice to the facts.

HPP considered units of analysis in a manner well ahead of its time. The analysts recognized that sampling had been at the teacher level. The unit for the study, then, was the teacher; classes of a given teacher were pooled to provide one mean on each variable. The main analyses compared the HPP mean-of-teacher-means with the control mean, a procedure that would be judged reasonable today if the control treatment were considered meaningful. Variation within treatments being large and teachers few, important differences could easily fall short of statistical significance, however.

In some substudies teachers were categorized according to the mean IQ of their students. The lowest category had mean IQs of 112 or below, and the highest ranged from 120 upward. "Low ability," then, is low relative only to the physics-taking population. Table 2 shows the number of teachers in each subdivision. The irregularities suggest that random assignment had not produced equivalent groups. (I believe that analysis of covariance, with mean IQ of class as covariate, would have been more powerful than the blocked analysis of variance that the investigators carried out.)

A multivariate analysis of variance with several cognitive posttests as dependent variables, ignoring the split of the control group, reported the interaction of treatment with ability level as nonsignificant. Readers were left, then, with the impression that treatment differences did not vary with ability level.

Nonetheless, it is possible that an interaction was present. An analysis of individual scores (classes pooled within treatments) showed low-ability students doing much better in

Table 2. Distribution of Physics Classes by Mean IQ and Course of Study

	Class Ability Level			
	Low	Middle	High	Total
All experimentals	13	12	9	34
All control	6	8	5	19
PSSC	1	4	1	6
Traditional	5	4	4	13

HPP than their counterparts did in the (mixed) control treatment. No difference between experimental and control achievement appeared in the upper range of ability. (This was reported only in a methodological paper by Walberg, 1970.) Current theory (Cronbach, 1976) would advise an evaluator having such data to plot the class means on achievement against IQ within each text and to plot pupil scores within each class, noting the text for the class. If there were enough teachers with two or more classes, a third level of analysis—classes within teachers—should be considered. Each set of plots has its own story to tell, and a nonsignificant trend could be practically important. Walberg's finding suggests that there was an interaction effect at the level of class means, or an effect within classes, or both.

Neglect of Treatment Variation. It will be recalled that teachers were encouraged to assemble the HPP materials as they chose, so that HPP was the very opposite of a standard treatment. The pilot phase had produced suggestive findings regarding classroom processes. A correlational analysis (Welch and Bridgham, 1968) showed, for example, that classes spent from twenty-five to sixty-two days on Unit 1 but that the slower rates were not characteristic of duller classes in particular. Time spent was not related to achievement on the unit. The project therefore strongly recommended that teachers stay on schedule, so that they would not slight the last part of the course. This is a nice instance of useful correlational research and also of a finding of no difference that is credible and useful. Another subanalysis of pilot data (Smith, Schagrin, and Poorman, 1968) found achievement conspicuously better in those HPP classes that used a rich variety of media than in those that did not go beyond the text. This lead was lost from sight; the main experiment could have confirmed or disconfirmed it.

Partly because of fixation on summative comparison, the main report stopped with the planned contrasts and did not track down the effect of variations in instruction. The decision to draw a representative national sample—hence a dispersed one—made it impractical to observe teaching pro-

cesses directly, though one member of the project staff did
some visiting of sites. Data from the Learning Environment
Inventory (to be described later) and from teacher logs would
have permitted a class-by-class analysis that was not in fact
made. Walberg (1970, p. 198) noted the shortcoming: "It has
not been possible to examine the 'fine structure' of instruction and investigate the individual options [regarding use of
media, for example] and their interactions with aptitudes and
environments. Comprehensive studies of this order of complexity are obviously difficult and time consuming, certainly
beyond our present resources if not ambitions." No doubt the
project's budget went into other justifiable lines of effort, but
it is my impression that the statistically minded investigators
were uncomfortable with case studies. As the number of variables far exceeded the number of teachers, it would be impossible for statistical reasoning to rule out the possibility that
whatever pattern appeared among the cases was a chance oc-
currence.

   Attitudinal Data. The HPP evaluation measured attitudinal outcomes—a valuable feature of the study. As most students in the project would not go on to scientific-technical ca-
reers, the planners wanted to give them a sense of physics as a
human adventure, not an affair of algebra and apparatus
alone. According to the main analysis, HPP classes tended to
show the desired attitudes to a greater degree than did control classes taken together. This was true especially of less
able students. A later breakdown (Ahlgren and Walberg,
1973) showed that the PSSC fraction of the control group accounted for most of the difference. Students following a traditional text differed little from HPP students in attitude.
This conclusion was almost uninterpretable, however. Differences in attitude fluctuated with the IQ level of the class and
the measuring procedure, and IQ level was confounded with
the PSSC/traditional subdivision of the control group.

   Students, filling out a Learning Environment Inventory (LEI), served as informants about classroom processes.
Morale, teaching styles, and so on were described in ninety-
eight statements, and in midyear the students indicated how
well each statement described the physics class. For scoring,

the statements were grouped into fourteen scales, such as Apathy, Favoritism, and Diversity [of activities]. Usually the class mean on a scale or item was entered into the analysis. These LEI variables play several roles. Teacher style could be regarded as a characteristic established prior to the experiment —that is, as a potential covariate and as a basis for deciding which persons would be likely to respond well to HPP. Alternatively, LEI scores of teachers could be regarded as an outcome of the treatment; thus, HPP would be considered beneficial if it induced teachers to adopt some desired style. Third, the LEI score could reflect a process that mediates treatment effects. Class apathy, for example, could be a consequence of initial motivation or of the treatment, and it could be a cause of a student's final attitude toward science. In various research reports, LEI scales were analyzed in any of the three ways: as predictive, intermediate, and dependent variables. In the evaluative reports, the LEI scores were treated only as dependent variables.

A matrix-sampling plan increased the variety of the data. Each class was split at random for each testing session; for example, one half responded to LEI while others filled out a biographical questionnaire. Adequately reliable class means were obtained on about twice as many variables as could have been covered with uniform testing.

Violence Study

Although fictionalized, the third example of evaluation design has a basis in an actual study that continued for some years. (Reports on one year of the study have appeared; see Social Action Research Center, 1979a, 1979b, 1980.) My fictionalizing is motivated partly by a desire to simplify; the planning took many twists and turns, and the study evolved far beyond the point where my story ends. But I also use this approach to bring out themes that surfaced during a series of seminars at Stanford. These themes are of interest even in instances where they did not become primary concerns in the actual investigation.

American high schools and middle schools are plagued

by morale problems arising from crime, violence, and fear of violence. A federal agency, judging it possible to train staff members within a school to analyze and solve such problems, set aside funds for a tryout. An announcement invited schools to apply. Any school chosen was to send a team from its staff and community to a training center. In the course of training, the team was to formulate ideas for introducing change when it returned home; and a small grant to facilitate activities at home was to be provided. A year-long follow-up study would assess effects.

The chief hope of the agency was that the training would equip school staffs to solve problems for themselves. The agency did not recommend particular tactics for dealing with violence, since little is known about the control of violence and the improvement of morale in the presence of violence. Moreover, a tactic suited to one school and community would not necessarily suit the next. The evaluators thus invested considerable effort in learning about each school and its setting, the character of its problem, the resources available, and the activities undertaken. The principal supplied much of the background information. A member of the school staff was asked to keep a journal of events as the year progressed; one of the evaluators did some visiting, but the evaluators relied more on periodic telephone calls to keep the central record of significant developments up to date. The evaluators checked closely with the team to learn of its activities and, later, its perception of its achievements, difficulties, and abandoned efforts.

It was believed that the program would have less effect on disruptive conduct than on perceptions and attitudes, but information on actual incidents was wanted. The principal's staff was asked to record every incident reported to the office during selected months. Questionnaires for the teachers and students called for self-description on a few demographic variables, opinions as to changes needed in the school, and a report of experience with violence and disorder. Thus, respondents were asked whether they had been victims of specific kinds of violence, and they were also asked about the school atmosphere. For several reasons it was decided not to identify questionnaires of individual students. The school as a whole was the experimental unit, and students were seen as informants. Anonymity was appropriate for a questionnaire of this character, and student-body turnover made it difficult or pointless to question the same students each year.

Sampling Considerations. It was originally planned to question a random sample of 200 students from the student-body roster each year, but a tryout of the questionnaire in a sample of schools challenged that approach. The schools varied considerably in their ethnic makeup, and a few schools had highly unbalanced sex distributions. Within a school the percentage of students endorsing some items varied strongly with the demographic category of respondents. If boys are less likely than girls to express fear, it is hard to interpret student-body averages: Does a low mean score in a predominantly male student body reflect less emotion or a reporting bias? The fact that pretests as well as posttests were to be available made this problem less troublesome than it might have been; student-body makeup changes slowly. But *random* samples of 200 could be ill matched on sex and other relevant variables.

The original plan was to rely on a morale score for the whole student body. When variation across categories of informants was discovered, the research question was revised. An intervention procedure might make one kind of student more contented while threatening or alienating others. Therefore, it seemed advisable to record *six* school-level scores for any variable: means for black males, black females, Hispanic males, and so on. Sampling plans had to be modified accordingly. In a school whose student body is 80 percent white, it is advisable to oversample nonwhites, so that each of the six means is based on, say, fifteen or more individual respondents. (A category including few members of the student body would perhaps be omitted entirely.)

School-to-School Variation in Activities. Experimental schools were expected to vary in the character of their activities. Variation in the vitality of school efforts was also anticipated. Not every team returning home with good intentions launches a viable program. Perhaps team members lose their impetus under the pressure of everyday responsibilities, or perhaps the remainder of the staff or the community find their plan unacceptable. Or perhaps they launch a student-staff review committee that never manages to find an agenda on which to work. How many teams actually initiate activities is, therefore, a reasonable first indication of the value of the central workshop.

Measures of effects on the school are harder to interpret. The average embraces schools where the team developed no activity, schools where an activity was tried but went largely unnoticed, and schools where at least some activities were highly visible. It seems almost perverse to judge the treatment by its average end effect, just as it would be perverse to judge whether exercise is good for heart patients by mixing records of patients who follow the advice to take exercise with records of those who do not. At most, one reaches a conclusion about the average benefit realized from the intervention, not an assessment of the power that the treatment has when followed. In the Violence study, the conclusion probably estimates conservatively the benefits that could be expected in the future. The staff that conducts future training can learn from the most successful experimental schools and do a better job with its trainees. Moreover, within any school one would expect a scheme to be improved after the first or "shakedown" year and to take firmer root as time passes.

The most valuable yield of a study of this character is likely to be a file of case histories. Comparison can suggest why one returning team initiated an activity and another did not. The reasons are probably too idiosyncratic to be captured by the "standard" variables that the investigator thinks of in advance. Activities given the same name will take on a local shape and will have a local trajectory of development. An isolated but dramatic incident of violence or an unexpected football championship will make a large difference in a school, at least for a time.

In a large study, it is prohibitively expensive to observe in every site. The evaluators in the Violence study therefore placed themselves in a position to prepare case studies by setting up telephone interviews. The narrative history so compiled provides a background for interpreting events and responses to questionnaires. Very likely it would be profitable to collect more detailed narratives retrospectively, after posttests are analyzed. School staffs could shed light on a large effect or on the failure of a promising idea. The school should be able to gain suggestions for its own future practice from the case study, and the training staff should be able to gain insights for its future work. Summary over the group of schools that initiated a certain kind of activity is also of some use. In how many, one may ask, did it prove viable? Among schools where that activity thrived, what effect on violence and morale could be detected? What were the characteristics of teams that functioned well and got results? Such a summary, combined with qualitative information on successes and failures, would bring out whatever generalizations the data permit.

No-Treatment Control. The schools where teams manage to initiate activities are probably not typical of the total sample, and schools choosing to work, say, on a new discipline code differ in unknown ways from schools adopting other plans. The approach to these questions is inherently correlational, whether the emphasis is on statistics or on integration of case studies. The relationships therefore allow alternative explanations. It was this concern that led to establishment of a control group of schools. After elimination of the least suitable schools and after blocking on certain school characteristics, blocks were divided at random. Half of the applicants were promised that, in return for participating in the control group, they would be placed in the program the following year. The most obvious price paid for randomization of this kind is that immediate service was not concentrated on the applicants most in need of and ready for assistance; the sample reached down to less urgent cases. But for evaluative purposes this is not undesirable; the larger pool represents the clientele for an expanded program better than the "neediest hundred" would.

Following summer training in Year 0, the experimental team worked with its local colleagues in the fall of Year 0 to form and try out a local plan. In each school, data were collected on certain variables in March of Year 0 (prior to the training) and in March of Year 1. (Later follow-up is possible, but the formerly untreated controls have become experimental cases in Year 2.) For any dependent variable, the formal experimental/control comparison can be made at the end of Year 1, with data from Year 0 providing covariates. The statistical comparison at the end of Year 1 is logically a strong one with respect to the variable "Was action initiated?"

But is the control group worth its cost? Without the program as a stimulus, surely few schools would spontaneously initiate, during any one year, activities similar to those of the schools in the experiment. Questions on the application form about a school's practices in the preceding year would provide adequate base-rate information on initiatives intended to reduce violence and fear. Suppose that 50 percent of the trained teams did initiate activities in their schools. Even if there were no control group, who would conclude that this percentage could be attributed to causes other than the program? Suppose that the initiation rate is 20 percent. That would be disappointing even if it were higher than the rate in control schools. The weakness of the treatment effect would be a more important finding than the simple conclusion that the treatment had an effect.

When the investigation moves on to socially important consequences, the equivalent control group buys little. The program sponsors hope that school staffs will gain competence in managing their affairs. This competence can be observed in the experimental schools but not formally measured, because the teams face different problems and act along different lines. Comparison with the controls is out of the question. In the control schools, no teams are formed. With no program initiated, not even anecdotal evidence of competence in management is available. One can compare competence only when units undertake equivalent tasks. Nevertheless, the no-treatment control does improve technically the comparison on disruptive incidents and on morale. Both the pretests and the data on the controls indicate the level of violence and fear in schools that had no special staff training. The control data guard against any secular trend during the year of the study that might otherwise be interpreted as a program effect. (Fine weather, for example, might have reduced the number of incidents by reducing the number of hours students spent in the school building.)

It is hard to manage a study with 100 experimental schools; yet even that is a seriously limited basis for a summative statistical analysis, especially after high schools are separated from middle schools, as is surely advisable. Perhaps the schools where teams started few activities should be left out of the calculation. The modest interventions contemplated are not likely to turn a troubled school into a happy one, and morale-affecting events that the school has little control over may mask effects of the program. Since small effects may be important in the long run, the study is lacking in power. Note the dilemma the planners faced. Trying to investigate both high schools and middle schools in the same year had distressing consequences for statistical power. However, since the agency wanted to learn about both kinds of school, there was a good case for proceeding on both fronts.

When we come to questions about the kinds of teams and kinds of activities that worked well (which surely varied over categories of schools), the control group gives no help. For the teams that were vigorous, or the schools that opted for a new discipline code, no reasonably equivalent control schools can be picked out. If the original design had formed pairs of similar schools and made the experimental/control assignment randomly within pairs, the analyst could use the pairmates as controls for those schools choosing to work on discipline. That design falls short of equating schools with their controls, however, since the matching may not have considered the characteristics that predispose schools to choose this activity. To see this more clearly, assume that triads rather than pairs were formed, one school becoming a control (C) and the other two becoming experimental (E). Suppose that, to learn if a new discipline code helps, we look at every triad in which one E school and not the other adopted that activity. Call the former school E_1, and call the school that adopted a different activity E_2. An E_1/E_2 comparison is a rather weak approximation to an experiment; schools selected themselves into category 1 on unknown bases. The E_1/C comparison is equally weak, despite the randomization, because the E_1 schools are not representative of the E sample.

While on the subject, I note—with disapproval—that pairmate controls have been recommended as a device for coping with attrition. If pairs are well matched and members assigned to contrasting treatments, some analysts would confine attention to pairs in which both members complete their respective treatments. When one member dropped out, the pairmate would be ignored in the analysis (Riecken and Boruch, 1974, p. 79). But this has obvious risks. If nonreaders make no progress in instruction, become discouraged and vanish, the experimental comparison is confined to a population of good readers. The ability of the treatments to serve learners who have difficulty is not entered into the balance sheet. The device, says Wortman (1978, p. 1146), "would add to the credibility of the findings by eliminating differential attrition as a 'plausible rival hypothesis.'" This comes perilously close to "Better the Devil you *don't* know . . . ."

In the following chapter, I turn to a general description of evaluations and the issues faced in planning. Several of the issues have been foreshadowed in the examples of this chapter. Self-selection played a role in each controlled experiment. The evaluators sought to rely on statistical inference but found it inadequate. They were uncertain how to deal with collective units because research traditions have developed almost wholly with individuals as the ostensible unit. The evaluators sought to assess treatment effects, yet their treatments were not unitary in delivery and sometimes not in conception. Each treatment was shaped by the responses of mothers, teachers, or school staffs, as would surely be the case if the treatment were accepted for operational use. Consequently, effects of the treatments depended on what appealed to whom, and simple questions about treatment effects unfolded into uncertainties about the interplay of innumerable variables.

3

❧ *Elements in an Evaluation Design*

The evaluation of a program leads to a statement about what to expect if a certain plan of action is adopted (or continued) in a certain site or class of sites. Such expectations have to do with program delivery, reactions of clients, their behavior or health or employment, a change in the level of a social indicator, institutional change, and so on. The designer of an evaluation would like the forecast to be definite, sound, and believable.

Whether a prediction is sound could in time be checked by observations if the action is in fact taken. Whether to credit the prediction has to be judged much earlier, however, when action is still pending. The judgment can best be made after critical scrutiny both of the logic that produced the inference and of the observations it took into account. The interpreter of a study makes a case for the validity of the interpretation; his hearers pass judgment.

Interpretation is held in place by chains (or cobwebs) of reasoning. Few of the links are formal and objective. Virtually any argument about real events is rhetorical in the sense that Perelman and Olbrechts-Tyteca (1969) use the term *rhetorical*. That is, the interpreter assembles information and assumptions to make a persuasive case. Chapters Four and Five will examine the process of drawing and defending conclusions, while recognizing the companion functions of deduction and persuasion. Recommendations on design will be derived from that theory of argument. This chapter sets forth a shorthand notation—awkward at times but economical overall—for speaking of the data available, the domain that the sample can be said strictly to represent, and the situation(s) about which predictions are made. My conception is much like that of Kruglanski and Kroy (1976), except that they are concerned with testing formal hypotheses whereas I treat exploratory inquiry as well. I remind the reader that I am concerned with the evaluation of programs that will be considered for adoption in many places, not with local evaluations or monitoring of ongoing programs. The scheme that this chapter develops could logically apply to evaluations of the here and now, but the application would be strained. The scheme does apply to naturalistic and case-study evaluations wherever the cases observed are regarded as instances of the working out of a generalized plan or policy.

Concepts Describing a Study

The trial of a program is to be described in terms of units, treatments, observing operations, and setting. These concepts apply also to the situation in which a program operates if it is adopted permanently. This scheme, one of many possibilities, is sufficiently complex for my purposes; a writer emphasizing different points might introduce other elements. My four elements will appear in various forms. Table 3, a summary of ideas to be developed in this chapter, will help the reader keep track of distinctions as they are introduced.

The basic orientation is one of sampling, with inference from sample back to the original domain or another domain. When a study is planned, that plan marks off a domain of

Table 3. Outline of the Notational System, with Examples from the Violence Study[a]

Character of Element	Symbol[b]	Units	Treatments	Observing Operations
Domain about which question is asked	$UTOS$	U The population of persons, sites, and so on, about which a conclusion is sought. *Urban schools troubled by violence and volunteering to receive T.*	T The plan for the program and its installation. *Schools are invited to send team to workshop, then to choose their own plan and install it.*	O The plan for collecting some kind of datum. *Questionnaire on fears and attitudes to be given annually to 20 percent sample of student body.*
Describable subset of instances in $UTOS$	sub-$UTOS$	sub-U *Schools that will decide to increase security measures.* *Black male students, in all schools with a certain sub-T.*	sub-T *All treatment plans considered to be security oriented.*	sub-O *Cluster of items inquiring about racial harmony.*
Instances on which data are collected	$utoS$	u Actual participant. (In some contexts u refers to any unit in U.) *A school volunteering and selected for the trial, or the set of all those schools.*	t Procedures actually applied to any u. Also, the set of t in the study. Rarely, all members of the set that T would have generated in U, from which the observed t are a sample. *Procedures followed in one school, including the handling of disruptive incidents.*	o The actual procedure representing O. Rarely, all members of the set of o that would have been consistent with plan O. *The particular items in a test, conditions of test administration, occasion.*
Situation or class about which a conclusion is wanted (if other than $UTOS$ or a sub-$UTOS$)	*$UTOS$	U^* A unit or set of units not regarded as fully representative of U or a sub-U. *A school not in the original sample that proposes to adopt a plan.*	T^* A plan under consideration that does not match T or a sub-T. *Adding to the security plan some training of teachers in how to resolve conflicts.*	O^* A variable not observed directly in the original study, or an alternative method of measurement. *"How do students really feel?"*

[a] Examples are set in italics.

[b] S refers to the times and cultural conditions in which the study is made—say, the United States in 1982. S^* refers to the times and cultural conditions when and where the findings are to be applied.

possible studies, all of which address the same question. The several studies that conform to the plan will differ as samples always differ: Each study will have its own set of subjects; there will be at least minor variations in the way the treatment is delivered to different subjects or groups; and there will be at least minor variations in the conditions of measurement and observation, if not in the formal procedures themselves. Specifying the treatment domain T, the admissible procedures and conditions O for obtaining data on a certain variable, and the population or domain U of units from which subjects will be drawn defines the intended domain of the study, $UTOS$. Any one of the actual studies consistent with the specification directly addresses the same question.

The setting S is the large social context in which the study takes place; it includes the prevailing social attitudes, political divisions, economic climate, and so on. Experience with a program in one decade will not necessarily be similar to experience with the same program in another decade. A 1969 evaluation of military conscription, for example, could not indicate what a similar study would have found in 1943 or perhaps will find in 1985.

The Sample utoS. The actual subjects are, as usual, thought of as a sample from U. Likewise, the treatment as delivered and the observing operations as performed are seen as representing their respective domains. Hence, when the particular study is denoted by the symbols *utoS*, that conjunction of specific samples is a sample from the domain of studies consistent with the definition of $UTOS$.

A study attends to certain units: individuals, perhaps, or classes or communities. A plan for rendering service—a treatment—is applied. The Harvard Project Physics (HPP) materials as obtained from the publisher constitute a treatment T; so does a formula for welfare payments. Each unit is exposed to a realization t of the treatment. In HPP each teacher selects and organizes lessons, and proceeds through them in her own lucid or confusing style. Even when a treatment supposedly has been standardized, realizations are certain to vary. For example, how the welfare formula is applied in borderline cases will probably vary from one locality to another. The term *operations* refers to the sources of data. The evaluator sends a certain visitor to a class to record certain kinds of impressions or collects responses from class members. Decision makers need descriptions of the units treated and of the agencies delivering service, as well as reports on outcomes. Some variables are observed before, some during, and some after the treatment.

The units, treatment realizations, and operations that generate the actual data of the evaluation are denoted by u, t, and o, respectively. These symbols can have a singular or plural meaning, as in "the unit u" and "the sample u." Each u is paired with at least one t and o to form an element of *uto*. This compound symbol refers to the study as realized; *uto* may refer to a single datum or to all the data of a study. Where the reader is to be mindful of the setting, I write out *utoS*. Where S is not written, its presence is to be understood.

The four elements are present simultaneously, and the identification of a feature with one of the elements may be arbitrary. Sometimes an observing operation functions as part of the treatment plan. Likewise, if schools operating on a nongraded plan are selected for investigation, it is pointless to ask whether nongrading is a feature of u or of t. Such ambiguities create no significant difficulty.

The Domain UTOS. The domains U, T, and O combine with S to define a domain of investigation *UTOS*. (I shall use the symbols in various combinations; thus, UT refers to U and T in combination.) *UTOS* is described by the investigator when planning begins. The description may be explicit and formal, amounting to an operational definition, or it may be exceedingly vague. The domain is likely to change during planning and pilot work, as issues come into focus and certain investigations are seen to be infeasible. *UTOS* may be redefined even after the data come in. For example, if few follow-up questionnaires come in from one kind of unit, conclusions have to be limited to a U that excludes that group.

The specification of *UTOS* identifies the direct question of the study. That is to say, if we are told what U, T, O, and S

are in the investigator's mind, we know what observations would be made in an exhaustive study of his question. (How the data will be manipulated to bring out relationships is a further part of the plan. I have chosen not to give that aspect a symbol, but Chapter Six is devoted to analytic operations and Chapter Eight treats them alongside observing operations.)

In specifying U, T, and O, however vaguely, the investigator has said what he intends to find out. "If the study is done in the near future in this culture . . ." is an opening clause referring to S. The question continues: ". . . and T is administered to all the members of U, what will observing operation O report?" The $UTOS$ for the Nutrition study had four elements:

U *Aldeas* of a certain size and degree of isolation.

T Establishment of a station to render service and supply *atole* or *fresco* prepared according to particular recipes.

O Application of the Matching Familiar Figures Test, in a specified form, by a trained member of the project staff in the testing room of the local station within two weeks of the child's third through sixth birthdays (this was one among many—rather, four among many—measuring operations).

S Rural Guatemala in the early 1970s.

This $UTOS$ implicitly states the research question: "What is the distribution of scores on this test, at each of these ages, in the group of children receiving *fresco* and in the group receiving *atole?*" Of course, the study is concerned with broader questions of why and how, but these are not under direct observation.

As the example shows, T as a general symbol may refer to two or more treatments, and O as a general symbol may refer to a set of several O—different procedures, different timing, and so on. I emphasize that O, as a general symbol, encompasses pretests, posttests, and intermediate variables.

U may be plural; in Chapter Two I suggested the usefulness of village-by-village case studies. In such substudies each village becomes a U in turn; U and u are then scarcely distinguishable.

Whether the planner specifies $UTOS$ in detail or sketches his vision in the air, it occupies a crucial position in design. The plan for collecting data is to be judged in terms of how well the data can answer the question $UTOS$ — and other questions to which we shall come shortly.

Two Implicit Elements. Many features are implicit rather than explicit in the $UTOS$ formulation; two deserve special mention. The first is the immediate, local situation or setting. The evaluator ought to inform himself about the setting of each treatment realization: community characteristics, organizational characteristics, characteristics of the staff that administers the treatment, and so on. A symbol to represent local conditions is not essential because settings and units are tied together. The evaluator does not plan to move persons from one site to another; hence, selection of a u also selects its site or setting. In defining U, the evaluator will characterize not only persons (or aggregate units) but also sites. The definition of U can be expected to limit the range of communities and institutions in which the treatment will be examined. The ultimate description of the u in the study should include, to the extent feasible, whatever information on the local setting is expected to help in interpreting results.

Social scientists have become increasingly attentive to the influence of immediate situations. Following the same person from situation to situation, one obtains varying indications of her confidence, persistence, talkativeness, and so on. The sampling of microsituations where data on the unit will be collected is an important aspect of the selection of o. The investigator ought to be attentive to the setting of an observation just as he is attentive to the larger setting for the treatment, but an added symbol would not improve the notation. Defining admissible units implies an admissible range of local settings where such units can be found; likewise, there are admissible situations for delivering a treatment element or for collecting a particular kind of observation.

The second major feature given no symbol is time. Time schedules are important in planning an evaluation and in recording what was done. The plan has to say something about scheduling—about the intended duration and frequency of treatment, for example. As the treatment realization proceeds, the evaluator will almost certainly record some of its temporal aspects: how a physics teacher distributed class time, or how often children came to the station where *atole* was provided. Once it is understood that such matters are part of the description of T and t, an extra symbol is not required.

The plan for measurement has to consider when in the course of treatment the various measurements will be made. In some studies follow-up will be scheduled for a date far in the future. Every test, observation, or interview takes place at a certain time; a similar procedure applied on other occasions around the same date would ordinarily provide equally acceptable information. The specification of admissible times for collecting each datum is part of O.

A few words are needed to anticipate a complication that will be clarified later. It is convenient for the moment to speak as if the domains U, T, and O are "completely crossed"; that is, as if every u within U could be paired with every realization within T and within O. That is often the case in laboratory experimentation, but it may be neither possible nor meaningful in a field observation. Part of the conceptualization of UTO has to do with the joint distribution of the elements—in particular, with whether to impose a certain pairing or to let the pairing (of u and t in particular) work out as it will. If former teachers of PSSC handle HPP physics differently, as a rule, than former Dull-Metcalfe teachers do, realizations t are correlated with that characteristic of the u.

The Domain *UTOS. Insights applicable to units, treatments, variables, and settings not directly observed are, I shall argue, the principal yield of an evaluation—more important than answers about the domain directly sampled. Traditional inference views the sample uto as a deliberate representation of UTO. The sample data are a basis for direct inference to the parent domain. But persons concerned with policy and program operations have questions about combinations of clients, services, circumstances, and variables that differ from *UTOS*. And, invariably, the passage of time changes the setting, possibly to an important extent. Any of these other questions covers its own span of units, treatments, operations, and settings. I represent a question other than *UTOS* by **UTOS* ("star *UTOS*"). At least one component of **UTOS* differs from its counterpart in *UTOS*. Combining the original *T, O,* and *S* with a new population *U** defines a **UTOS*. Combining the original *U, O,* and *S* with a modified treatment *T** poses another question, another **UTOS*. (The asterisk is placed first because an asterisk at the end might suggest the reading "*UTO* in *S**.")

The educator who asks what will happen when a locally planned procedure for coping with violence is applied to a specific school is asking about a **UTOS*. That code applies even when this school and treatment plan fall within the domain *UTOS*, because an answer about *UTOS* is a summary over a heterogeneous domain. But why is this **UTOS* identified by capital letters rather than small letters? The forthcoming decision applies to a single school and realization. This **UTOS* is a domain, though a limited one, because a policy decision has to do with a class of events. Policy makers who choose a treatment *plan* may work it out in detail, so that most characteristics of the realization are known in advance; even then, however, the realization will take on unforeseen characteristics. Hence, the judgment has to be about a universe of realizations that the plan might generate locally. Moreover, the policy set in June is to apply to the school next year. Next year's staff and student body will have characteristics that cannot be completely foreseen. The actual constitution of next year's school is a sample from among the student bodies that in June are envisioned as possibilities. The school's prediction, then, is about a domain of possibilities, one of which will be realized.

Subdivisions of UTO. The domain *UTO* can be subdivided and a conclusion can be drawn about one of the sub-*UTO* as if it were the whole *UTO* under study. For example, communities may be categorized according to size, and pupils according to sex. These sub-U combine with T and O into sub-UTO; one can draw a conclusion about cities with populations of 100,000, or about girls, or about girls in cities with populations of 100,000. A treatment T may be tried in various forms—for example, by carrying on training for two, four, or six months. Each specification identifies a sub-T about which a question sub-$UTOS$ is asked. Subdividing U in advance can improve sampling and can indicate more clearly whether various sub-U respond differently to T. Splitting T has similar advantages. HPP, it will be recalled, examined a control group. At the start of the planning, it would have been worthwhile to subdivide "existing physics courses"— making PSSC, for example, a distinct sub-T. Some tests in the HPP evaluation were organized to represent specific categories of knowledge or kinds of thinking. These categories were sub-O.

The common two-group comparative study is generally spoken of as investigating two treatments. I shall call the experimental and control treatments sub-T, the capital letter emphasizing the reference to treatment *plans*. At times it will be convenient to write T_E and T_C or T_1 and T_2 for contrasting sub-T.

It is possible to subclassify after the fact, as was done when the u in the INCAP study were classified according to the amount of food they received. Similarly, HPP classes might have been sorted according to the liveliness of discussions in them. Liveliness could be a result of student characteristics or of the teacher's procedures; hence, the group of lively classes is better identified as a sub-ut than as a sub-u or a sub-t. A direct inference would speak about a sub-UT of classes with lively discussions. The kind of sub-U that is defined in advance, even though units perhaps cannot be classified until events in the field are observed, is to be distinguished from the classification picked after the fact (from innumerable logical possibilities) to account for the variation among the units in response to treatment. Only the former kind of categorization is allowable in confirmatory research;

the latter kind summarizes an exploration. I do not speak of sub-U^* and the like. A question, for example, about the possibly distinctive effects of HPP on boys and girls within U^* is easily treated as a pair of questions, each about a different population.

Fixed and Random Elements. The concepts of fixed and random elements, borrowed from analysis of variance, will be useful to us. Fisher's original designs focused on a set of fixed factors: varieties of oats or three dosages of a certain fertilizer. Nuisance variables were left random; variation associated with single plants or plots thus entered the error term. Later it was recognized that random factors could be of interest, as in plot-by-fertilizer-by-variety interaction. In studies of rat psychology, animals were a random factor; a rat was representative of the colony, and no particular rat was the subject of a conclusion. In time, psychologists exposing rats to two or more treatments found it profitable to assess subject-by-treatment or strain-by-treatment interaction. Statistical theory was extended so that sources of variation could be treated as fixed or as random, depending on the intended interpretation.

I shall treat S as fixed; each study has only one setting. In the New Jersey income maintenance experiment, the setting was the state of New Jersey in a particular period; New Jersey had its own level of employment opportunities, its particular collective attitudes regarding work, and a new program of welfare benefits that unexpectedly appeared midway in the study. The investigation reported on New Jersey events in the years 1968 through 1972; its evidence does not give direct estimates of what to expect in any other state or in any other year.

I shall treat u, t, and o as random elements in most of my presentation. It is common enough to think of the subjects of an experiment as sampled from those about whom a conclusion is drawn. Also, the familiar concept of "error of measurement" recognizes that independent o representing the same O would not agree and, hence, that any one test or observation is only a sample of the behavior that is of interest.

Because of the Fisherian tradition, it is common to regard the treatment as fixed. When two varieties of barley are planted, for example, the contrast is between two well-identified, essentially uniform kinds of seeds. The grains within a variety will not be identical, but the variation can be ignored for most purposes. When social institutions are manipulated, however, the treatment is fixed only superficially. What *is* fixed is the list of steps the investigator intends to take and the resources he intends to supply.

No matter how completely the field investigator elaborates the plan for a service, that specification does no more than bound a domain of admissible realizations. INCAP's physically standardized food supplement was delivered at local stations whose social atmosphere reflected characteristics of the local clientele as well as of the staff, and neither the social stimulation nor the food intake could be standardized. Consequently, the treatment realizations varied. It makes sense to view the observed set of treatment events t as a more or less random sample of what would have been observed if the same general rules had been followed in applying T in many more sites. Although one ordinarily regards a site as a sample, it is possible for an investigator to confine his conclusion to the site studied. In such a case study, u is the same as U and is interpreted as fixed. Within the HPP evaluation, for example, a junior investigator made a case study of an urban black classroom in a poor neighborhood. The domain U was that classroom, a single unit.

Sampling may be controlled to any degree; judging how much to invest in such controls is a critical aspect of design. In survey research at its best, the one making the poll defines the collection (U) of units that is of interest, carefully draws a representative sample from the chosen population, and tracks down nonrespondents as best he can. In contrast, some investigators sample haphazardly. A questionnaire may simply be mailed to schools near the investigator's base to learn about, say, their experience with adult hall monitors as a means of maintaining order. Sampling from O and T may similarly be careful or casual. For example, a child might be observed by a psychologist, who rates her degree of dependency. That report would be taken to represent what would have been reported by other psychologists seeing the child on other days. Those admissible ratings would constitute the set O. If cost were not a barrier, however, data from many more raters on many more occasions would be wanted.

The treatment realizations observed are a systematic or unsystematic sample from the domain. Treatment realizations are almost never sampled directly. Rather, sites (or other units) are sampled. In a manipulative study, someone is induced to apply plan T to the unit. The realizations are, it is hoped, representative of all the t that such inductions would generate in US. In a nonmanipulative study, it is possible to take a census of whatever t have developed under current policies, and use that as a sampling frame. A statewide survey could find out what practices schools are using to deal with threats of violence and fear of violence. Then a sample where practices of special interest are in place would be studied. Sampling of sites without first inquiring about their t is far less expensive and can produce an equally representative sample of realizations. The advantage of the survey is that the sample can be structured to draw as many instances of a distinct sub-T as desired.

It will be recalled that when HPP sampled teachers, the planners chose not to identify teachers using the Dull-Metcalfe text. Had they done so, they could have discarded teachers who used uncommon texts, and pitted a homogeneous control group using the Dull-Metcalfe text against an experimental group of teachers shifting from Dull-Metcalfe to HPP. This would have been a change in UT, not merely a change in procedure.

UTOS, The Domain of Admissible Operations

UTOS tells what observations the investigator desires and, hence, what operations he would like to carry out. It refers to three operations in particular: the identification of subjects or units, the identification of treatments, and the procedures for collecting data on events and reactions. (S is not under his control.) In stating what $UTOS$ is, the investigator describes a domain he would like to study exhaustively—every u exposed to T or a sub-T and observed on each O. The actual study is a practicable substitute for the hypothetical study that would answer his question directly, without inference.

$UTOS$ is the domain of admissible observations. The definition of U, for example, excludes some possible objects of investigation and admits others. If it were possible, the investigator would obtain a report from every one of the admissible uto. That being impossible, he still wishes the uto he studies to fall within UTO; then all uto would be within the scope of the question. The definition of U amounts to a set of rules for recognizing which u are admissible. The definition of O amounts to a set of rules for creating admissible o. As for T, the rules may be used for creating t or for recognizing admissible t already in place. The rules, then, tell how the investigator must operate for his data to bear on the intended question.

In emphasizing that $UTOS$ states an operational question (even if vaguely), I deliberately echo Campbell's papers. Later I shall identify *internal validity* with the validity of a conclusion about $UTOS$ or a sub-$UTOS$ stated operationally. Internal validity "has nothing to do with the abstract labeling of a presumed cause or effect" (Cook and Campbell, 1979, p. 38). For example, to say that each class will be scored on the "morale" items of the Learning Environment Inventory is distinctly different from saying that morale will be assessed. Many other procedures can provide indicators of morale; these other indicators are O^*, and so is the conceptual variable "morale," which no indicator measures perfectly. The evaluator may or may not find detailed operational definitions appropriate. Campbell (1969a) has inveighed against "definitional operationism," which at its most doctrinaire denies that one meter stick is the equivalent of another. In his usage and mine, an operation refers to a *class* of objects or actions. The requirement for a useful communication is that

UTO be described well enough for readers to agree in judging which *uto* belong to the domain.

The planner decides what unit-treatment-operation combinations fall within his range of interest. Thus, he may refer to daycare programs that meet certain specifications (*T*) and are intended for children from a defined class of families (*U*). He will mention evidence (*O*) of particular kinds: a health rating by a physician, a mother's report on her use of the time that the service releases, and what some community group says about the worth of the service. Unless the investigator makes an error, any *uto* observed falls within the stated domain. An observation recognized as falling outside the domain is discarded.

At least in principle, we can test whether *UTO* is clearly specified. Some persons likely to use the results of the study can be asked to read the definition and then sort units, realizations, or operations to indicate which ones fall within it. The better the sorters agree, the clearer the definition. The clearer the definition of *U, T,* and *O,* the easier it is to defend the internal validity of a conclusion; confidence that another investigator would reach the same conclusion increases.

In this chapter I am emphasizing what it means to specify *U, T,* and *O*—that is, what decisions the planner should face consciously. I shall incidentally touch on the fact that particular specifications make an evaluation more suitable for one purpose and less suitable for another. That, and further discussion of the contribution made by clarity of specification, will be taken up in Chapter Eight.

Units. In an educational study, the unit could be a student, a class, all classes of a teacher, a school, a community, or perhaps a larger area. The unit *u* in my scheme is the smallest group or institution that is treated independently and responds independently. A unit should be complete and autonomous enough so that its experiences and responses are not influenced by the experiences and responses of persons in other units—at least, not influenced to an extent important for the effect under examination.

Independence is hard to define rigorously unless the

situation is highly controlled. Persons treated together form a single unit unless the treatment is realized separately for each. If the staff member delivering the treatment to Person 1 receives her instructions directly from headquarters and does not communicate with the staff member treating Person 2, the two realizations are presumed to be independent. But two persons who experience independent realizations are not independent if the response of the second is affected by reactions of the first.

In the Violence study, for example, one would expect students in a school to gossip about an incident of violence and thus to influence each other. They should therefore be regarded as members of a unit, not as separate units. (The community would probably have been a better unit for study than the school, since schools within a community are sensitive to the same news about such occurrences as racial flare-ups.) In the other illustrative studies of Chapter Two, the unit was also a collective: the community in the Nutrition study, the set of classes of any teacher in the Physics study.

A person or an animal is the unit (subject) in the typical experiment in the psychological laboratory. In the typical classroom, however, students are not independent; a confusing explanation by the teacher affects every student present. That implies that the class is the unit treated (Campbell and Stanley, 1963, pp. 192–194). But classes may also be influenced by communication among teachers. Then the school or the community becomes the unit (Lindquist, 1953, pp. 172–189; Cronbach, 1976). Thinking about the size of the unit early in the design process is essential if the study is to investigate the intended question. Identification of the unit derives from working hypotheses about the way the treatment will operate and about the process by which persons and institutions will respond. It is a mistake to say that *because* persons were sampled, the person is the unit in the inquiry. The logic runs the other way: The sampling plan should reflect careful consideration of links possibly inherent in the situation to be studied.

The New Jersey experiment made payments to scattered residents who had been invited to become test cases. No one knows whether the same data would result from an operational plan in which payments went to all eligibles (Rivlin, 1974). That kind of procedure could generate a new community ethic about employment. When a larger fraction of the population or a larger area is treated, social resonances are likely to magnify both good and bad effects.

Frequently the objects under investigation have a nested structure; for example, the question may be concerned with pupils within classes within schools within districts within states. Which level is regarded as the unit treated depends on how the treatment is thought to operate. When Plan A for teaching reading is to be investigated, for example, the evaluator may ask, "What percentage *of first graders* taught by this method reach a score of 80 on Test X by the end of the year?" Or "Among representative classes taught by Plan A, in what percentage *of classes* do three quarters of the pupils reach a score of 80?" Or "Among school districts using Plan A, in what percentage *of districts* do three quarters of the pupils reach a score of 80?" Questions about means, variances, correlations, and so on, are likewise definable at each level. These are not trivial variants. If the success of Plan A depends strongly on characteristics of the teacher and the success of Plan B does not, the two plans might look equally good when pupil scores are thrown into one grand calculation. Yet Plan B might look much better than Plan A if class success is the criterion; its results presumably will be more uniform over classes.

The school district is likely to be a suitable unit when communication among teachers and common supervision are thought to tie schools together. Then some of the forces generating effects are district-wide. Putting a treatment into all the schools in an experimental district points the inquiry to one question; installing the innovation in a few selected schools points the inquiry to a quite different question. The teachers in the second study will lack the normal district-wide colleagueship. The designer has to prejudge how important that is.

Suppose it is agreed that Plan A for reading has class-level effects and that there is no contagion or common influence across classes. One might reasonably sample a modest number of districts and several schools per district. One class per school could be assigned to Plan A, any or all the others remaining available as controls. For costly operations such as interviewing parents or testing pupils individually, sampling pupils within the class is sensible. Even so, the class remains the unit for analysis and interpretation. This design represents the population of classes better than would an equal number of classes concentrated in a few schools. If, however, those planning the inquiry are persuaded that a teacher's success depends on what other teachers in the school are doing, they must put all the teachers on Plan A or acknowledge that *UT* is defined eccentrically—that is, as schools-with-one-Plan-A-teacher.

Taking a large collective as the unit obviates the assumption that smaller elements are independent, yet study of the smaller elements remains possible. A design that takes school districts as units supplies information about school-level, class-level, and pupil-level effects (both main and interactive). Pupil effects are nested within classes, and school effects within districts. A case study of a single class can keep an eye on school and district characteristics that influence the class. For statistical power it is important to observe as many collectives as possible. A variable affected by community characteristics is assessed much more precisely if one observes forty schools in forty communities instead of forty schools in ten communities. Irrelevant community factors average out better in the extended sample. The result covering more communities (holding number of schools constant) is more stable from sample to sample.

Treatment Plans and Realizations. In amplifying on the concepts *T* and *t*, I start with the manipulative study. The investigator or administrator sets down in words what the program staff is to do. The treatment *specified* for the unit is *T* (or a sub-*T*). The specification is a verbal statement, an operational definition that gives body to the eventual conclusion:

"We tried T and these were the consequences." The same label may be given different specifications in different investigations; these studies then bear on different T.

In the natural sciences, treatment T can be almost wholly specified; judgment plays only a minor role in the manipulation. The specification includes such things as sterile glassware, chemically pure reagents, and standard conditions of temperature and pressure. Even the stirring of ingredients can be made mechanical and its duration specified. Experience and theory indicate what is irrelevant and need not be mentioned in the operational definition. But room for significant variation remains; Rutherford discovered the element thorium as a consequence of inadvertently moving an electroscope from a corner of the laboratory to a breezier location.

Specifications for a social intervention can also be elaborate, although the control is much less complete than in the physical laboratory. The plan may include directives and guidelines, supervisory procedures, qualifications for personnel delivering the treatment, instructional materials, and more or less detailed schedules for treatment events. In an experimental evaluation of parent-teacher conferences, for example, someone has to decide what the schools will be told in order to elicit their cooperation, what instructions for installing the program will be mailed to teachers and supervisors, and what instructions are to be given to persons sent to help the schools with the project. Anything not specified in T is decided as part of the realization.

The treatment events (t) in a manipulative study are unlikely to be entirely consistent with the investigator's intention. Some rules of delivery may be violated, and there is sure to be variation in respects not specified. When instructional materials are field-tested, for example, a full description of the actual t would include the pace at which the teacher schedules the work, the exercises assigned, the rewards made available to students, and so on. A good after-the-fact description of t would include what is generally spoken of as "delivery"; the description would make clear which elements of the planned treatment each unit u actually received.

The specification for a pilot run of a program usually covers a few gross aspects of the treatment. The planned manipulation may be no more than an order awarding so many dollars per pupil to eligible school districts that intend to improve reading instruction. In the realization, awards may not be distributed evenhandedly; moreover, the districts will purchase different resources for reading instruction with the money, and not all the funds will actually go into reading instruction. It is appropriate to omit from the specification any aspect of the situation that the planner does not intend to control. Such omissions properly broaden the characterization of the T under study. Features brought under control as part of the investigative plan are sometimes inadvertently omitted from the statement; that is a major error because the description then extends beyond the domain investigated.

The treatment is not limited to the planned intervention. Much else matters. Any stimulus of which participants are aware affects behavior; this is true even when the stimulus is an accustomed part of the environment. Measuring operations, for example, often constitute part of the treatment. In industry, routine records of production are often in place prior to an experiment. The workers probably know that such records are continually being made. When a leadership style is introduced, the treatment is that style in conjunction with the record-keeping operation. The same style applied to workers unaware that production records are being kept would constitute a distinctly different treatment.

Measurements introduced by the evaluator are part of the treatment whenever they are "obtrusive"; that is, whenever the clients or the staff administering the treatment are aware of them. Not only the overt measuring operation but anything that is said about what *will* be observed is to be seen as part of the treatment; so is any signal that tells the community that an investigation is going on and hints at its purposes. Those concerned with experimental comparison may call this issue of "obtrusiveness" irrelevant to the comparison, arguing that both treatment groups (experimental and control) would be equally aware of the measurement and equally affected. But communications may have different meanings for experimental and control subjects. Asking a participant in the income maintenance study "Are you seeking work?" reminds her of a moral obligation; reduce that pressure, as would happen when the evaluation ends, and the treatment would be altered.

Treatments take on meaning from participants' past experience; hence, significant aspects of a manipulative study cannot be manipulated. How much, and in what respects, a treatment differs from procedures previously in place is an important part of both the theoretical interpretation and the operational character of an investigation. The injunction to follow a certain plan does not mean the same things to teachers accustomed to that method of instruction as it does to teachers who find the plan novel, and these differences affect what they do (McLaughlin, 1980). I identify the past experience of the participants with u rather than t, but this is only a convention.

The status of t is ambiguous. The realizations are an effect of the manipulation, not a truly independent variable (Cook and Campbell, 1979, p. 62). The swine flu vaccination campaign of 1975 included, in the planned manipulation T, certain kinds of publicity. The vaccination was not the independent controllable manipulation; the announcements about the program played that role. In some cities the target clientele stayed away in droves. Figures on percentages vaccinated in the several sites tell what the local realizations were. Delivery of vaccine was the effective t, but it was a dependent variable, a response to the publicity. In a study of instruction, classroom processes have a similarly ambiguous status. They are a treatment variable, but also a dependent variable, as the discussion of the Learning Environment Inventory in Chapter Two illustrated.

Logically, T is to be identified with the specified manipulation—thus, in the study that supplied funds for reading, any district covered by the order "received the treatment." The investigator may, however, consider as admissible only those realizations that met certain standards—for example, schools where the money clearly did augment the usual instruction in reading. Such after-the-fact selection of *ut* on the basis of a dependent variable limits the definition of *UT*. It is probably wise to treat districts meeting the narrow specification as a sub-*UT* and to examine the facts on other districts also. The sub-*UT* was not directly established by the manipulation.

Some studies are nonmanipulative. The investigator studying a kind of treatment that he cannot or prefers not to install must locate instances of the treatment in the field. *T* then refers to the range of local arrangements that he is willing to examine. The control treatment of HPP was of this kind. The *UT* was simply the then-current population of physics teachers and courses in American high schools. In a nonmanipulative study, the description of *T* is sometimes extremely loose, perhaps no more than a global specification such as "team-taught classes" or "court-ordered busing." Each and every realization that someone labels that way is admissible.

Plans for Observing. Observing operations include tests, interviews, classroom visits (and the instructions given to the visitor), tape recordings of classroom dialogues and procedures for coding the remarks, and searches of archives. There may be observation of background characteristics, of initial and final status on abilities and attitudes, and of intermediate or process variables. In laboratory science, procedures are likely to be so standardized that the distinction between the class *O* and the instance *o* matters little. But field procedures are hard to standardize; fixing the test questions or other ostensible stimuli is only a partial control. A particular testing situation, interviewer, or observer may produce systematically higher or lower scores. Generalization over a universe of observers or interviewers is almost always intended.

The consumers of an evaluation are most often interested in a broadly defined construct such as "reading achievement," but that is too indefinite for research planning. The investigator may best represent the interests of his clients not by choosing one test but by defining a range of diverse reading tasks: reading of classified advertisements, highway signs, poems, instructions for assembling a toy, and so on.

The class O ought to be specified with as much care as U and T. Even to point to a booklet of test items, unduly narrow as that O would be, leaves much unspecified. When will the test be given? By whom? What will students be told about the reason for the test and its importance to them? Until these questions are answered, the range of admissible procedures remains wide. Moreover, procedures presumed to be equivalent and bracketed into O without thought may in fact not be equivalent. A comparatively weak third-grade class, for example, may appear to be much inferior to the average third-grade class on the reading test intended for grade 3, but may appear very little inferior when judged by a less difficult level of the same battery of reading tests (House and others, 1978).

UTO *as a Joint Distribution.* The specification of UTO refers not merely to the separate distributions of admissible u, t, and o but also to the ways in which the three are combined. The joint distribution of u and t within UTO is especially important to consider. The investigator might ideally want to know what would happen, on the average, if every u experienced every treatment realization t (and was measured exhaustively on every o). In such a design, there would be no correlation between characteristics of u and the t that the unit receives. We can say, as shorthand, "the U,T correlation is zero." The correlation remains at zero if, instead of imagining that every u receives every t, we imagine that the u and t are paired at random. If the U,T correlation is zero, then any variable describing the u correlates zero with any variable describing the t. If every u is observed on every o in O, or on a suitable sample, the U,O correlation is zero. Likewise, if there is no systematic relation of characteristics of t to the o chosen for it, the T,O correlation is zero. A zero correlation means absence of confounding.

In social research it is often appropriate for U and T to be correlated. Payments under a welfare plan, for example, may vary according to earned income and marital status. The plan thus confounds sub-T with sub-U. Likewise, a plan for ability grouping in schools would presumably call for different instruction in each ability stratum—again, a nonzero U, T correlation. In these examples the correlation is to be manipulated as dictated by the program plan.

Sometimes the correlation already exists, or arises naturally. When a program is made available to many units, they use the opportunity to various degrees and in various ways; most likely, utilization varies with characteristics of u. We speak of this naturally arising correspondence as an ecological correlation of U and T. In a study of a vaccination program, for example, one might ask about the effect when the vaccine is injected into a randomly selected 10 percent of the community; this calls for a zero U,T correlation. The UTO with an ecological correlation poses the more realistic question "What will happen when the vaccine is made available (in a specified manner)?" When persons are free to accept or reject it, who receives vaccine is correlated with psychological and social characteristics. (Note that the treatment itself changes in strength when delivery changes, since contagion depends on how many persons have been immunized within each circle of persons likely to encounter one another.)

It is natural to think of applying the same measuring operation to all units; this procedure creates zero correlations of O and U and T. There are justifications, however, for planning to collect different data in the sub-U or sub-T, establishing U,O and T,O correlations. For example, schools in the Violence study adopt activities of several types (sub-T); a set of questions and observations on the implementation and consequences of a particular activity might well be developed for those schools where it is installed.

*UTOS, The Domain of Application

When an evaluation is reported, no more than a fraction of the audience is mainly interested in the $UTOS$ that defined the study. The hearers are instead concerned with a *UTOS that differs from the original. The evaluation can serve them if they are able to extrapolate from the observations to the circumstances of *UTOS*. Evaluation results thus have greatest value when they reduce uncertainty about the *UTOS* on which policy discussions center after the data come in. In designing the study, the evaluator ought to anticipate as best he can the U^*, T^*, and O^* that someone will want to know about. The domain *UTOS* may be a broad one that includes the original *UTO*. It may be a domain that lies wholly outside the original or that overlaps it. It may also be narrow —a single community, perhaps, or a single child. My argument applies equally to all these cases.

"Will it work with *our* students?" expresses concern for a comparatively narrow U^*. A difference between two methods of teaching physics, found in a representative national sample, may not hold up in the wealthiest or the most isolated school districts. Whether a finding in Newark will apply even to New York City is an open question. U and U^* differ, and the importance of the differences has to be weighed when actions affecting U^* are being planned.

Interest in an O^* may arise because the original outcome variable covers only a fraction of the relevant outcomes. For example, a science course is quite likely to "succeed" when O is tailored to the lessons covered (Cook, 1974). But because science is always advancing, a sophisticated critic will ask how well graduates of the course are able to reason about research reports not matched to the lessons. Again, a college course in remedial English, found effective in decreasing errors in syntax, will be challenged by a professor who asks whether the quality of ideas in the students' papers also improved. In another instance, a token economy may make classes orderly and work oriented while it is in operation. But a supervisor of teachers can reasonably ask whether students so taught learn to use their energies widely when not under that regimen—that is, when working with no monitor and no direct reward. Finally, when a study reports that "parent participation" makes a difference in quality of education, the indicator of participation may be challenged. The mere presence of parents at an open house or a community meeting, for example, will not fit everyone's definition of "participation." A skeptic may want to know whether parents expressed conflicting opinions and values at the open house or meeting. If only the head count was recorded, this latter question refers to an $O*$.

A main thesis in *Toward Reform* regarding the political uses of evaluation is that the audience is rarely faced with a proposal to adopt the experimental T of the original study. By the end of the study, alterations in the plan will have been suggested. Each variation produces a $T*$, and so does any generalized interpretation of the result. Public comments on the first large trials of compensatory education, for example, were not confined to the UTO for which data were collected. One famous comment will serve as an example: Jensen (1969) said only that compensatory education had failed. He did not mean "and always will"—but political participants who wished to read his comments that way did so and thus passed judgment on all manner of $T*$. Those favoring a compensatory effort contemplated a change in treatment, arguing in this vein: "It is all very well to report negatively on Head Start results after one year. But does not the *especially* bad showing of 'summer only' programs imply that compensatory treatment needs to continue beyond even the regular school-year treatment?" A multiyear program was a $T*$ in that discussion. Later, in the Follow Through Planned Variations study, it became a T under direct study.

The treatments delivered in $*UTOS$ can depart from those in $UTOS$ even when the operational specification of T remains unaltered. When U changes to $U*$ or S to $S*$, some realizations become more frequent and others less frequent; this is true because realization of a treatment depends on the local settings and participants and on the climate of the times. The population of realizations changes with events even when the intervention remains the same. To give a simple example: Adding iodine to salt was introduced to prevent goiter. It worked. But nutritional literature is now warning about the effects of salt on the vascular system; if people decide to use less salt in foods, iodine-in-salt will become a less potent treatment for goiter.

Decisions subsequent to the evaluation take place in a

new setting. In the United States, the headlines of the past two decades have recounted innumerable changes in family life, in the economy, in social institutions, and in the psychology of the public. To name only a few lines of change, some transient and some lasting: the press for excellence in science and mathematics, the birth-control pill and the emergence of new sexual norms, the growing alienation of youth, the countermovements of desegregation and resegregation, the appearance of the energy crisis, the demand for increased community participation in government, and the women's movement. Changes such as these cannot but make a difference in the effects of related social programs. The policy-shaping community trying to use the evaluator's evidence must therefore ask: How much difference for the program does the change from S to S^* make?

A change of outcomes connected with a change in setting is illustrated by a finding of Whinery and colleagues (1976). In a two-phase study of a type of counseling intended to reduce delinquency, they collected data over several years. Early in the work, the counseled males showed gratifyingly little delinquent behavior. Later, however, considerable delinquency occurred. The investigators concluded that lessened opportunity for employment was responsible for the change. Taking conscience as a guide is a luxury for the young person who cannot find a job. Going back to previous studies, Whinery's team found indications of a relationship: Crime rates seemingly lagged one year behind unemployment rates. The behavior of Whinery's cases also was found to be in step with lagged employment rates.

To pose a question to be *directly* investigated is to ask for a description, numerical or verbal, of an aspect of *UTOS*. Any other question in effect requests a similar description for a *UTOS*. Generalized interpretations anticipate the latter questions. Each is a statement about a *UTOS*. "Placing slow learners in special education classes does not (on the average) improve their educational progress" is such a statement. U^*, T^*, and O^* are all broad; the interpreter presumably wished to make just this sweeping statement. "Special education classes" might mean (1) such classes as they are conducted at the time the assertion is made or (2) special classes conducted in any manner. The first interpretation is more cautious, but some hearers might automatically make the second interpretation. Generalized interpretations of this kind clearly refer to a domain of application. If trusted, they could guide policy decisions affecting the whole domain, or decisions about any proposal falling within the domain.

There is no fundamental, logical difference between such categories as "poor readers," "children with learning disabilities," and "autistic children." These labels are all constructs. The only major difference is that "reading ability" is a comparatively well-defined term. Constructs also characterize situations, communities, and institutions—"suburban" and "comprehensive secondary school" are examples. Constructs are used in describing treatments ("client-centered counseling," "protein supplementation") and explanatory processes ("sense of political efficacy," "trust in the therapist"). Conclusions in such abstract terms clearly go well beyond the data and refer to broad $*UTOS$.

Comparative Studies

Either at the time of the original inquiry or later, a comparative question may be asked regarding two or more treatments, populations, or measurements at successive points in time. For the moment, let us think only of a question about two treatments, T_E and T_C, both represented in the original study. The $UTOS$ is subdivided; in effect, there is a domain of experimental subjects and a set of observing operations for T_E; likewise for T_C. The comparative study is, first of all, a study of the two domains separately; conclusions are to be drawn about each sub-$UTOS$. The contrast is secondary. At times I use the symbol Δ to refer to the contrast; a conclusion, we can say, is to be drawn about the contrast $\Delta UTOS$ or —elliptically—about ΔT.

My first reason for considering analysis within treatments as prior to comparison is that the conclusions are meaningful in themselves. If the outcome of T_E is judged to be unsatisfactory, that is important even if T_E outdid T_C. Moreover, the experience with T_E in various sub-U is important for explanation and for planning the next steps. A similar economic concern makes it desirable to record data on the separate treatments for future use. Suppose that treatments 1 and 2 are compared this year and that T_1 triumphs. When T_3 is suggested next year, it will make sense to collect data on T_3 and judge them against the data already recorded for T_1. A purist might call for fresh data on T_1, but cost will be a strong counterargument.

　　The fact that I am not prepared to rule out designs that study a single treatment is a more basic reason for my one-treatment-at-a-time formulation. One-treatment designs are viable, they reach conclusions, and the conclusions are instructive. To help the evaluator decide whether to set up a formal comparative study, a theory of design must discuss noncomparative studies. Many writers on evaluation, including Cook and Campbell, limit themselves by assuming that the difference between T and not-T has already been identified as *the* central research question, to which other questions should be subordinated. I start further back, considering a wider field of possible investigations. I invite the planner to ask whether data on a contrast have sufficient policy importance to deserve the extra investment required.

　　In my notation the comparative study pits one sub-$UTOS$ against another. This has two implications. The first implication is that the contrast is not between the sub-T and does not provide evidence on an effect "of treatment." A complex argument is required to defend the view that the effect depends on the treatment contrast and not on U or S. The second implication is that comparative studies are by no means restricted to treatment contrasts. A contrast, for example, between sub-U or between one sub-UT and another may also be a legitimate evaluative concern. Contrasts of sub-O also appear. Thus, in the Violence study, teachers' statements about the amount of tension in their schools correlated only moderately with the scores derived from similar responses in the student body. This discrepancy became a question to study in its own right. The logic of inference regarding *UTOS* and **UTOS* applies to all such studies.

Consider the following question: "Does the Law School Admission Test (LSAT) predict grade average within the student intake in this law school?" An investigator would draw samples of incoming students at two or more levels of the LSAT, would later collect their grades, and would then calculate a correlation. Differences between sub-*U* are at issue; only one treatment *T* is identified. That this kind of correlational study is not logically different from a contrast of treatments becomes rather obvious when we consider a second question: "Among persons with similar LSAT scores, is college graduation relevant to law school performance?" To get data it would be necessary to admit to law school some persons without B.A.s who do well on the LSAT and to compare them on grades or other criteria with persons possessing B.A.s, LSAT scores being held constant. This study—intervention and all—manifestly *is* an experiment. Samples from two populations are exposed to the same ostensible treatment, they are assessed in the same manner, and their scores are compared. A conclusion can be reached that in the law school as it is (including whatever prejudices instructors have about students without B.A.s), success does or does not correlate with B.A. status when LSAT scores are held constant. This is a report on an effect of baccalaureate training.

Considering the contrast formally, we see that one *UT* has been pitted against another. The first is a population of persons who enter and survive college, apply to law school, and produce acceptable LSAT scores, all as a result of an unanalyzed mixture of self-selection, response to the treatment administered to undergraduates, and institutional selection. The second is a population that received some mix of educational experience short of the B.A. degree (again for entangled reasons) but still applied to law school and produced acceptable LSAT scores. In a court test of the baccalaureate requirement, the judge would have no interest in disentangling all these causes. The judge would want to hear arguments that would help him to decide whether—among persons with the same reported LSAT scores—those with B.A.s do or do not deserve preference over the others. It can readily be seen that the question about the LSAT is formally the same as the question about graduation. The LSAT is an indicator of past development in test form; the bachelor's degree is a similar indicator, even though baccalaureate training is, in effect, a treatment.

Internal and External Inferences

This last section introduces the subject of the next three chapters: the process of making inferences from evaluative data and judging their validity. Understanding this process enables the planner to increase the usefulness of an evaluation. The distinction between *UTOS* and **UTOS* is fundamental because research tactics that generate sound statements about *UTOS* may generate comparatively weak statements about **UTOS*, and vice versa. But the distinction is not sharp, especially when the planner of an evaluation can choose a *UTO* in a way that brings it close to **UTO*.

A statement about *UTOS*, made on the basis of observations on *utoS*, can conveniently be called an internal inference. The inference is internal to *UTOS* in the sense that *utoS* is a subset of observations from that universe. An inference from a sub-*utoS* to the sub-*UTOS* within which it falls is likewise an internal inference. Questions about the trustworthiness of the inference are questions about *internal validity*, as I use the term. Validity attaches to a conclusion and, indeed, to the specific wording of a conclusion (Kruglanski and Kroy, 1976). To speak of "the validity of this experiment" or of "a valid design" is inappropriate because many conclusions can be derived from the same data and these conclusions are not equally warranted. When the same inference is worded more cautiously or less cautiously, validity changes accordingly.

The social research community has been much influenced by the linchpin statement of the Campbell and Stanley monograph (1963, p. 175): "Internal validity is the sine qua non." Some followers have given the doctrine a weight that was never intended, even using it as warrant for rejecting out of hand research designs that do not include a randomly assigned control group. My recommendations are chiefly concerned with heightening external validity. Chapter Four will explain why I reject the Campbell-Stanley priority.

A statement about *UTOS is obviously an external inference, and its trustworthiness is a question of external validity. I shall often speak of the external inference as an *extrapolation*. This term refers to a deliberate projection to a situation outside the range where information was collected. Some examples of external inference are, strictly speaking, interpolations, but I shall not treat them separately.

The internal and external categories were introduced in Campbell's paper of 1957. Cook and Campbell (1976, 1979) made further distinctions. They separated the validity of statistical inference ("statistical conclusion validity") from the validity of "internal" causal inference. I keep the validity of all inferences internal to UTOS in one package; likewise, for reasons that Chapter Four will explain, I do not separate construct validity from external validity as they do. I point out that both external validity and internal validity are matters of degree and that external validity does not depend directly on internal validity. Whether a change in design that increases the validity of a specific internal inference improves or impairs the validity of a specific external inference depends on the content of the two conclusions and on the factual situation. Internal and external validity are not emphatically different. The distinction comes down to whether a conclusion refers to a domain that was deliberately and systematically represented in *utoS* or to some other domain.

Internal validity will generally be greater than external validity when *UTO is broad and UTO is a subset of it (Kruglanski and Kroy, 1976). Otherwise, the conclusion about UTOS may be irrelevant in reaching a conclusion about *UTOS. Methodologists, myself included, have hitherto written as if internal validity "comes first," as if, in other words, a conclusion is first established as true of UTOS and then extended. That is not always the case. My present conception is that a conclusion about a *UTOS extrapolates the evidence on utoS in the light of other experience. The extrapolation is best made from the facts, not from the synoptic conclusion about UTOS. Only under special circumstances would the two paths of inference come out at the same place.

Statistical inference extends the result in the sample to instances similar to those studied—for example, to villages similar to the aldeas studied in the INCAP evaluation. But the term similar is ambiguous. If the villages in *UTOS were part of a roster from which the u of the study were drawn, the inference would be strictly statistical. Also, if there is a clear definition of a class of villages U instead of a roster, a generalization about villages within that class can be internally valid. A statement about a single village within the class can have internal validity if it is weak and probabilistic. (Strong probabilities may be justified if villages are homogeneous in their response to treatment.) When the village falls outside the class or the class is heterogeneous, similarity to the typical village or to specific u has to be judged on substantive criteria. External validity is at issue.

External inference, of course, is not limited to statements of the form "similar case, similar forecast." An extrapolation is a prediction that takes into account known differences between situations. The evaluator asked to say something about *UTOS should draw on all available knowledge, including studies of phenomenally different UTOS and sub-UTOS. The answer will be a conjecture, a best judgment. The prediction may be that experience in *UTOS will differ markedly from that in UTOS. An extrapolation as memorable as any had to do with withdrawing graphite rods from the first atomic pile. The inference was by no means a generalization from a past instance to a class of further instances. The inference was to a first instance.

Validity depends not only on the data collection and analysis but also on the way a conclusion is stated and communicated. Validity is subjective rather than objective: The plausibility of the conclusion is what counts. And plausibility, to twist a cliché, lies in the ear of a beholder.

Science, it is agreed, is consensual; most scientists in a field come to accept the same findings and formulations. Evaluation research is even more social in its uses than basic research; and while consensus about politically laden matters may be only a dream, an evaluation must aim to reduce disagreement about its subject or, at least, to produce a shared understanding of those matters that it is able to clarify. But persuasion begins at home. Unless a chain of evidence and reasoning is credible to the person who advances it, it can scarcely be expected to persuade the critical listener. Cook and Campbell (1979, p. 55) appropriately stress the investigator's responsibility to judge validity. In basic research, which they have chiefly in mind, the investigator must be his own best critic in deciding on the next step in a research program and in deciding what to publish. In evaluation, obviously, the important matter is whether the evidence will persuade the onlookers.

Associating internal inference with "deduction" suggests that internal validity might somehow be made *logically* compelling. Campbell and Stanley (1963, p. 187) have contrasted the looseness of inference to *UTOS* with the deductive and final character of argument to *UTOS:* "Whereas the problems of *internal* validity are solvable within the limits of the logic of probability statistics, the problems of external validity are not logically solvable in any neat, conclusive way" (see also Cook and Campbell, 1979, pp. 55, 86). I shall argue that an interpretation based on a tight design brings in substantive assertions to reach a statement even about *UTOS*. Ennis (1973) makes the point that a causal statement limited to events in the sample requires substantive presumptions. Importing prior knowledge moves internal inference from the realm of pure logic into the realm of rhetoric, of persuasion.

The Platonic and Cartesian notion that a conclusion can be really true or really false is of no help to us. It is, however, appropriate to speak of a conclusion as "justified" or "warranted"—that is, it can be highly plausible to critical-minded, open-minded listeners. Moreover, the evaluator has to consider audiences that are not open-minded. Insofar as his evidence and argument can influence citizens who already hold strong opinions, the value of the study increases. House (1980) has developed this line of thought:

> Expecting evaluation to provide compelling and necessary conclusions hopes for more than evaluation can deliver. Especially in a pluralistic society, evaluation cannot produce necessary propositions. But if it cannot produce the necessary, it can provide the credible, the plausible, and the probable. Its results are less than certain but still may be useful.
>
> Proving something implies satisfying beyond doubt the understanding of a universal audience with regard to the truth. To produce proof that a universal audience comprised of all rational men would accept requires overcoming local or historical particularities. Certainty requires isolating data from [their] total context, as, for example, in the terms of a syllogism. Logical certainty is achievable only within a closed, totally defined system like a game [p. 72]. . . .
>
> Explanation implies a person who is understanding the explanation. It does not exist by itself. The understanding is ultimately reducible to something familiar in the mind of the audience doing the understanding—or else it is not an explanation.
>
> Similarly, unless an evaluation provides an explanation for a particular audience, and enhances the understanding of that audience by the content and form of the arguments it presents, it is not an adequate evaluation for that audience, even though the facts on which it is based are verifiable by other procedures. One indicator of the explanatory power is the degree to which the audience is persuaded. Hence, an evaluation may be "true" in the conventional sense but not persuasive to a particular audience for whom it does not serve as an explanation. In the fullest sense, then, an evaluation is dependent both on the person who makes the evaluative statement and on the person who receives it [p. 89].

One phrase above is taken from Perelman and Ol-brechts-Tyteca (1969), who identify the domain of argumentation with "the credible, the plausible, the probable, to the degree that the latter eludes the certainty of calculations" (p. 1). In his *Discourse on Method,* Descartes ([1637] 1910) set a pattern of thought that dominated philosophy for three centuries. He disparaged argumentation, finding deductive reasoning the only perfect reasoning, and very nearly took the position that whatever was short of certainty (*vraisemblable*) should be regarded as false. But argumentation, according to Perelman and Olbrechts-Tyteca, is required for persuasion, and persuasion for action. What will persuade depends on what the hearer already believes. A proof compels assent in that special case where all participants have agreed to circumscribe the domain "formally, scientifically, or technically" (p. 46). That might possibly happen with respect to a factual question about a treatment; it cannot possibly happen with regard to a political issue.

4

↜ *The Limited Reach of Internal Validity*

This chapter amplifies the concept of internal validity introduced at the end of Chapter Three. After reviewing the claims that have been made for its importance, I shall argue that internal validity is of only secondary concern to the evaluator.

The causal statements for which internal validity can be claimed are peculiarly restricted. Causal conclusions are conditional, and conditions may severely limit the application of such conclusions. In Chapter Five it will be seen that the reasoning leading from *utos* to *UTOS* is not exclusively formal or statistical. Many statements, only a few of them explicit, link the formal reasoning to the real world; their plausibility determines the force of the argument. Internal inference, then, is much less deductive and rigorous than others have suggested.

The real and apparent conflicts between my position and Campbell's will be examined closely. Readers who are content to skim that analysis should note in particular my identification of internal validity with reproducibility rather than with causal inference. The argument is directed particularly to readers who have been interested in what Cook and Campbell (1979, chap. 1) say about causal inference in social research.

Key Terms

What does it mean to say that "internal validity is the sine qua non" of research? Here is the context in which Campbell and Stanley (1963, p. 175) placed the famous statement:

> Fundamental . . . is the distinction between *internal validity* and *external validity. Internal validity* is the basic minimum without which any experiment is uninterpretable: Did in fact the experimental treatments make a difference in this specific experimental instance? *External validity* asks the question of *generalizability:* To what populations, settings, treatment variables, and measurement variables can this effect be generalized? Both types of criteria are obviously important, even though they are frequently at odds in that features increasing one may jeopardize the other. While *internal validity* is the sine qua non, and while the question of *external validity,* like the question of inductive inference, is never completely answerable, the selection of designs strong in both types of validity is obviously our ideal. This is particularly the case for research on teaching, in which generalization to applied settings of known character is the desideratum.

Although Cook and Campbell (1976, p. 246; 1979, p. 82) say that external validity is of special interest in applied work, they continue to assign priority to internal validity. This entire line of thought originated in a 1957 Campbell paper on *basic* psychological research; later writings extended the argument to applied studies but never examined directly the requirements of work that has a practical orientation. Increasing one kind of validity may jeopardize the other, according to the passage quoted above. I agree with that and with the following Cook-Campbell statement (1976, p. 246): "'Common sense' is obviously called for in trading off internal and external validity in any research project." What I do not accept is the general precedence given to internal validity.

The enthusiasm for internal validity and randomized comparative experiments followed from a special perspective that the writings of Campbell and his allies, down to 1979, failed to make explicit. At last, in 1979 Cook and Campbell did carefully but briefly delimit the value claimed for internal validity, saying that they were *assuming* that their readers were centrally concerned with causal inference (Cook and Campbell, 1979, p. 91). Further along, this demurrer appears: "Though random assignment is germane to the research goal of assessing whether the treatment may have caused any observed effects, it is conceptually irrelevant to all other research goals" (p. 343). They also note that "the case for random assignment cannot be made on the grounds that it is a general facilitator of high-quality research" (p. 384). The "other research goals" and aspects of "quality" have to do with the relevance of the information to prospective users. Randomization may be achieved at the expense of relevance. But relevance is surely the sine qua non in evaluation. Cook and Campbell (1979, pp. 344–345) themselves say that in evaluation random experiments may be *inadvisable,* not merely hard to arrange.

The concept of internal validity expressed by Campbell in 1957 lost shape as it passed from hand to hand during the next two decades. The 1979 monograph of Cook and Campbell gets back to the original logic, but only the meticulous reader will realize just how narrow a meaning the term is given. Internal validity and "statistical conclusion validity" together are said to warrant one particular kind of end statement—a statement that some action had a causal effect in the operationally defined *UOS*. The statement may be elaborated into an interval estimate for the magnitude of the effect. The identification of the cause does not have internal validity; the action that made a difference might not have been mentioned in specifying *T*. Cook and Campbell are constrained by the way they state the problem. They intended to limit their book to causally oriented research and so were prepared to discuss the validity only of a conclusion that is explicitly causal. I must extend the term *internal validity,* because the validity of *any* statement about *UTOS* is a proper concern of the planner and the user of an evaluation. Indeed, I shall simply identify internal validity with the ability of a statement about *UTOS* or a prespecified subset of it to withstand challenge. Most of the issues remain identical whether internal validity embraces statements about *UTOS* or only statements about *utoS*. Campbell could object that I have taken liberties with the term because he associated internal validity with a *causal* assertion about *utoS*. But a present-tense causal statement is inherently counterfactual, extending beyond the events observed; it has to be supported by external inference.

My thought comes down to this: Evaluative conclusions are descriptive. They may be elaborated into explanatory or causal propositions, but the elaboration comes second. For evaluators, the validity of descriptive information is of prime importance. Moreover, my argument about evaluation and the comments on design that follow from it could be extended to more "basic" research. Reasoning about the nature of inference and the role of boundary conditions is pertinent to research of all kinds; but at some points in an extended program of basic research, internal validity is more significant than it is likely to be in evaluation. When exploratory work has pinpointed a question, *then* one calls for a well-controlled study of a fixed treatment.

Many aspects of a theory about natural and social events—atomic theory, for example, or linguistic theory—could be forced into a causal mold. But "How . . . ?" and "Why . . . ?" questions do not all reduce to "Does X have a demonstrable effect on Y?" The effect-size question is a way of testing hypotheses about process when explanation has advanced to the point where it implies a specific consequence of a manipulation. Not all explanations evolve in this way, and there are many other kinds of hypotheses and tests that can confirm and infirm explanations (Cronbach and Meehl, 1955).

Meanings of "Generalization." The traditional association of external validity with the equivocal term *generalization* can be confusing. In logic a generalization is unqualified: "All crows are black." Empirical generalizations are weaker: "Giving additional calories to expectant mothers whose diet would otherwise be substandard will produce stronger, brighter children." That type of conclusion (which could be put forward on the basis of the INCAP study) ought to be taken less as a law than as a working hypothesis: "In future instances I shall expect that result and act accordingly until the expectation is contradicted." The result is not expected for every mother or for every instance of intervention. Even though the generalization does not carry the qualification "tends to," professional readers and most lay readers will know that the trend is statistical. A local contradiction will be recognized if a reasonably large series of cases of some type run predominantly counter to the hypothesis, not otherwise. Then the statement will be hedged by noting the exception.

To generalize is to extend a statement. In the simplest case, one observes a number of instances of a class, finds that X happens, and concludes that X would also happen if other instances of the class were observed. I would include this statistical generalization within internal validity whenever the class was identified in advance. Inference from sample to population is generalization; and if the sample was not drawn strictly at random, inference must be justified by nonstatistical arguments (Edgington, 1980).

Cook and Campbell (1979) seem to limit internal generalization ("statistical conclusion validity") to generalization over persons (or units) only—from *utoS* to *UtoS* and not to *UTOS*. But if *t* was not identical to *T* (and *o* to *O*), the broader generalization would be wanted by those who posed a question about *UTOS*. The planned *T* was no more than a hopeful specification. Human actions translated it into an intervention, accurately or inaccurately. The realizations were a sample of what *T* leads to in setting *S*. Only when the realizations adhered perfectly to the plan can one be unconcerned about the way the *t* were sampled.

Generalization over *o* is similarly ignored in conventional analysis. To be sure, an investigator can limit his conclusion to Form B of the Metropolitan Test administered on May 7 by the class teacher, but he is not likely to do so. Recognizing the generalization from *o* to *O* has major consequences in evaluation. Insofar as specific features of *o* systematically raise or lower scores in a way that a second *o* would not confirm, the data can be seriously distorted. It is notorious that small changes in the wording of a question can produce a large shift in reported public opinion on an issue. Random error, too, makes a difference, especially in predictor variables. The regression of outcomes on a pretest *o* is invariably shallower than the regression onto the true score that would be obtained by averaging all admissible *o*. Unless the investigator deliberately states the research question in terms of an incompletely measured variable, he surely has the true score for operation *O* in mind, if not some broader construct *O**.

Generalization need not simply carry forward the summary that describes the sample. A formula can construct an estimate for *UTOS* whenever *utoS* is formed by systematic sampling. In surveying a community, for example, one might elicit reactions from an age-stratified sample. Drawing the same number of persons from each stratum is probably a good idea. Proper weighting converts the sample information into a picture of the population. The sample then can be called "systematically representative" even though the makeup of the sample was not that of the domain.

Internal generalization is not always to the prespecified *UTO* as a whole. If a sub-*U* of a particular kind gives a response atypical of the main data, it is fair enough to consider this category separately. Generalization can then be stronger. But special inferential difficulties arise in after-the-fact identification of the target. (A study by Berman to be discussed early in Chapter Five provides an example.)

Unless the class defined by *UTO* is homogeneous in all relevant respects, a conclusion is a summary statistic. It speaks of an average or of the proportion of instances where something happens. This kind of statistic is directly useful to a synoptic policy maker whose actions will affect a large number of units; for her, the payoff is described by the average (or other suitable index). But the person whose actions will affect only a single unit or treatment realization is concerned with the payoff in that instance. For her, the overall statistic is only an indicator—and a crude one if the class is heterogeneous. Paradoxical as it may seem, the required "generalization" is from a statement about the class to an instance within the class. The assumption has to be that what is true on average is true (within certain limits) for the case in point.

I illustrate with Coleman's report on public and private schools (Coleman, Hoffer, and Kilgore, 1981). This report was based on a carefully drawn sample of public schools, Catholic schools, and "other private" schools. The statistical comparisons treated these as separate domains, but many of the verbal conclusions and virtually all the news accounts and public comments merged the two "private" categories.

Of course, a defense can be offered for this kind of merging. A member of Congress deciding on a tax credit to offset private school tuition wants to know if such tuition buys good education; the average student achievement, calculated over all eligible schools, addresses that concern. In contrast, consider the non-Catholic parent deciding whether her child will be better off in a private school. She does not care about the grand average, and the average for "other private" schools embraces military academies, schools serving the learning disabled, elite prep schools, Bible Belt schools, and so-called progressive schools. Even if far more than Coleman's twenty-seven schools had contributed to the average, the average would have no direct meaning for the parent. The inference from the aggregated report to the individual decision is to be justified, if at all, on the grounds of *external* validity. This would be true even if the private and public schools down the street from this particular home had entered Coleman's sample, and it would be true even if the data had been generated by random assignment of children to schools.

To recapitulate: In my formulation internal validity is the concern when a *UTOS* is defined, a *utoS* that supposedly conforms to the definition is observed, and inference back to the designated *UTOS* is made. Internal validity is best assured when *uto* is systematically representative of *UTO*. (Sampling of all three aspects, jointly, has to be suitably planned.)

When a statement is made about a **UTOS* of which *utoS* is not thought to be systematically representative, external validity is at issue. This is better called an extrapolation than a generalization. It is a prediction that takes into account the known differences between situations. A planner in Gambia who hears that *atole* in Guatemala raised a certain test score by five points (on the average) has somehow to take into account the likelihood that Gambian villagers will accept food delivered in a similar manner, that a food supplement produced with Gambian raw materials will have similar nutritional effects, that the test in question is close enough to the experience of Gambian children to be meaningful, and, most important, that the baseline nutrition of the Gambians is enough like that in Guatemala for the nutritional needs to be similar qualitatively and quantitatively. If the similarities are sufficient, she may generalize in the simple sense of expecting to equal Guatemala's record in Gambia. Insofar as she perceives changes in milieu or treatment operations to be important, she will predict a result different from the original.

Cook and Campbell (1976, 1979) distinguish external validity from "construct validity," identifying the former with "generalization." But it is unreasonable to say that the Gambian generalizes when she predicts the same result and not when she adjusts the Guatemalan figure on the basis of knowledge about the two countries. Either inference is situation specific; the Gambian **UTOS* can be as operational in conception as *UTOS* in Guatemala. A World Health Organization official may extend the conclusion to countries where the average caloric intake of mothers is within a given range. The inference to Gambia and the inference to the class of countries are logically similar. The official makes allowances on the basis of her beliefs about nutritional, developmental, community, and administrative processes. These beliefs are a construction of reality. That is why I do not separate construct validity from external validity. Cook and Campbell rightly emphasize the role of constructs in extrapolation; they are mistaken, I think, when they separate conclusions *worded* in somewhat abstract language from extrapolations to concretely identifiable U^* and S^*. Statements about them often depend on substantive theory—on generalized knowledge—for support. I shall return to the topic of external validity in Chapter Five.

Internal Validity as Reproducibility. An investigator hopes to reach the same conclusion that other competent scientists would reach if they set out to study the same specific question at the same time. Unlike Campbell and his co-workers, I identify internal validity with reproducibility. The report on *UTOS* derives from a sample of events in a particular period of time. Essentially, the inquiry is to be seen as a "completion test"; the research plan is a description in blank of the phenomenon, and the blanks are to be filled in on the basis of the data. To ask about reproducibility is to ask whether another investigation would have filled in the blanks with the same answers.

The issue is not how well investigations in different times and places agree. When a design is highly controlled and well executed, a conclusion may fail to replicate because conditions change. The Scranton income maintenance experiment was patterned on the Trenton experiment, but it was a parallel study rather than a replication. Scranton data were collected in a different labor market at a different time. Only implausibly strong assumptions (or a very loose statement of the research question) could justify saying that the two trials investigated the same *UTO*.

Reproducibility is to be judged by a thought experiment—that is, by a hypothetical replication. When a design is proposed, the investigator tries to anticipate sources of unwanted variation that would decrease reproducibility (see Chapter Eight). When the conclusion about *UTOS* is reported, a critic asks, "Is it to be believed that every other investigator would have filled in the blanks in the same way?"

Internal validation, then, requires an exercise of imagination (Cook and Campbell, 1979, p. 55). Imagination enables one to consider the reproducibility of a statement about a historical event that could not possibly be repeated.

A statement about *UTOS* may be definite or indefinite. Obviously, weaker statements are more likely to be confirmed. "Slow delivery of supplies _____ (was/was not) a frequent complaint" is more likely to be answered the same way twice than is "_____ was the most frequent complaint." There is an obvious reciprocity between definiteness and validity; a definite statement, being a stronger claim to knowledge, is more questionable (other things being equal) than an indefinite one. Some will say that if reproducibility is the test of internal validity, then validity has been reduced to reliability. This is not a weighty objection; reliability is a part of validity (Cronbach and others, 1972, p. 378).

It will be objected that a false finding can be reproduced if an erroneous procedure is successfully duplicated. It is obvious that errors of procedure—arising, for example, from a wrongly calibrated instrument—may impair reproducibility. When several investigators make the same errors of observation, however, these are almost always errors of verbal interpretation, not of procedure. A challenge to interpretation comes under the heading of *external* validity, as when a skeptic proposes a different set of operations and asks whether the resulting report would be consistent with the original interpretation. Interpretations that invoke constructs can be checked only in this way (by thought experiments, or by actual evidence when cost and time permit). But the critical check cannot be started until someone manages to step outside the original investigator's belief system and invent a challenge to it.

Reproducibility is obviously related to the adequacy with which investigative procedures are described. Student scientists are told that the reason for describing research operations meticulously is to enable others to replicate the study; but in the behavioral sciences replication, even of laboratory research, is rare. Thus, the primary reason for the advice is that if an investigator is explicit about the steps he took, a qualified referee can judge the reproducibility of the conclusions. To reach a positive verdict, the critic has to believe, among other things, that the original investigator honestly described what he thought he did. A reader who accepts a conclusion as reproducible without reading all the procedures and thinking hard about them is accepting the conclusion on the basis of prior beliefs. Either that, or she is expressing enormous faith in journal referees and in the investigator's capacity for self-criticism.

Lykken (1968), writing on standards of excellence in psychological research, spoke of three kinds of replication. I shall build on his thinking, with modifications. Lykken defined the three kinds of replication according to what a second investigator does, since he was writing about studies that can be cheaply replicated. However, he had both thought experiments and actual replications in mind. In contrast, I define levels of reproducibility according to the information supplied to the second investigator. That enables one to judge reproducibility without carrying out the second study.

Lykken's first two categories match mine; his third has to do with checking on the abstract or generalized hypothesis of the first study by *deliberately* altering the procedures. For present purposes I substitute a third category that remains closer to internal validity. Fiske (1978, p. 182) discusses the validity of research on personality with a scheme much like Lykken's, referring to "replicability," "reproducibility," and "generalizability" as successively broader concepts. Indeed, when a research report or plan uses ambiguous language in describing U,T, or O, my third category does shade into external validity.

If we assume S to be unchanged in the replication, my three levels of reproducibility will then correspond to three questions:

1. How closely will the results of a second study agree with those of the original study if the procedures of the first study are exactly repeated on fresh samples from U, T, and O?

2. How closely will the results of additional studies agree with those of the original study if each additional investigator tries to carry out the original procedures according to the best available description of them?
3. How closely will the results of additional studies agree with those of the original study when each additional investigator is given the description of the target *UTO* and chooses procedures for himself in a reasonable manner?

Obviously, reproducibility$_2$ and reproducibility$_3$ depend on the original investigator's communication of procedures. The more operational his statement of the question to be studied, the less distinction there is between the three kinds of reproducibility.

An evaluation has a life cycle. When the task is first considered, only reproducibility$_3$ is possible and *UTO* is loosely conceptualized: "We want an evaluation of this new physics course, and we want it to cover both knowledge of and attitudes about science." It is a reasonable guess that two teams, sent off independently to do such an evaluation, would plan rather different studies. Some relationships would be checked by both studies; others would be touched on in one study only. Even where the two addressed the same questions, the designs might differ enough to change the result.

Once the design is firmed up, reproducibility$_2$ becomes possible, and two teams could carry out more or less the same study. In working out procedures that the plan left unspecified, an investigator creates a particular inquiry that would perhaps have a very high degree of reproducibility$_1$ if he could keep in mind all the details of his procedures. Many of them, however, were spontaneous adaptations never systematized. A careful statement of the *systematic* procedures would nonetheless enable others to judge reproducibility$_2$ or, with a stable phenomenon, to carry out an actual replication. The message that reaches a nontechnical audience, however, will be a compressed and generalized statement, rather like that with which the evaluation effort began. For such a broad conclusion, only reproducibility$_3$ is possible. Unless terminology and appropriate research procedures for the topic have been crystallized, investigators are unlikely to conduct equivalent studies. They may, in fact, study fundamentally different variables under the same name. When that is suspected, the distinction between reproducibility$_3$ and external validity vanishes.

As Lykken (1968) points out, reproducibility$_1$ is best achieved when the *original* investigator collects additional sets of data, drawing on the same pool of subjects. The intended procedures are repeated, and so are many acts that were not deliberate. (Lykken refers to the cues the trainer unwittingly gave to the mysteriously intelligent horse Clever Hans.) Any bias, any systematic error in statistical reasoning, and any shortsightedness in interpretation contribute to reproducibility of this kind. The variation over the several reports could be represented in a numerical index of reproducibility. It would include far more than the ordinary statistical sampling error, particularly if the original data were collected in a batch; then an inadvertent change of procedure would affect an entire treatment group. Reproducibility$_1$ no doubt seems extremely limited, but it is no narrower than internal validity in Campbell's strict sense, as we shall see.

Reproducibility$_2$ is close to the ordinary conception of strict replication of another scientist's work. The original investigator writes down everything he recognizes to be important in his procedures. These procedures describe the classes U, T, and O rather than u, t, and o as such. Thus, a report may say that a Gerbrands tachistoscope was used or that a 5 percent area sample of Toledo was drawn. It does not give the serial number of the instrument or the house addresses of the respondents in Toledo. The study was concerned with some larger UTO, within which those examplars fit. If the original investigator is cautious in his wording, his conclusion will severely restrict the range of procedures legitimate for the replication. For example, the definition of a narrow UTO would begin: "When single 12-point Bodoni Bold capital letters are exposed in a Gerbrands tachistoscope . . ." But to begin, "In tachistoscopic exposure of letters," broadens the domain, and the result is less likely to be reproduced. How much less? That is a substantive question.

Reproducibility$_3$ envisions that investigators will address a question that is not definitely operationalized. If they share a common understanding of the words in which the question is stated, they can hope that their studies will be equivalent even though their designs differ. In the absence of such companion studies, whether the terms are ambiguous remains a matter for judgment.

A narrow *UTO*, explicitly described, makes each level of reproducibility easier to attain. The definition of *UTO* need not be explicit, clear, or operational; the degree of reproducibility can be considered even if the description is loose. For a conclusion worded loosely, however, reproducibility is likely to be slight, and external validity becomes the chief concern.

Hearnshaw on Burt. An extended example may be instructive. I take up an evaluation—qualitative and historical —of a man and not of a program. That choice makes the story easier to tell and illustrates the reach of the concepts of reproducibility. The late Cyril Burt was a controversial figure, especially because of inconsistencies in his reports on twins, which supported the thesis that mental ability is largely determined by heredity. Hearnshaw's (1979) biography evaluated the man and his work. In reviewing the book (Cronbach, 1979), I had to decide particularly about reproducibility$_2$. But reproducibility$_3$ is a better starting place for this account.

If another qualified and honest scholar had set out to investigate Burt as man, scholar, and public figure, not neglecting the disputed research, would his main conclusions have matched Hearnshaw's? To think through this question, one works out possible lines of inquiry and compares them with those of Hearnshaw. The differences would be few, I believe. The replicator might have interviewed some Burt acquaintances that Hearnshaw did not, or might have given more attention to citations and reviews of Burt's work prior to the controversy. But I could not think of major sources that Hearnshaw failed to use, and I would expect an independent investigator to have done what Hearnshaw did: examine

diaries, interview persons who had known Burt, read the
public documents to which Burt had contributed, check archives of institutions where Burt had worked, and so on. Assuming impartial choice of informants and conscientious
reading by all parties, reproducibility$_3$ would presumably be
good. This, of course, implies reproducibility at the two lower
levels.

Turn for a moment to reproducibility$_1$. That amounts
to asking, "Suppose that Hearnshaw had turned up a different set of informants, correspondence, and archives and had
based his conclusions on them; would the conclusions have
differed?" (I assume use of the same published sources and
the indispensable diaries.) My judgment at this level of analysis was also favorable. Hearnshaw's sources spanned the
spectrum from detractors to admirers of Burt. To believe
that a different sample would have changed the story importantly, one has to imagine the existence of documents radically at variance with the extensive file Hearnshaw used. A
document that could not be reconciled with the present file
can be imagined; that one would turn up seems improbable.

For reproducibility$_2$, whether another reader-inter-
viewer-interpreter would have selected differently and
reached a discordant summary of facts is central. A study like
Hearnshaw's allows far more latitude for bias and carelessness than a technical, quantitative study. How serious such
failings may be is a matter of speculation unless one is prepared to redo a good fraction of the work. The clues suffice
to support another favorable judgment—for example,
Hearnshaw was ready to display Burt's achievements, along
with his shortcomings, and to side with a critic of Burt on one
point and not another. (On matters of explanation—that is,
with regard to the inference from observed facts to Burt's
mental states—I have less confidence in Hearnshaw. For example: Did Burt engage in deliberate deception, inventing or
falsifying the twin data? Counsel for the defense would arrange the facts sympathetically and fill gaps with imaginings
that differ from Hearnshaw's. Likewise, on Burt's psychological makeup and its origins, I cannot disprove what Hearn-

shaw says, but I believe that there could be alternative explanations.)

To examine internal validity, I had to imagine alternative inquiries. I considered the internal consistency and size of the sample of documents and informants, along with the objectivity of data processing. But imagination has limits. We will never know whether Hearnshaw's story is the one that would have been told by an observer—an o^*—looking over Burt's shoulder at certain crucial moments.

Campbell's Minimal Inference. The final topic in this definitional section concerns the strict and severely limited meaning that Campbell has assigned to internal validity. My understanding—based on Campbell's early papers (1957; with Winch and Campbell, 1969), Cook and Campbell (1979, pp. 37, 38, 80), and personal communication from Campbell—is that he seeks to enhance the internal validity of a minimal inference. From the outset Campbell was interested in causal interpretations of treatment comparisons. But surely most readers were thinking of the question "Did T make a difference?" and interpreting it as the statistical question "Does the outcome mean in the treated population differ from that in a similar population exposed to another kind of treatment?" As a matter of fact, Campbell's ostensible intent was *not* to ask about a population or about a class of treatments. Indeed, he did not make even reproducibility$_1$ a requirement for internal validity.

All too easily overlooked in the quotation from Campbell and Stanley (1963) at the start of this chapter is the phrase "in this specific experimental instance" and their deliberate use of the past tense at a key point. They define internal validity as pertinent only to an interpretation of a particular historical event. The interpretation is not a prediction about other instances, not a lawlike statement. Only in a trivial sense is it "explanatory." In the history of a true-experiment *uto*, some action by the experimenter caused a subsequent measurement to have a value other than the one it would have had if the experimenter had acted in another *particular* manner (perhaps no action, perhaps an alternative action). That is the whole interpretation. The sentence is a counterfactual statement: "If this intervention had not occurred, there would have been no difference." The statement is a twin of: "Had the nose of Cleopatra been shorter, the whole face of the world would have been changed."

Campbell does not say and seemingly does not mean that something the experimenter was *conscious* of doing produced the difference. It could be that his study lacked reproducibility$_1$. If the experimenter himself could not obtain the effect a second time, the finding would be pointless (as Kruglanski and Kroy, 1976, protest). To demand minimal reproducibility is thus to set a standard higher than Campbell's.

Jouvenel (1967, pp. 85, 96) emphasizes, as I shall, that the effect of an intervention depends on initial conditions, and that without a close analysis of those conditions one's experiment teaches nothing. To drive home the point, he reconsiders the alchemists of bygone centuries. They must have succeeded in producing gold or silver, by Jouvenel's reading of their history, but presumably they did it by accidentally starting with crude raw materials that contained the noble element. Hence, their result depended on unidentified conditions. Thus, James Price, "after making gold and silver in the presence of reliable witnesses in Oxford in 1782, was ordered by the Royal Society to reproduce his experiment under the supervision of three specially appointed men of science. Price poisoned himself on the day they were to appear. One may suppose that he had simply made a mistake, having used impure substances, and that, his supplies exhausted, he was driven to despair by his inability to obtain the same results with a new batch of minerals" (p. 96).

Deeply buried in Campbell and Stanley (1963, pp. 193–194) and in a rarely cited paper by Winch and Campbell (1969), we glimpse what Campbell apparently has always meant the term *internal validity* to refer to: an inference devoid of generalization. I shall first state Campbell's idea in abstract form and then put it concretely. Thus, we find N units willing to accept random assignment and remain to the end of the study. We allocate them randomly to subsets of size

$N/2$. We expose each member of subset 1 to condition t_1. The necessary minimum is that the investigator instruct himself to provide some stimulus (for example, words, drugs, or food) to all units; then the t_1 will have some feature in common, though perhaps not the intended one. The treatment need not be uniform over units and need not conform to the instruction. The investigator instructs himself to expose subset 2 to condition t_2 (possibly "no special treatment"). This too can be a mix of events, but only by happenstance would a realization include the stimulus identifying a t_1. Every unit is measured similarly when the treatment period ends. A difference in outcome mean Δ_e is observed for the particular realized experiment e.

Random division of the fixed sample could produce $N(N - 1)/2$ distinct subsets u_1; hence, any of the $N(N - 1)/2$ equivalent studies might have been carried out on these N units. Let Δ_E stand for the mean of these numerous possible Δ_e. Δ_E will be zero if t_1 and t_2 have the same effect on every unit or if their effects average out the same over *these* units.

Suppose that Δ_e turns out to be .6 points. The statistician is able to check whether this result would be likely if Δ_E is truly zero. To do so, he distributes the final scores from the original experiment into two *random* subsets and calculates another Δ_e. Repeating the procedure over and over, he ultimately has a set of values of Δ_e whose mean will be very close to zero. If the observed value of Δ_e is well out toward the tail of the distribution of the constructed Δ_e, the statistician says that the observed difference probably did not arise from a lucky split. This is a "randomization test" of a conclusion about the sample (Edgington, 1980). (Technically, it would be better to convert Δ_e to the t statistic than to stop with the difference in means. This kind of test is pertinent only to the randomized comparative experiment, and it may report significance when use of the tabled t or F distribution does not, or vice versa.)

To make this idea concrete, I turn to the INCAP experiment discussed in Chapter Two. The small number of units (four villages) permits a full demonstration. Two vil-

lages were assigned at random to *atole* and two to *fresco*. Take
the following suppositious numbers to be the mean weights
of boys in the study at age three:

$$
\left.\begin{array}{l}
\textit{Atole } \text{village A : mean} = 12.2 \text{ kg.} \\
\textit{Atole } \text{village B : mean} = 12.6 \text{ kg.}
\end{array}\right\} 12.4 \\
\left.\begin{array}{l}
\textit{Fresco } \text{village C : mean} = 12.0 \text{ kg.} \\
\textit{Fresco } \text{village D : mean} = 11.6 \text{ kg.}
\end{array}\right\} 11.8
\qquad \Delta_e = .6
$$

Since there are only four units, we can list all the possible divisions of the data, arranging them in the order of their Δ_e:

Atole AB, *Fresco* CD;	means	12.4, 11.8 kg; Δ_e	.6 (observed)
BC	AD	12.3, 11.9	.4
AC	BD	12.1, 12.1	.0
BD	AC	12.1, 12.1	.0
AD	BC	11.9, 12.3	−.4
CD	AB	11.8, 12.4	−.6

The observed Δ_e is at the tail; the statistician would therefore
say, "There is one chance in three that a difference this large
in either direction would occur if Δ_e is zero." With four units,
of course, no outcome could counter the null hypothesis; but
with slightly larger Ns, the difference has a chance to reach
conventional levels of significance. (The actual INCAP study
was able to compile indirect lines of argument to support the
relation of weight to food intake.)

The conclusion capable of having internal validity in
Campbell's sense is. "Something made a difference." Cook
and Campbell (1976, 1979) are careful to say that labeling the
cause raises a question of construct validity and that the interpretation cannot be purely deductive. *Identifying* the cause is
not part of the claim for internal validity. For example, a difference found in the Harvard Project Physics (HPP) experiment on behavior could be due entirely to the heightened
morale of experimental teachers and students rather than to
the quality of the course of study; still, the "made a difference" report is internally valid.

Campbell's "made a difference" inference is minimal.

The villages in the INCAP study are *not* regarded as a sample from a population of villages. Rather, the allocation to subsets is regarded as a sample from a finite population of assignments. Inference is from Δ_e to $\Delta UtoS$, where U consists of the N units in the study and only of them. Inference is restricted to the sets of t_1 and $_{t2}$ actually in the study, though it embraces all possible ut pairings. Campbell thus has given $UTOS$ a restricted meaning. U, T_1, T_2, and O (as well as S) are all defined by the research operations *as realized*. With this understanding, my $UTOS$ schema includes his special case. He claims internal validity for his design because a statistically rare difference would imply that Δ_E very probably is greater than zero (assuming a positive sign for Δ_e).

A small modification of the statistical procedure produces a kind of confidence interval. We could conclude that a Δ_e as small as the observed .6 would be expected by chance no more than one time in 6 when the true treatment effect is 1.61 or larger. (I obtain this significance level by subtracting an arbitrarily postulated Δ_E of 1.61 from the means for two *atole* villages and then regrouping villages as before.) An interpreter might now assert that a difference of 1.60—the largest value consistent with the data (at $p < .16$)—is not worthwhile. But such a value judgment would be external to the experiment.

Although a large Δ_e presumably shows that "something made a difference," a tiny Δ_e does *not* show that what the experimenter did made no difference. I am not making the timeworn point that one cannot prove a null hypothesis; rather, I refer to the possibility of genuine effects that balance out one another. This is illustrated in the Transitional Aid Research Project (TARP) study (Rossi, Berk, and Lenihan, 1980) on whether cash payments to released prisoners would reduce their rate of return to prison. The design was close to Campbell's ideal, with randomly assigned groups and a large sample. At the end, the finding on key outcome measures was that there were no significant differences among groups; arrest rates varied only slightly from one group to another. But the investigators rejected the conclusion that the treatment made no difference and argued instead that the effectiveness of the intervention was masked by unanticipated side effects (p. 91). How they established this point is a story for Chapter Eight.

Cook and Campbell's (1979, pp. 51–55) listing of threats to internal validity violates Campbell's own logic. Notably, the list mentions several ways (such as compensatory rivalry) in which the control units might react on hearing that experimental units had received special treatment. In such studies, Cook and Campbell write, "it would be quite wrong to attribute the [between-groups] difference to the planned treatment. Cause would not be from the planned cause, A, given to the treatment group" (p. 55). Indeed, it would not. The experimental intervention is, in the first place, not identical to the plan; inference from t to T is a generalization. Second, the intervention had two parts: an action A directed toward one group and a different action (measurement and perhaps a placebo) in the other group. The design included an arrangement that allowed each group to know of the other. "What if arrangements had been modified so that A was given to everyone, or so that neither group suspected that things were different outside its microcosm?" That counterfactual question reaches outside $UTOS$. Insofar as there was a threat to validity, it was one of incorrect identification of the effective cause; it was not a threat to the validity of the claim that "something made a difference."

Causal Inference: How Important?

The primacy that others assign to internal validity arises from two nearly inseparable suppositions: that the object of the inquiry is causal inference and that a conclusion about wholly manipulable effects is wanted. Campbell's stress on causal inference requires me to explain carefully the circumstances that should make an evaluator reluctant to sacrifice other considerations in the hope of achieving secure causal interpretation.

Causal Inference in Basic Social Science. In most of his

writings, Campbell was thinking of long-term scientific advances. His preference for well-controlled studies, even unrealistic and/or unrepresentative ones, is to be understood in that light. Two excerpts from his earlier writings particularly represent his ideal for pure social science. The first statement was made just before he gave the Soho-water example discussed later in this chapter: "Sociologists' emphasis upon randomization [of sampling] to achieve representativeness of some specified population . . . is so out of keeping with what we know of science that it should be removed even from our philosophy of science" (Campbell, 1969a, p. 360). Earlier, arguing that knowledge evolves through a kind of natural selection, Campbell wrote: "Science will develop fastest where the selective apparatus is sharpest, . . . [growing fastest] in the social sciences around fortuitous circumstances that make experimentation possible. . . . *For building a social science, a trivial problem* which is amenable to the experimental probing of hypotheses *is to be preferred* to an important problem area where selection from the glut of alternative theories is impossible. With the tremendous pressures for an immediately useful social science, this has been, and will continue to be, a difficult decision to accept" (1959, p. 165; italics added).

Evaluation *is* to be useful in the short run, and trivial problems are not its proper subject. After their earlier writings had been criticized for insufficient sensitivity to these questions, Cook and Campbell (1979, p. 91) qualified their position: "Timeliness is important in policy research. [If the investigator] decides to place a primacy on internal validity, this cannot be allowed to trivialize the research." This shift, welcome from the point of view of evaluation, is supplemented by other statements (for example, at pp. 345, 369) that favor choice of significant problems. The questions most amenable to elegant design, Cook and Campbell acknowledge, may not be those most relevant for scientific *or* practical purposes. Kruglanski and Kroy (1976), Kruglanski (1975), and Gadenne (1976) specifically challenged the suitability of the Campbell-Stanley (1963) advice for basic research. One complaint was that internal validity is an operationist concep-

tion and that science is built in terms of constructs. Campbell
has been fully aware of the crucial role of constructs and is a
harsh critic of naive operationism; the 1979 monograph of
Cook and Campbell takes care to reduce the hint of positiv-
ism that brought criticism earlier.

The value of causal interpretation, especially of the
narrow kind that achieves internal validity in Campbell's
sense, is an open question in basic science. Note these remarks by Kaplan (1965):

> The importance for methodology of the con-
> cept of causality has been grossly exaggerated for
> many decades. . . .
> The heyday of causal explanation occurred
> about a century ago. It was marked by the insis-
> tence on mechanical models as not just ideal expla-
> nations but as the only models that really explain [p.
> 145].
> Statistical explanation is other than causal be-
> cause, although it introduces the asymmetry that
> causality allows for, it lacks the determinism essen-
> tial to causality [p. 150].
> The usual view is that statistics gives us a
> practical approach to matters, but if we really want
> to understand "how come," we should look at a me-
> chanical, which is to say a causal, explanation. Since
> each of us has his prejudices, I opt for the prejudice
> that causal or mechanical regularities are impossi-
> ble to understand until they are seen as the mass ef-
> fect of random statistical operations [p. 151].
> The centrality of the notion of control (or in-
> tervention) in relation to causality is revealed by the
> fundamental distinction between so-called causes
> and conditions. It is impossible to make sense of this
> distinction except by reference to the possibility, or
> desirability, of intervention by the experimenter
> (or, in general, the observer) [p. 147].
> Causality is significant in the philosophy of
> science chiefly when science is seen as an instru-
> ment of control over phenomena. Causality is intro-

duced just insofar as we are concerned with the effects of the intervention of the investigator. The concept of causality belongs not to the subject matter . . . independent of the observer's perspective, but to the concept of the subject matter that is related to a particular perspective of the inquirer [p. 147].

Kaplan's statements explain the asymmetry in conventional writings on social experiments. Why, in writings about social experiments, is the effect associated with $\Delta UTOS$ labeled a treatment effect rather than an effect of the four components working together? The electric current in an electrolytic apparatus is a treatment, but decomposition comes from the combination of the current with the forces within the molecule of water. The current is *the* cause only for someone who proposes to run a current through water. The policy maker cannot manipulate U or S, and to manipulate O is trivial for her purposes. Therefore, she wants to hear about *treatment* effects.

Meehl (1977) describes how the methods of construct validation refine and ultimately win acceptance for the identification of a disease entity that is associated with a set of physical symptoms. Having discussed how one isolates a cause in a strongly connected system, Meehl goes on to say that the argument fits disorders having a coherent course of development, but not those whose origins are multifaceted, with no *necessary* condition. The second kind of phenomenon is "so common . . . in the biological and social sciences as to make one wonder upon reflection whether it may not even be the modal type" (p. 47). According to Meehl, these "nonspecific etiologies" were best explicated by Mackie (1965, 1974). I shall review Mackie's analysis later.

Social and developmental psychologists have for sometime been debating whether they can arrive at lawlike generalizations. Gergen (1973, 1980) emphasizes that in a changing community the boundary conditions for a phenomenon are transient. For him, psychological conclusions are so

bound to the times that the usual inquiry is essentially historical. Others—for example, Manis (1975)—defend the traditional effort to establish lawlike propositions by observing
under controlled conditions. Still others (Spiker, 1977; Epstein, 1980) expect to obtain solid main-effect generalizations
by sweeping many diverse conditions into a grand average.
The debate has served to remind psychologists of the limitations on propositional knowledge and will perhaps reinstate
naturalistic methods to full partnership in what was becoming a primarily experimental discipline (Cole, Hood, and
McDermott, 1979).

    Causal Inference: Trivial and Nontrivial. The unlabeled
causal inferences for which internal validity can be claimed
are not very significant for evaluation. Obviously, discussions
of social problems and programs have a causal flavor when
words such as *outcome* and *benefit* are used and when explanations rather than mere predictions are offered. But these discussions are carried on in plain language, not in operational
language, and they stretch beyond *UTOS* in many directions.
They therefore are not the kinds of circumscribed inferences
that can be rendered highly plausible by an isolated, strongly
designed study. Campbell and Stanley (1963, p. 173) pointed
this out, but the message was overlooked by the evaluators
they inspired.

    Over many centuries scholars have struggled to clarify
the meaning of the term *cause*. Some of the disagreements
are reviewed in the first chapter of Cook and Campbell
(1979); I have no reason to restate what they say there or to
quarrel with it. It is appropriate, however, to cast a different
light on their position. Eight of their conclusions acknowledge the existence of multiple and reciprocal causation and
the usefulness of molar causal statements that cannot (yet) be
explicated in terms of microprocesses. Crucial for social research are these sentences (italics removed): "Molar causal
laws, because they are contingent on many other conditions
and causal laws, are fallible and hence probabilistic (p. 33).
Field research involves mostly open systems. . . . (p. 34).
The more open the system, the more fallible will be causal in-

ferences. Until contingency conditions are more fully specified, which is a process that can take many, many years, molar
causal relationships in society may not be reproduced easily"
(p. 35).

I consider it pointless to speak of causes when all that
can be validly meant by reference to a cause in a particular
instance is that, on one trial of a partially specified manipulation t under conditions A, B, and C, along with other conditions not named, phenomenon P was observed. To introduce
the word *cause* seems pointless. Campbell's writings make internal validity a property of trivial, past-tense, and local statements.

It seems, however, that Cook and Campbell want to say
something about all instances that are similar to the particular
instance observed. Why else do they speak of laws? They intend to conclude: "If conditions A, B, C . . . t occur, then P
follows [with some likelihood]." In this present-tense statement, the compound ABC . . . t is a less-than-sufficient condition for P. To speak of A or t—or ABC . . . t—as "the
cause" is a misleading oversimplification.

When an event is nonrecurrent, to identify the cause is
to make an untestable, counterfactual statement. Example:
"The cause of the extensive damage to the American fleet at
Pearl Harbor was that the staff at the radar warning station
did not trust its new equipment." The implication is that if
this circumstance had been reversed—if we postulate a
UTOS—the bombers would have done much less damage.
The assertion may be plausible. It could be proved or dis-
proved only by identifying it as a member of a class of events
for which a nonprobabilistic law has been established.

With regard to conditions that recur or can be arranged at will, a causal statement may be weak or strong.
Consider the statement "Long absence at sea caused the sailors to develop scurvy." That statement is weak; the past tense
makes it no more than a statistical inference. The claim is that
scurvy would have been observed in others sampled from the
same UT and setting. Only internal validity is required. The
claim is believable, but the word *caused* adds nothing. Any fac-

tor associated with the long absence could have produced the effect.

Reworded in the present tense ("causes scurvy"), the statement is strong: "T is a sufficient condition for scurvy in sailors." The statement is not restricted in time or setting; external validity is at issue (Ennis, 1973). Many factors in addition to absence at sea were part of the t originally investigated. The sailors lived in ships of a certain kind; maybe the tar of the ropes was the efficient condition. If so, scurvy would appear in men imprisoned on the ship, not absent at sea but tied alongside an enemy's dock for a long time (T^*). The ships carried a certain range of provisions; maybe the absence of a particular kind of food was critical. If so, scurvy would appear in cadets eating from ship's stores while undergoing a long period of shore-based training (another T^*). It is accumulated experience with widely varied conditions that enables us to attribute scurvy to lack of a certain food and nothing else; even so, evolution may in time change human metabolism so that people can go two years without vitamin C.

Within an isolated system, the sufficient conditions for a phenomenon may be few; one can speak of a bacillus as causing a disease. The boundary assumptions (for example, the bacillus must enter a living human body) go unmentioned, being implicit in the nature of the inquiry. A social phenomenon, however, does not reside within a stable, isolated system. Causal language is loose at best. What does it mean to ask the cause of the women's movement of the last decade in the United States? It is only tautological to say that conditions in society were right for it. One might point out a few events or demographic trends and say, "If it were not for these, the movement would have died." But such a claim appears to be unprovable. The issues raised in an educational evaluation are more like questions about the women's movement than like questions about a bacillus.

Mackie on Causal Reasoning. Let us turn to Mackie's formulation of causal logic. I shall paraphrase and summarize Mackie's chapter on causal regularities (1974, chap. 3), em-

phasizing sufficient conditions and omitting his similar remarks on necessary conditions. Mackie starts by accepting
Mill's view (1872, pp. 378–394) that a phenomenon P may
originate in many ways and that any one of those ways is the
conjunction of several antecedents, not a sole cause. Moreover, writes Mackie (1974, p. 63), "the 'antecedents' and 'con-
sequents' will not, in general, be events that float about on
their own; they will be things that happen to or in some
. . . setting [S], . . . the background against which the causing goes on." With regard to sufficient conditions, a law
would then take such a form as "In S, all (ABC or DEF or
JKL) are followed by P." A, B, and C refer to kinds of events
or situations, or possibly to the absence of some action or object.

Now ABC is a minimal sufficient condition; none of its
elements is redundant. A single element such as A or an incomplete set AB would not produce P. Thus, A, or AB, is neither necessary nor sufficient for P. The element A (analogous
to the Δt of the true experiment, or perhaps to the ΔT) is described by the acronym *inus:* "It is an *i*nsufficient but *n*onre-
dundant part of an *u*nnecessary but *s*ufficient condition"
(Mackie, 1974, p. 62). What can actually be established are
"elliptical or gappy universal propositions" (p. 67). That is to
say, instances of character X exist that, in conjunction with A
and S, will generate P—but the characteristics that identify X
are unknown.

The value of the "gappy" causal conclusion is this: *If we
have reason to believe that X often occurs, we can introduce A
into S with the expectation that P will follow in many instances* (Mackie, 1974, p. 68). The probabilistic character of
the law arises from the gaps. The elliptical generalization
does not in itself say what normally or even often happens;
the guess regarding the frequency of X comes from experience and is outside the law. Moreover, the generalization pre-
cedes and supports the causal statement, not the other way
round (p. 78).

Progress in causal knowledge consists partly in arriving
gradually at fuller formulations. As some of the gaps are re-

duced, the uncertainties represented by X become correspondingly less. Progress is made through such methods as the application of Mill's Method of Differences in before-and-after measurements and in controlled experiments. When P appears in one set of observations and not the other, whatever differences there are between the contrasted situations contain something that is an *inus* feature. This feature may be the entire cluster of differences or some subset of them, and the finding does not imply that elements common to the two antecedents are irrelevant. The approach, then, is a start on the long road of "progressive localization of a cause" (Mackie, 1974, p. 73).

Causality in Evaluation. Evaluators need not and ought not sort inferences into a more honored category of causal statements and a less honored category of correlational statements. The pertinent distinction is between a black-box study that reports an association of input with remote outcomes, ignoring intermediate events, and a study that looks inside the box.

Could a strongly controlled experiment on HPP have yielded a worthwhile causal statement? Suppose that teachers in many schools were randomly assigned to teach either HPP or the text by Professor Oldhat. Suppose that the HPP classes averaged significantly higher on major outcomes than the Oldhat classes did. This proves a trivial causal statement: Something done to the experimental subjects made a difference. But *what* is the cause? It could be the new text, it could be the laboratory equipment provided to the HPP classes, it could be the training provided HPP teachers, or it could be the glamorous publicity used to recruit students into HPP classes. All these were legitimately part of the program evaluated, of T. Causal language is superfluous. When a school proposes to use the HPP program as a T^*, without investing in equipment, without sending its teachers for special training, and without glamorous publicity directed toward students, the benefits may or may not vanish. No one knows. Nor did the experiment rule out the suspicion that deficiencies in the Oldhat text or in the way it was used, rather than any feature of HPP, accounted for the experimental finding.

"[We] can regard as aspects of the experimental treatment *all* features which differ between experimental and control groups"; Campbell (1969a, p. 358) thus concurs with Mackie. "All features" include differences in realization as well as differences in treatment plan (unless one believes that differences in realization were entirely unsystematic and the sample of independent units was large enough to even them out). Suppose that the u and o for the contrasted treatments differ only by chance. Then, if a difference between samples is observed, the assignment to T_1 or to T_2 was what mattered. But interpretation is still problematic, as assignment generates consequences in many ways. The experimenter who knows when he is administering T_1 may handle t_1 rats differently from t_2 rats; the police applying a new strategy to a community of potential delinquents may incidentally put fewer minor offenses into the record; telling students that their physics course is concerned with humane values may be enough to shift their ratings of physics from "technical" to "humanistic."

The much-debated choices about assignment of subjects to treatments and about control groups bear on only the outer shell of a set of inquiries. Within the shell an investigator has endless options in studying subprocesses that might suggest explanations. Processes can be studied within a manipulated shell or within a naturalistic shell. It is not practicable to vary many aspects of the treatment systematically. Even within a strong design, much of the explanatory (causal?) interpretation will capitalize on the uncontrolled variation among realizations.

There is no inherent conflict between a concern for interactions and a concern for experimentation. Thus, Gilbert and Mosteller (1972), who recognized that a reform—for instance, of police administration—might work out differently in different cities, could reasonably call for a series of within-city experiments. But this approach works only if the reform

can be applied to a fraction of each city. If each city has to be
treated as a whole, then the experimenter would group cities
and make assignments to treatments within clusters. The experiment would then become a series of contrasts in successive sub-U. If the features of cities expected to condition
results are identified, the relevant experiment can test that
prespecified interaction hypothesis as logically as it would test
the main effect. Controlled assignment, however, gives no
special support to post hoc explanations of site-to-site differences.

   The previously quoted statements of Cook and Campbell on causal laws are consistent with those of Mackie, but the
word *probabilistic* merits a closer look. For a logician to speak
of the incomplete, elliptical generalization as fallible is to put
the statement in the form "Some XAS imply P". When a controlled experiment produces a statistically significant difference, the implication may be phrased in distinctly different
ways. One takes the form: "In setting S, for some u in U, ΔT
makes a difference in O." That is a causal remark: In conjunction with S at least, ΔT is relevant to O for some u. An
alternative puts the statement this way: "T_E works better
than T_O." As the report by Coleman, Hoffer, and Kilgore
(1981) on private schools illustrates, this quantitative statement means one of two things (Bakan, 1967, p. 35): All realizations of T_E are superior for all u in U, or (more modestly)
realizations of T_E help more of the u than they hurt. The first
version would reach far beyond the evidence in most social
research, and it surely is not in the investigator's mind when
he draws a substantive conclusion in any one field study. The
second version is probabilistic in the usual sense, and so is the
statement that positive differences outweigh negatives on the
average. That kind of sentence is the usual product of a
quantitative comparison of treatments.

   A probability refers to a proportion of instances and
means nothing without a reference group. The reference
group for the experimenter's strong inference is US or a designated sub-US. If U matches the population to which the
policy is to be applied, the probabilities and the resultant aver-

age are a basis for decision. If there is a reproducible outcome, the decision maker concerned with *US* can do without causal language—indeed, without an explanation (Riecken, 1979, p. 366). If the end result is good when *U*, *T*, and *S* come together, the sensible action is to bring them together in the future. If the alchemist has been able consistently to extract gold from certain *identified* supplies, the finding is useful no matter how it is mislabeled. It is only when one wishes to apply *T* to a **US* that causal language adds something to an evaluative conclusion; external validity then becomes the issue.

I am confident that Campbell would agree with the preceding paragraph, contrary though it is to his statement (1969a) about removing "representativeness" from the philosophy of social science. Campbell is now prepared to say *almost* the opposite of what he said then. He clearly favors extending investigation over diverse *uto*, to more adequately cover the range of **UTO* envisioned as pertinent; and Cook and Campbell (1979) mention conditions where "relevant research demands representativeness" (p. 88). But reservations enter on the next page, where they respond to an earlier draft of views I present in this chapter: "We have no quarrel *in the abstract* with the point of view that, where causal propositions include references to populations of persons and settings and to constructs about cause and effect, each should be equally weighted in empirical tests of these propositions. The real difficulty comes *in particular instances* of research design and implementation where very often the investigator is forced to make undesirable choices between internal and external validity. Gaining a representative sample of educable, mentally retarded students across the whole nation demands considerable resources" (p. 89). I agree that research plans must be practicable, so we have no quarrel here. But Cook and Campbell then strike a discordant note. After chiding me for approving "timely," representative, but less rigorous studies" (p. 90), they comment that in *non*experimental studies causal inference is problematic. They urge evaluators to ponder "whether the costs of being wrong in one's causal inference are not greater than the costs of being late with the results" (p. 90). Alas, they miss my point: The causal inference even from a true experiment is problematic when the statement extends beyond a trivial summary in operational, past-tense wording.

Cook and McAnany (1979, p. 63) carry the rejoinder a step further: "Unfortunately, results from weak designs are not always wisely interpreted, and the sources of bias are often not made explicit. Even when all the assumptions are expressly stated, . . . by the time results become part of the popular or policy debate, the qualifications to the conclusion have [frequently] been forgotten or . . . omitted from summary reports for general audiences." Can these authors believe that strong designs are immune to such mishandling? The section that follows shows how vulnerable truth can be when a strong design seems to deliver a welcome message.

The True History of The Bail Bond Experiment

To support the thesis that internal validity is insufficient for purposes of evaluation, I turn to the Manhattan bail bond experiment. This study is idealized by those who want evaluations to demonstrate treatment effects conclusively. The very first page of *Social Experimentation* (Riecken and Boruch, 1974) is devoted to the bail bond experiment, and it is also the lead-off example of controlled experimentation for Wholey (1979). I find, however, that internal validity cannot be claimed for its main conclusions, that the randomized design added little force to the conclusions, and that most accounts of the findings are misleading. Still, the bail bond study is commendable in its motivation, its execution, and its social consequences, whatever the inadequacies of the investigators' reports and others' echoes of them. The primary report, on which others have relied directly or indirectly, is that of Ares, Rankin, and Sturz (1963). But the facts do not match the impression that a hasty reader takes from that report and from the other direct reports on the study.

The summary in *Social Experimentation* (Riecken and Boruch, 1974) provides a suitable point of departure here:

In 1961 the Vera Institute of Justice, in collaboration with the criminal court judges of the Borough of Manhattan, New York, began the Manhattan bail bond experiment. The experiment was motivated by a desire to alleviate the situation of a great many criminal defendants who remained in city jails for many months while awaiting trial simply because they were too poor to make bail. Judges and lawyers generally believed bail to be the only satisfactory method of binding the accused person to an agreement to appear for trial, which might occur as much as a year or more in the future. On the other hand, some criminologists contended that an accused person who had substantial links to the community through employment, family, residence, friends, or social institutions could be successfully released prior to trial *without* bail. The Vera Institute proposed an experimental test of this contention. The experiment defined a target group, namely, persons accused of felonies, misdemeanors, and certain other crimes (but excluding individuals charged with homicide and other serious crimes). The defendant's records of employment, residence, family structure, personal references, and criminal charges were reviewed to make a judgment about eligibility for pretrial release without bail. The next step was to divide the total group of eligibles randomly into an experimental and control group. All members of the experimental group were recommended to the court for release without bail, while members of the control group were not so recommended. Judges were, of course, free to accept or reject the recommendation; it was accepted in a majority of cases. The results were clear cut [pp. 1, 2].

Judges in the first year granted parole to 59 percent of the recommended defendants, compared to only 16 percent in the control group; recommendations based on information then served to increase the rate of release without bail. Sixty percent of the recommended group were either acquitted or had their cases dismissed, compared to

23 percent of the control group. During 1961–
1964, less than 1 percent of the experimental group
failed to show up in court for trial, suggesting that
the relaxation of the bail requirement did not result
in unacceptable default rates [p. 292].

The writers add that the default rate was lower than that for
similarly charged defendants who had posted bail.

One fact genuinely does have reproducibility$_2$ or re-
producibility$_3$: Judges paroled far more of the recommended
prisoners than of the randomly equivalent controls. But
quasi-experimental evidence would also have shown the recommendation to have that effect. Judges gave parole more
often during the experiment than in the preceding year. If
there had been no control group, some of this increase might
be attributed to a changing climate of opinion and to the
probable leniency of judges agreeable to the experiment. But
that threat to validity was not bothersome. The investigators
planned from the outset to do away with the control group
after the first year, and did so. (This fact is mentioned by
none of the advocates of comparative design.) The time-series comparison for all three years against the baseline parole
rate seems to have had reproducibility just as the experimental comparison in the first year did, though it lacked internal
validity in Campbell's sense.

The comparison between experimental subjects and
control subjects on parole rate is hard to interpret. "Something the experimenter did made a difference." But what? In
the courtroom the project representative would step forward
with a file of data and a "Do parole" recommendation for the
experimental cases while remaining silent about all other
prisoners. Might not the judge hear this silence as an unfavorable signal? Three categories of prisoners faced the judge:
recommended for parole by the project, judged equally suitable for parole but not recommended, and judged to be unsuitable for parole. The latter two groups received the same
treatment: silence from the project staff.

The threat is to external validity—that is, to identification of the cause. The parole rate for experimentals was 59

percent; that for controls was 16 percent. If the baseline parole rate in these courts (something not explicit in the reports) had been around 40 percent, we would think that the silent treatment of the controls made as much difference as the positive recommendations. If the base rate had been 50 percent, we would conclude that "no treatment" was what made most of the difference. It is experience outside the experiment that gives meaning to the numbers from this internally valid study.

Moving on to the second conclusion, that generous parole did not produce unacceptable default rates, we see that the random assignment now is irrelevant, since the control group was ignored in reaching this conclusion. One percent of the experimentals who were paroled defaulted; this was at least as acceptable as the base rate of 2 or 3 percent default among persons who raised bail in previous years. A sixth of those in the control group were paroled without the project's recommendation. No report tells how many of them appeared for trial. Suppose that they defaulted more often than experimentals on parole. Would this finding have internal validity? What would it mean? The following inference has some degree of internal validity: If the project staff made a positive recommendation and the judge followed it, the outcome tended to be better than if the judge granted parole on her own. Is this a treatment effect or a selection bias? The obvious implication would be that the project interviewers and the judge, acting together, made better judgments than did the judge acting alone. But (surprise!) the difference could be a treatment effect.

The finding of a low default rate turns out to be a perfect example of the weakness of a conclusion that "something made a difference." One line in the Ares, Rankin, and Sturz report (1963) tells us that when a paroled experimental subject failed to appear in court, someone on the staff at Vera telephoned the person and explained the importance of appearing, then persuaded the judge to accept the excuse offered and reinstate the parole. Only in another source (Sturz, 1967) do we learn that the staff also took several steps *prior* to the scheduled appearance to increase the likelihood that the experimental parolee would show up. The default rate would obviously have been higher, perhaps unacceptably so, without the follow-up aspect of the treatment. But since that aspect goes unmentioned in secondary accounts of the project, readers trying to reproduce the treatment would leave out important elements.

Turn now to the disposition of the cases: "Sixty percent of those recommended for parole were found not guilty, while only 23 percent of the equivalent control group were found not guilty" (Wholey, 1979, p. 153). The primary reports tell us that the tally compares those recommended for parole *and* granted it with controls for whom no recommendation was made *and* who were neither paroled by the judge nor able to make bail. These groups were grossly nonequivalent if the judge's criteria for granting parole and the bondswoman's criteria for choosing her clients were appropriate. Only in an obscure manner does the Ares, Rankin, and Sturz paper (1963) say that it is leaving out of account the experimental subjects that the judge did not trust and the control subjects that she did trust. (It is not strictly true that the defendants who went free were "found not guilty"; most of them were "dismissed or dismissed on their own recognizance," the latter phrase implying that the prosecutor recommended release without conceding the person's innocence.)

In the legal literature, the facts about the trial outcome, based on noncomparable samples, received much attention. This leads me to question the following assertion in *Social Experimentation* (Riecken and Boruch, 1974, p. 243): "Experience suggests that experimental evidence may be just what is needed to overcome resistance from strong vested-interest groups—for example, the Manhattan bail bond experiment, where professional organizations of bail bondsmen actively opposed the selective relaxation of bail requirements." If it is true that reports on the project overcame resistance, that is because the label "experiment" (which everyone has applied to the entire three-year activity and to the comparisons of nonequivalent groups) had propaganda value. The only figure calculated from equivalent groups was the parole rate, and even its meaning is clouded. Inferences from loose, biased, and poorly described contrasts loomed as large in reports and must have carried as much weight in the bail reform movement as those meeting Campbell's strict standard.

Alternative Views on Interactions

Experiments can be designed to identify effects of treatments on the average over *UOS* or can be framed to check on interactions of the treatments (or sub-*T*) with sub-*U*. Most writings on strong designs regard interactions as unimportant, as a minor nuisance, or as food for *after*thought. In *Social Experimentation* (Riecken and Boruch, 1974, p. 5), for example, we read: "In a true experiment the differences . . . can be attributed entirely to the effect of the treatment plus an accidental (random) error. . . . All other factors which augment or suppress the outcome variable occur evenhandedly in both the experimental and control groups." These statements are true, but they are misleading in two ways.

First, the opening sentence is much too emphatic. The accidental error may be enormous. One textbook speaks of a change of organization that was tried on one of two floors in a hospital. The other floor was the control; and, the book says enthusiastically, the assignment of treatments to floors was random. This does circumvent deliberate, biasing placement of the innovation on the floor where the staff would probably be more cooperative; cooperation is left to the luck of the draw. Evenhandedness does not mean evening out, however, unless the sample is large or the investigator is in a position to cumulate experience over many studies.

Second, there is a subtle error in reference to "the effect of the treatment." The effect is that of a treatment plan (label?) *in context*. An interacting factor will augment the apparent effect in *UOS* of one treatment relative to the other. "Other factors," then, may be responsible for the so-called treatment effect. Saying that "*T* had an effect" underplays the conditions under which the effect appeared; an effect of another magnitude and perhaps of opposite direction would arise under other circumstances. A statement that "T had a negligible main effect" allows for a strong effect in another *UOS* context. (In present-tense form, it does not.) Important interactions can be present in *UTOS* and yet balance out so that no main effect is found. If a treatment enters into interactions—and who can say that it does not?—a decision maker will not be much interested in the main effect unless her decision is limited to the *UTO* studied. Even within that *UTO*, the interaction may imply that some sub-U thrive on T and some suffer under it.

Advocates of strong designs fall into a trap; the problem lies not in their understanding but in the rhetoric they adopt as advocates. Recognizing that a treatment may affect persons differently, *Social Experimentation* (Riecken and Boruch, 1974, p. 52) nonetheless gives priority to seeing "whether or not a treatment does have an effect." *If* a main effect is established in U, it is said, one can go on to look for interactions of T within the range of units in U^*. Similarly, Cook and Campbell (1979, p. 39) would become interested in external validity (that is, in examining the effect of changes from U to sub-U or U^*) only *after* finding a treatment effect significant. This seems reasonable if U is highly relevant, but negative evidence from U should not be persuasive to someone who cares about a U^* that has limited resemblance to U.

Interaction as a Fact of Life. Interactions exist. Any inference about *UTO* has a distinct possibility of being wrong for policy makers acting on U^* or T^*. That is why the qualification "other things being equal" is attached to empirical generalizations. When the same T enters *UTOS* and *UTOS*, it is a good bet that U^*, O^*, and S^* will interact with T to modify the effect. The magnitude of the change in conditions and its effect on the outcome can be large or small. In field research substantial changes are not unlikely. Harvard Project Physics quite possibly had one outcome with able students and another with ordinary students. In the INCAP study, the benefit from extra calories depended on the age of the child and on the family's usual diet.

The confusion generated by giving priority to testing of main effects is seen in the argument of Gilbert, Light, and Mosteller (1975, p. 52; compare with Deming, 1975, quoted in Chapter One). "Slam-bang" effects, say Gilbert and his colleagues, can be accepted on the basis of evidence comparing the treated group with a baseline of general experience, with no formal controls at all. In fact, however, not even an unmistakable effect is to be carried directly over to *UTOS*. In 1922 the British discovered that bombing tribal villages from the air was sufficient to put down a revolt in Mesopotamia (Taylor, 1965, p. 229); there's a slam-bang effect for you! What came to be called "area bombing," then, would overcome opposition. This causal inference was one of the roots of British insistence on using that strategy against Germany from 1940 to 1945, even in the face of considerable evidence that the Germans were not reacting as the desert tribesmen had (Wilensky, 1967, pp. 24–34). Treatment interacted with *U* and *S*. No amount of true experiment on brushfire wars would have established a causal effect applicable to Germany.

The strong effect that Gilbert's team offers as an example is of a hypothetical treatment that cuts the death rate from a killer disease from 100 percent to 70 percent. One cannot hope for such a striking effect from the usual social innovation, they argue, and to isolate a weak effect requires formal controls—preferably random assignment. The difficulty with this argument is that, in the presence of a weak main effect, outcomes are likely to vary considerably from one experimental unit to the next, as Gilbert and Mosteller (1972) had noted elsewhere.

In the physical sciences, microsystems are likely to be sufficiently independent that local circumstances make little difference. Campbell (1969a) cited the discovery of hydrolysis as an example of the robustness to be expected of "main effects." In Soho in 1800, the investigators' laboratory supply of water was surely impure and not representative of all water. Even so, the result was reproducible. Other laboratories obtained hydrogen and oxygen by passing a current through *their* atypical water, with volumes, voltages, and temperatures varying over a wide range. The electrolytic apparatus evidently acts as an isolated system; events outside the container can be disregarded most of the time. I draw attention, however, to a contention that even the decomposition of water can be affected by remote events (Feyerabend, 1978, p. 93).

Few social events are or can be so isolated. Interactions are ubiquitous—that is "the Achilles' heel of the behavioral sciences" (Cook and Campbell, 1976, p. 237; see also Campbell, 1975d). Yet Campbell has minimized the role of interactions, as is especially to be seen in his "Reforms as Experiments" (1969a, p. 359): "The potentialities [for interaction] are so numerous that we pay attention only to explicitly elaborated and plausible hypotheses of this nature. More than that, we are even more likely to disregard or judge implausible an interaction effect than a main effect. Perhaps part of the reason for this is that main effects are more easily handled. Probably more important, . . . main effects are more probable than interaction effects. . . . Even if this is not descriptive of nature as we find her, it is descriptive of the knowable aspects. . . . If the highest-order interactions . . . are always significant, then no generalization is possible, and hence no knowledge and no science."

The issue is not statistical significance but influence. The influence of an interactive effect can be large. For example, Irle (1975) examined psychological responses to noisy aircraft landings. One third of the variance came from interactions of noise with characteristics of listeners, and many of the latter were manipulable. I tabulated (Cronbach, 1975a) many analyses in experimental social psychology, most of them studies with laboratory control. First-order and second-order interactions had about the same strength as the main effects under investigation. (I did not count main effects so gross and familiar as to be of no research interest—practice versus no practice, for example.)

There is no reason to expect effects to decrease in magnitude as one moves from main effects to lower-order interactions to higher-order interactions. Indeed, there is no distinction in nature between main effects and interactions or between orders of interaction; the distinction is a technical one applicable in the context of a given experimental design. When I have explained the second sentence, the first will be seen as a corollary. The magnitude of an effect depends on the range of conditions in a study. Irle could have varied noise conditions more than he did, if only by manipulating the distance of the hearer from the runway. The variance from the main effect would have increased correspondingly; interactions of noise with any second factor depend on the ranges of both factors.

Again, if the Soho investigators had run electric current through the various liquids to be found in a chemical laboratory, their largest finding would have been a substance-by-treatment interaction: Some substances would have given off gases, and some would not have. It was limiting the inquiry to water that made the decomposition into hydrogen and oxygen a main effect. The social or behavioral scientist who restricts investigation to one culture, one age group, one perceptual task, and so on, is more likely to detect what he can call a main effect. But the effect is sure to be conditional on age, task, or other aspects of *UTOS*. An *inus* condition thus appears in the disguise of a sufficient condition, a main effect.

This disguise is provided by the design. An effect can be main in a statistical, probabilistic sense, in which case it has little scientific meaning but has practical meaning for those who care about *UOS*. An effect is main in the stronger scientific sense when a system has been identified within which the variable "always" makes a difference and the boundary conditions are appended (perhaps unvoiced) as part of a "sufficient condition" conclusion. I put quotation marks around "always" as a reminder of the need for additional words: "for nearly all u, in S that arise in several consecutive years or decades or centuries."

Bounding the inquiry lowers the apparent order of effects. The investigator turns a puzzling "higher-order" interaction into a "lower-order" interaction or a main effect by teasing out a subclass of conditions in which relations are homogeneous. Natural science proceeds in that way. Chemistry grew out of the alchemist's classification of substances. Materials responded differently to fire—this was a report of interaction. In time, materials were grouped into classes within which fire produced much the same result (calcining, melting, or whatever). *Within* such a class, fire had a main effect. We return, obviously, to a point that Mill (1872, p. 354) made: "The universe, so far as known to us, is so constituted that whatever is true in one case is true in all cases of a certain description; the only difficulty is to find what description."

Discounting of Interaction Hypotheses. Interactions have received less attention than they deserve in social science. One reason is that no large proportion of F ratios for interaction reaches statistical significance. For interaction hypotheses having more than one degree of freedom, however, rather large samples are required to show even sizable effects as significant (Cohen, 1977). Absence of influential interactions is therefore hard to prove.

A further difficulty arises for the investigator whose heart is set on establishing statistical significance. Each additional interaction acknowledged brings in a new hypothesis for testing. The more tests, the more relations reach significance when *all* effects are due to chance. Significance, then, has to be discounted. Similarly, the investigator testing the fit of a formal model to data opens himself to embarrassment if he builds speculative complications into the model, because a more complicated model is more likely to be disconfirmed. With these difficulties in mind, Campbell (1969a, p. 366) argued that *basic* research should proceed as if interactions were negligible. It is parsimonious, he said, to regard as a main effect even a result that may have arisen from an interaction of treatment with conditions. Proving otherwise is left to whatever critic cares to postulate a particular interaction and collect fresh data to test it. Ultimately, the scientific community will mark out the boundaries of the effect.

Though Campbell's advice may be acceptable when time is unlimited, evaluators should not play down interactions. They must within a short time help the community decide what actions to take—and making social changes as if an observed effect is independent of circumstances is foolhardy (Campbell, 1975b). Experience serves as a basis for a *conjecture* about the practical situation (Jouvenel, 1967). That is how a higher organism copes with any day's new situations. It is the way medicine, agriculture, fiscal management, and all other applied sciences proceed. The conjectures direct *provisional* actions. Since more relevant experience, more carefully interpreted, can be expected to produce more valuable conjectures, systematic knowledge is still worth a considerable price.

Trading Off Strength of Design for Relevance

Insofar as one wants to adopt as general policy whatever works best on the average, the fact that the average over u may not match the average over U^* is troublesome. Equivalence of groups within a comparative study is *not* more important than representativeness when effects are weak. It is not impossible to run a controlled experiment on a representative sample of a significant U, but it is difficult to satisfy both ideals at once (Riecken and Boruch, 1974, pp. 33, 52). The trade-off between the two must receive serious attention.

Recognizing the peril of the leap from *utoS* to **UTOS* changes the perspective on design. A well-controlled and unambiguous experiment may not be the best way to gain insight into **UTOS*; studying a diversified set of *UTO*, each less thoroughly, or breaking out sub-*UTO* within the *UTO* may serve applied purposes better.

This point of view is illustrated by Witmer's (1952) comments on the Cambridge-Somerville Youth Study. In this tightly designed study, a population of boys at risk was sorted into matched pairs; one member of each pair, chosen by lot, was to receive seven years of service from counselors. The planner had expected the experimental control/contrast to result in less delinquency among the treated boys. In fact, no such overall difference appeared, and those who received the

most attention from counselors tended to have the worst subsequent records. But this was explained by the tendency of
busy counselors to work harder on those boys who seemed to
be in greatest need. Witmer, who had taken major responsibility for the attempt to dig beneath the original formal analysis, called the overall comparison "dubious reasoning":

> The "treatment" was diverse and unrelated,
> in many cases, to the boys' needs. It seemed to us
> that to give a great variety of services to a great vari-
> ety of people, each practitioner doing what he
> thinks best without reference to any commonly
> held body of theory, is no more a scientific experi-
> ment—control group or no control group—than a
> medical one would be in which different kinds of
> medicine were given to patients suffering from dif-
> ferent kinds of disorders by doctors who held dif-
> ferent theories as to the causes of the illnesses.
>   If the study had shown that the "treated"
> boys did become delinquents much less frequently
> than the control boys, we might have been beguiled
> into thinking that the value of this kind of service
> had been demonstrated. Perhaps that would have
> been a correct conclusion. Since it did not (the pro-
> portions of delinquents by any test were about the
> same in the two groups), we were forced to consider
> other ways of determining the connections between
> the services and results, for careful reading of the
> records made it clear that the counselors had been
> helpful in some cases.
>   As a second way of showing causal relation-
> ships, reliance was put on a comparison of boys
> rated as "clearly aided" with those rated as "possibly
> benefited" and those rated as "not helped," the
> cases in which the boy had never been in need of
> assistance being eliminated from consideration. It
> was reasoned that if the boys in these three catego-
> ries were found to differ in ways that made good
> sense theoretically, the apparent difference in ben-
> efit derived was probably a real one. Such differ-

ences were found, on the basis of which conclusions
were drawn as to the kinds of boys that can be aided
by a program of this sort and the kinds of services
such boys require [1952, pp. 159–160].

As a matter of fact, the formal statistical comparisons—both
Witmer's and those of the recent follow-up by McCord
(1978)—were unable to provide a rigorous conclusion despite the use of random assignment and the great success in
obtaining follow-up records. In 1941 a number of boys were
dropped from treatment, chiefly because of staff attrition; a
few more left the study for their own reasons. In each case
the pairmate was also dropped, thus preserving a superficially tight control. But the cases dropped from treatment
were in general those judged not to be at risk (Powers and
Witmer, 1951, p. 346). Therefore, as was explained at the
end of Chapter Two, comparing this select group with their
pairmates is not an unbiased test of the null hypothesis. The
formal control is even less useful when one compares the
later fate of a subset such as boys who had juvenile police records with the fate of their pairmates.

5

✍ Models for Internal and External Inference

This chapter examines the reasoning process by means of which an investigator arrives at conclusions—a process that, as Mosteller and Tukey (1977) have said, is far more subtle and judgmental than most social scientists realize. Formal statistical reasoning has been so much emphasized in writings on social and behavioral research that even some experienced investigators are not conscious of the use they make of substantive assumptions. Inferences about *UTOS*, which were the subject of Chapter Four, will be considered briefly; then attention will shift to the kind of reasoning that justifies conclusions about situations not directly studied.

Reasoning by Means of a Model

Reasoning substitutes for direct inquiries that are inconvenient or impracticable to mount. The process is simplest in a direct, focused investigation. But even when the situation about which information is wanted has been observed directly, prediction about the future has to draw on less immediate experience and to bring in presumptions as well as evidence. This is true even of the simplest generalization from sample to population. We have no way to study the future and no way to examine an entire population.

A concrete question can be answered straightforwardly by manipulating objects and inspecting the physical outcome. Suppose one wants to know how many cars a four-lane highway can carry at peak load under certain rules—say, that no car goes faster than forty miles per hour or comes within four lengths of the car ahead. Cars equipped to give a warning when either limit is reached are crowded onto the highway until it is saturated, and the cars are then counted. A model carries us to an answer at far less expense—but perhaps not to the same answer. A simple calculation tells us that at forty miles per hour a car travels two thirds of a mile per minute. Dividing that distance by five car-lengths and multiplying by four (lanes) indicates how many cars should, in one minute, pass a given point. But because drivers change lanes, fall below the speed limit, and do not keep a uniform distance, the model is too regular. A more realistic, hence more complicated, model could produce a number closer to the result of the physical experiment. The following analysis is adopted from Coombs, Raiffa, and Thrall (1954).

Figure 1 represents, at the left, the concrete direct inquiry. The remainder of the figure represents the indirect approach: A model that simulates the concrete situation is constructed, then manipulated to reach a conclusion. That conclusion, expressed in the symbols and scale of the model, is translated into a statement about reality. The model may be physical, mathematical, or logical—or even a metaphor. The manipulation too may be physical, mathematical, logical, or imaginative. A blueprint is a model. Measuring a distance on the blueprint of a house indicates how much pipe is needed to reach a certain plumbing fixture. The measurement forecasts what would be found if the required amount of pipe

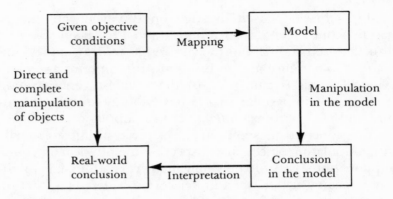

**Figure 1. Reasoning in a model as a substitute for
real-world investigation**

were determined by physical trial and error. A model, being
simplified or schematic, maps just part of reality. The blueprint reports only a fraction of what could be said about the
house—a fraction carefully selected for relevance.

Consider a further example, a mathematical model
used with an opinion poll. Different sectors of the population
have different views. The pollster wants to learn, from a
small set of respondents, what would be the composite opinion if everyone in the population were questioned. To justify
the inference, he relies on a model constructed of abstract
statements such as these:

1.   There is a collection of elements i.
2.   Each has a probability p_i of entering the sample.
3.   The p_i are equal.

This may in fact describe the real selection process falsely; for
example, the interviewers perhaps neglect to track down
members of the specified sample not found at home on the
first call. The pollster has to face another, broader question:
Which of several sampling plans will work best? Imperfect
though the model is, it generates adequate, inexpensive answers to the broad question. The pollster might appraise
sampling error directly, by interviewing many samples drawn
under one plan and noting how much the reports from the
samples disagree. Then he could repeat with another plan,

and another. But because such direct inquiry would be prohibitively expensive, reasoning by a model is the only way to compare several sampling plans.

The line at the base of the diagram in Figure 1 represents the translation step; thinking shifts from the model to the world. When the translation process simply reverses the initial mapping, no new difficulty is to be anticipated. The calculated length of pipe is likely to fit into the physical house. Problems arise when information is lost in translation or is added. The blueprint leads, say, to an estimated length of 87 feet, 7 inches of pipe (including an allowance for joints). The user who purchases precisely that length may have to return to the store, paying a price for having ignored the margin of error in the original mapping and in blueprint reading. The social science counterpart of this error in translation arises when a report of no significant difference leads to actions that only a finding of zero difference would warrant.

A person who fully understands the nature of indirect reasoning will not trust the final conclusion unless she finds all the mapping sentences credible *and* finds credible this further sentence: "Nothing that matters in the real world was left out of the model." A conclusion is credible enough if the person who acts on it thinks she runs little risk of painful consequences—that is to say, if events contrary to the assumptions are thought to be rare or not very influential. Statements gain their credibility from the hearer's experience. For a chain of reasoning to be accepted, hearers must accept each link. An argument everyone accepts at one time in history will be implausible in another era. At any time, statements acceptable to one sector of the community may be questioned by another sector. This is true of statements about fact and definitional statements, as well as value premises. Conclusions about either *UTOS* or **UTOS* rest on credible reasoning.

The model used to reach from *utoS* to *UTOS* I shall call a Model I. Several such models might be applied to the same file of data to answer various subquestions. A model used to infer to one or another **UTOS* is a Model II. As we shall see, Model I can be abstract or mathematical, but much of Model II is substantive.

Inference to *UTOS*

To consider the logic of inference to *UTOS* returns us to the subject of internal validity. What is said about *UTOS* would apply equally to a sub-*UTOS* and to a very limited inference about a single case. The ideal direct experiment on *UTOS* can be imagined but not executed. One would have to locate as many equivalent populations *U* as there are possible treatment variations *t*, apply every *t* to one of the *U*, and measure *O* exhaustively. A statistical model purports to tell how this unrealizable experiment would turn out. It substitutes mathematical manipulation of numbers for intervention on a grand scale.

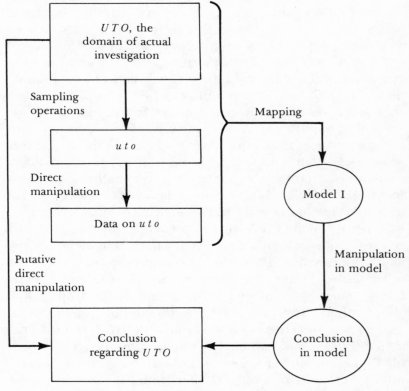

Figure 2. The process of reaching a conclusion about *UTOS*

The generalized model of Figure 1 is specialized and elaborated in Figure 2. Ideally, the investigator frames a question; that is, he chooses a *UTO*. Then he selects *uto* and collects data. Next he specifies a Model I and uses it to derive a conclusion. Finally, he claims that the statement applies to *UTOS;* that is, he claims that the statement reports what would have been true (in *S*) if observations had covered the whole of *UTO*.

The claim that a conclusion applies to *UTO* is beyond question if the mapping into the model is accepted, the manipulation within the model is free from error, and the translation back to the real world is also accepted. Little need be said about errors in manipulation (such as reading the wrong number from a table of *F* ratios). Nor need more be said about errors in going from model to real world; they are much like errors in mapping.

Any doubt about the mapping increases doubt about the substantive conclusion ultimately reached. The conclusion *in the model* is statistical or operational, as distinct from substantive (Tukey, 1960). The investigator could stay close to the operational in stating the conclusion about reality. The connection to reality rests primarily on the belief that the reported facts on *uto,* whether complete or incomplete, are dependable. In effect, the question is: Would an auditing angel who had hovered over the scene of the investigation presumably confirm that the procedures and responses were as described? But that would involve an extremely limited form of reproducibility. Generalized, nonoperational, but substantive language almost always enters the description of *UTO,* and then reproducibility$_3$ is wanted. Almost never can the operations that generate *u*, *t*, and *o* guarantee a match of *uto* to the labels in all significant respects. This mismatch should be a source of distrust.

The stated research question may refer to a population that during certain years gravitated into a certain treatment. Consider an inquiry about the number of scientists with doctoral degrees to be found, a decade after graduation, among alumni of undergraduate colleges of various types. When the investigator examines a fair sample or an entire cohort, he can summarize what did occur. A quite different question is "How many scientists would Mudhen State produce if its student intake matched that of M.I.T.?" Since there is no practical way to assign students so as to equalize the two student bodies, direct study of that counterfactual world is impossible. But sometimes an investigator can construct evidence on an unnatural *UTO* in which the usual ecological pairing is eliminated.

A mathematical model embodies premises. By way of (still partial) illustration, I expand on the assumptions regarding sampling and assignment:

3'.   All *utoS* within a stratum (sub-*UTOS*) had an equal chance of entering the final sample.

4.   Except as correlations of *U* with *T* and *O* are implied in the definition of *UTOS*, the *t* and *o* for a particular *u* were selected independently of the choice for any other *u*.

Whoever applies the model acts as if all its assumptions fit the concrete instance he seeks a conclusion about. These assumptions apply to the sampling of *t* and *o* as well as to *u*, but I concentrate on the sampling of *u* in what follows.

Take random sampling within strata as an example. To judge whether Assumption 3' is credible, one needs a description of the sampling operation that produced the data. If the description says that the schools in the final sample were drawn from a full roster of schools, with the aid of a designated table of random numbers, Assumption 3' will be credible to most of the audience. But even with so tight a degree of control, questions can be raised. On occasion a check has shown that a random number generator is not random (Cook and Campbell, 1979, p. 350).

The data are representative only if the *uto* providing data has the same characteristics as the *uto* originally drawn. Data usually are lost, and not at random. Units drop out. Some subjects fail to return a questionnaire. An observer becomes ill, and a visit is rescheduled. Some losses can be regarded as unimportant, some not. It will often be suspected that the missing data are atypical. The *uto*-to-*UTO* inference then becomes problematic. For example, the "Sesame Street" evaluation formed comparable groups of children who did and did not view the program. The number of units was small, and apparently many children were lost before final data came in. Reviewing the study, Cook and associates (1975, p. 109) did not believe that the treated and untreated groups were comparable at the end, even though classes or neighborhood blocks had been randomly assigned to treatments. In one of the several sites (Philadelphia), they had reason to trust the comparison. Certain data suggested that the contrast subjects who provided complete data had been similar initially to the surviving experimental subjects (though neither set was representative of *U*). Thus, a close look at the data made the claim to equivalence in that one site more credible than in others.

Under particular circumstances deliberate violation of assumptions may be reasonable. But this undermines the process of formal inference and greatly enlarges the role of persuasion and judgment. In a study of counseling of parolees, for example, Berman (unpublished; described by Conner, 1977) chose experimental and control subjects at random within the case load of each parole officer. The sample contained only ninety cases, and, by chance, all the narcotics offenders fell into the control group. Strict sampling produced, paradoxically, data that were patently unrepresentative by commonsense standards (Kruskal and Mosteller, 1979). Berman therefore discarded the narcotics cases. The mathematics of probabilistic inference do not apply strictly to samples censored in this way, however. Berman in effect shifted from a study of *U* (all parolees in the locality) to a study of a *U** (no narcotics cases) that resembles the fortuitous *u*. As he had not sampled from *U**, the inference lost some rigor. The inference would have been more rigorous—but hard to interpret—if the narcotics cases had been retained, because the long-run probabilities for true samples are known. Berman's failure, of course, occurred at the planning stage. The random model treats units as indistinguishable. Berman believed that types of offenders differ, so he should have mapped the typology into a stratified model of U.

If the conclusion in the model is judged not to fit UTO, the conclusion about the real world should be framed to recognize this. For example, if the sampling of persons and operations was satisfactory but the planned T was not delivered, the only proper substantive conclusion refers to the treatment realized. The T proposed for investigation, not having been realized, becomes a $T*$. Likewise, in the Philadelphia data on "Sesame Street," the direct comparison applies to a universe of survivors, not to the original U.

Inference to *$UTOS$

Inference to *$UTOS$ is a multiple-track, if not a trackless, process. Evidence from a newly finished study is assembled along with other experience. The argument is likely to be loose jointed: "Here is another thing to bear in mind." Members of the audience arrive at their beliefs through conversation. The interpreter's straightforward brief supporting a conclusion about *$UTOS$ is no more than an opening move. Doubts, challenges, and counterinterpretations will be voiced. The ensuing discussion may even modify the character of the *$UTOS$ considered, as when a substitute program plan is put forward.

Choosing a Starting Point. The interpreter of research may arrive at a conclusion about *$UTOS$ by reasoning from the conclusions of the original study—conclusions that would ordinarily refer to the whole $UTOS$. He is generally wiser to be selective. He may use information from a sub-$utoS$ marked out by the original investigator—a category of persons, perhaps, or a particular variant of T. He may even concentrate on particular instances in the data set that seem most similar to *$UTOS$, writing his own specification for a sub-$UTOS$. Or he may take up similar cases one by one. Deciding which data to emphasize is difficult.

The summary statistics on the sample, or the estimates for *UTOS* or a sub-*UTOS,* are usually not an adequate base for inference about **UTOS.* Insofar as there is diversity in the data, the consumer should be told about that diversity and any factors associated with it. An archive may be a more useful basis for thinking about **UTOS* than a summary of the original study. One then can look at information on processes and events in whatever sites are moderately similar to $U*$, to judge *why* the local t worked well or badly. Then one tries to judge what modified treatment will serve $U*$. An interpreter is likely to work back and forth between the gross statistical analysis and the differentiated, select cases, taking one level of analysis as background for the other.

A school board cannot reasonably expect the result of a program in its district to match the average in a nationally representative sample, but the board could reasonably concentrate on districts similar to its own. Reports on five similar districts may be available. The sample is small, however, and if the five case reports are not consistent, the uncertainty will be great. The school board might therefore do better to look at several sub-*UTOS* in turn: small cities, cities with a large Hispanic minority, cities with well-trained teachers, and so on. Several interpretations-by-analogy can then be made, each relying on more than five cases. If these several conclusions are not too discordant, the board can have some confidence in the decision that it makes about its small city with well-trained teachers and a Hispanic clientele. When results in the various slices of data are dissimilar, it is better to try to understand the variation than to take the well-determined— but only remotely relevant—national average as the best available information. The school board cannot regard that average as superior information unless it believes that district characteristics do not matter.

Consider a similar decision following completion of a randomized experiment. Burnham High School, let us say, is considering a switch from Physical Science Study Committee (PSSC) physics to Harvard Project Physics (HPP). The staff could request from the HPP evaluators the results for whichever schools, among those that taught PSSC in the preexperimental year, most resemble Burnham with respect to teacher experience. A comparatively small body of data would be available, and the subsample that resembles Burnham with respect to teacher experience would probably be unlike Burnham in some other equally significant respects. Matching in one respect may thus force a mismatch in another. For that matter, a true match may be impossible. In some HPP schools, teachers lagged behind schedule. Suppose that the science supervisor at Burnham insists that she will make certain that teachers stay on the planned schedule. What results, she asks, did HPP yield among teachers who stayed on schedule? But there is a fundamental difference between teachers on whom an administrator forces a standard pace of instruction and teachers in the original set who held *themselves* to the schedule. The intended match would not be achieved.

Suppose that a plan for bilingual education is considered for citywide or statewide adoption. Data from a dozen trial communities are available. Some of these communities realized the plan as intended. (Was this a result of committed leadership? Of self-consciousness under the researcher's eye?) In other communities delivery fell short of intentions. An administrator will not be much interested in the average over the whole *UTO* unless she thinks that events in *her* city or state will be subject to the same vagaries. The sensible procedure would be to examine how much difference in outcomes was associated with variation in delivery, to decide what is adequate delivery, and to invent an administrative plan to achieve that. Similar reasoning would be needed if the original results were consistently unsatisfactory; the administrator would want to know what went wrong in sites roughly like her own, in order to formulate a significantly different T^*.

Consider another example of a subtle difference between *UTOS and the data base. If classes with twenty-five or thirty pupils constituted U, a question about outcomes in classes of thirty-five seems only to require straightforward extrapolation. But a gap is left for imagination to fill. What negotiations with teachers are required to get them to accept larger classes? If the negotiation is stressful, how will the residue of emotion affect teachers' practices? Even with the same definition of T and the same controlled manipulation, the distribution of treatment realizations in the larger classes may differ from the original distribution. For example, if the plan asks teachers to make praise contingent on performance, teachers may comply less as class size increases.

Counterfactuals. A proposition about a world in which some feature is contrary to experience is a counterfactual proposition. The counterfactual is treacherous because the situation has to be created by unmentioned interventions that have their own consequences (Meehl, 1970, 1971).

In everyday circumstances treatments tend to be correlated with characteristics of units, often for good reason. The analyst seeks to describe a world in which the correlation is lacking. What is this counterfactual world like? Recall the question about Mudhen State—that is, about a world where student quality is not correlated with other characteristics of colleges. If M.I.T. turns to open admissions, instruction at the new, nonselective M.I.T. will be so changed that information gathered in former times cannot properly forecast its production of scientists. If, thanks to an enormous grant from an alumnus, Mudhen State brings its student body up to the M.I.T. level, that money will change the faculty and the instruction at Mudhen; extrapolation from the old Mudhen is beside the point.

To adjust for selection, statisticians turn to mathematical manipulations; their devices include partial correlations and regressions (as in structural-equation models), post hoc matching, and covariance adjustment. Such extrapolations are logically suspect, says Meehl (1970, 1971) (and Chapter Six will show that there is mathematical difficulty also). Meehl raises provocative questions for the evaluator who entertains propositions about imaginary worlds in which "socioeconomic status is held constant" or in which blacks and whites complete equal amounts of schooling.

Even for random experiments, interpretations often refer to imagined worlds. For example, a controlled experiment tests contraceptives on volunteers who accept random assignment. With suitable checks the investigator could convince himself that everyone in the experimental group did use the intended technique. "What would the rate of population growth be if everyone in the population were to use the technique faithfully?" That question asks about a world that has never existed and perhaps never will. The shifts in sexual practices and attitudes that have occurred since the basic clinical experiments on steroids illustrate how changes in setting, clientele, and treatment realization complicate extrapolation.

The importance of the volunteer bias in experiments warrants one more example. Suppose that HPP had limited its invitation to teachers who taught from PSSC materials in the year prior to the study and that no teacher who agreed to accept random assignment dropped out of the study. That study offers a firm comparison of PSSC with HPP on teachers willing to accept HPP as an alternative treatment—that is, on teachers who are *not committed* to PSSC. If the outcome favored HPP, simple extrapolation would say that students will learn more physics when PSSC teachers in general switch to HPP. One wonders about the generalization, however, since the original teachers not committed to PSSC had perhaps been comparatively unsuccessful teachers of PSSC physics. Besides, one would want to know what caused a teacher committed to PSSC to switch to HPP. If the switch was produced by an administrator's fiat, *UTO* would not be psychologically much like *UTO;* teachers complying with an uncongenial order would not resemble the experimental teachers.

Reasoning with Model II. It is instructive to extend Figures 1 and 2 into a schematic representation of the inference about *UTOS. This reasoning is less systematic and stylized than the statistical inference of the usual Model I, but again there is mapping, manipulation of symbols or abstractions, and translation into substantive terms. It is to be emphasized that many strands of evidence and reasoning are ordinarily combined in tying down a conclusion about *UTOS. For ease of presentation, the diagram is limited to a single strand.

At the upper right of Figure 3 is a box referring to a selected body of data; the cell below it indicates that infer-

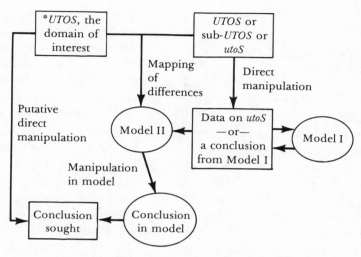

Figure 3. Route to a conclusion about *UTOS

ences start from raw data or from processed data. The information is mapped into a Model II that will be described in a moment. The interpreter may work from field notes, scores, and similar raw files, ignoring inferences made with Model I about *UTOS* or a sub-*UTOS*. Alternatively, or at another moment, the interpreter may take such a conclusion as the starting point. The arrow pointing downward toward the cell labeled Model II represents differences between *UTOS and the source of the data. Ideally, all differences would be considered explicitly. In practice, one falls back on the claim that nothing that matters was overlooked.

Allowing for differences by means of a model is a familiar process: The length and temperature of a copper rod are measured, and a long-established equation predicts the length of the rod at another temperature. The reliability of a certain test is determined by retesting a sample of children; an equation predicts the reliability of a test with ten more items. In each of these examples, a simple difference was mapped into a model; a conclusion was derived from the model and interpreted as applying to the real world. Indirect reasoning substituted for experiment. This procedure is cheaper and yields results more quickly than heating the rod and remeasuring it or constructing the longer test and trying it out. Though formal quantitative extrapolations are more easily discussed, the logic of qualitative differences is similar. The bombing in Mesopotamia, reported by a historian who interviewed witnesses, is a *uto*. The huge error in inferring from Mesopotamia to Germany makes the inference seem to be of a different order from that about the copper rod. The essential difference is that, in the former case, a burden was placed on Model II that it could not sustain.

Quantitative models can be just as wrong. Mark Twain knew the Mississippi River as only a steamboat pilot could. It was forever cutting new channels across sandbars. The distance from Cairo to New Orleans was 973 miles when Twain wrote *Life on the Mississippi* in the 1870s; but, he averred, the distance had been 1,215 miles in 1699, prior to certain cutoffs that river historians had recorded:

> Now, if I wanted to be one of those ponderous scientific people, and "let on" to prove what had occurred in the remote past by what had occurred in a given time in the recent past, or what will occur in the far future by what has occurred in late years, what an opportunity is here! Geology never had such a chance, nor such exact data to argue from!. . .
> In the space of one hundred and seventy-six years the Lower Mississippi has shortened itself two hundred and forty-two miles. That is an average of a trifle over one mile and a third per year. Therefore, any calm person, who is not blind or idiotic, can see that in the Old Oölitic Silurian Period, just a million years ago next November, the Lower Mississippi River was upward of one million three hundred thousand miles long, and stuck out over the Gulf of Mexico like a fishing-rod. And by the same token any person can see that seven hundred and forty-two years from now the Lower Mississippi will be only a mile and three-quarters long, and Cairo and New Orleans will have joined their streets to-

gether, and be plodding comfortably along under a single mayor and a mutual board of aldermen. There is something fascinating about science. One gets such wholesale returns of conjecture out of such a trifling investment of fact [Clemens (1875), 1901, p. 136].

Mark Twain was having his fun. For a serious counterpart, witness an evaluation of the American political experiment by Thomas Jefferson, surely one of the foremost thinkers of the Revolutionary Era: "We have had [by 1787] thirteen states independent for eleven years. There has been one rebellion [that of Shay]. That comes to one rebellion in a century and a half, for each state. What country before ever existed a century and a half without a rebellion?" (quoted in Padover, 1956, pp. 55–56).

Model II is built on constructs—that is, on categories or abstractions. In the copper rod example, temperature is a construct; the key relation is stated in terms of this abstraction rather than in terms of a specific measuring operation. The user of an evaluation commonly thinks about outcomes in abstract terms—"motivation to achieve" or "literacy," for example. A measuring operation corresponds only approximately to the inquirer's construct. Treatments also are discussed in general language: "private schools," Laetrile," and so on. Cook and Campbell (1979, pp. 60–70) develop this line of thought, mentioning among other constructs "aggression," "close supervision by a foreman," and "expertise of communicator." Such terms enter into explanations and into summary statements about the class of treatments or observations over which a relation is thought to hold.

Constructs play a similar role in characterizing settings and units. A setting may be characterized in such terms as "matriarchal society" or "period of high unemployment." Units are referred to as "learning-disabled children," "Hispanic families," "suburban communities," and the like. Choice of such a category as Hispanic families implies that those it encompasses—whether recent immigrants or longtime residents, whether from Mexico or Puerto Rico—are sufficiently homogeneous for the term to provide a useful medium of intellectual exchange.

Contents of Model II. In a Model II for interpreting an evaluation, statements have to do mostly with the nature of social processes and human response; this model, then, is largely substantive (Cornfield and Tukey, 1956; Bracht and Glass, 1968, p. 441). Interpretations are sometimes casual: "From California's experience with community colleges, we know what to expect in New Jersey." The logical basis for even that simple remark is a whole theory about the nonimportance of demographic, economic, and organizational context for the effects of such colleges. At the opposite extreme are the elaborate mathematical models that econometricians use to forecast the effect of, say, a 1 percent increase in the nation's money supply. Their equation systems, which link money supply to capital spending and price levels, encode substantive patterns perceived in past experience. The omission of certain variables and interactions from the model reflects experience too; those influences are judged to have been so small in the past that they can now be ignored.

Model II is a belief system, an analogue to, if not a primitive form of, an evolving scientific theory (Cronbach and Meehl, 1955). The network consists of propositions connecting constructs, along with sentences that tell how to identify concrete instances to which the constructs apply. The propositions are not proven truths; no matter how mature the scientific network, they cannot be. They are consistent with so much prior experience, however, that scientists trust them in their day-to-day work. The social scientist has few definite principles to call upon. Model II is likely to consist of weak statements about trends, correlations, and norms. Even highly structured models, as in econometrics, consist of working hypotheses.

In a belief system, some propositions express convictions; others are speculative. Evaluators generally use low-level abstractions (such as "urban schools") rather than refined constructs. As with a scientific construct, the label refers to distinctions that experience has indicated to be consequential and paints over distinctions thought not to be consequential. The experience that goes into a belief system comes mostly from everyday living, from experience filtered through common sense and cultural tradition (Campbell, 1974). The system is continually being reshaped, and scholarly findings and interpretations contribute to its evolution (Rein, 1976; Weiss, 1977; Lindblom and Cohen, 1979).

The scientific community is in better agreement about most of its theoretical networks than is the general community about its belief system, but consensus supports a large fraction of the beliefs in either type of system. There is a prevailing view of schooling, drug addiction, or unemployment and—within a specialist community—of such a narrow topic as computer-aided instruction. These views are taken for granted until a challenge commands attention.

The argument leading to a conclusion about *UTOS has to be abstract. There is no direct way to convert findings about schools in California into a prediction about schools in New Jersey; only by bringing to bear concepts about kinds of communities, or curricula, or taxation systems can the transfer be made credible or criticized. A strict defense of Model II would require an impracticable effort toward construct validation. In the natural sciences, the validation of propositional networks proceeds slowly. The pace of social events is far too swift to allow a comparable sharpening of thought about proposals for intervention. The networks used in considering social programs have to deal with ever new institutions and conditions; hence, much of Model II will always be conjectural. It would be wrong, however, to dismiss either common experience or accumulated social research merely because it is undependable. Current experts on contraception or delinquency or early education are vastly better informed than those of a generation ago. Much of the added knowledge consists of complications, of additional factors for planners to consider. Such knowledge rarely signals what is right to do, but it can warn against numerous shortsighted courses of action. Replacing unwarranted certainty with uncertainty is a contribution.

External Validity as Credibility

In the context of program evaluation, a conclusion about *UTOS is a prediction. This is true of a local conclusion —for example, "Violence and fear will decrease considerably if we have guards to keep nonstudents off our school premises." It is equally true of a general statement: "Plans for reducing violence are likely to succeed when there is active community support, not otherwise." Either statement predicts what will be found if a certain action is taken and the outcomes are observed.

If the data cast a warm light on a course of action, the action is likely to be taken. The predictions will then be confirmed or disconfirmed. When a discouraging prediction about a course of action is accepted, that action will not be taken, and direct evidence will never come in. The evaluator cannot await empirical confirmation or refutation of even an optimistic prediction about *UTOS, especially if ever changing settings make *UTOS a moving target. He must combine judgment and formal reasoning to reach a conclusion. Whatever he says, the client ought to make her own assessment after the investigator presents his case.

As with Model I, the force of the reasoning rests on the credibility of the sentences in the model, of the mapping sentences, and of the statement that nothing left out of the model matters much. The credibility of a conclusion depends on the degree to which the working hypotheses command acceptance within the relevant community. Thus, the acceptance of a conclusion rests on a social-psychological process.

The following remarks on technological decisions (Branscomb, 1977) demonstrate that external inference is not peculiar to social science:

> Increasingly, public decisions will be based on *predictions of risk that cannot be verified through empirical data.* Impacts on nature of technological activity are initially difficult to detect when masked by the normal and unpredictable natural fluctuations. By

the time these consequences have grown to the point that man-made influences exceed natural fluctuations, it may well be too late to mitigate irreversible effects. The injection of carbon dioxide into the atmosphere with a possible effect on climate is an example. In situations like this, it may be necessary to make very important decisions (such as whether to place primary reliance on coal as an energy source for the next twenty-five years) in the absence of empirical determinations of the consequences (in this case, of increased concentration of carbon dioxide). In such circumstances, *public decisions must be based on simulations, theoretical predictions, and sophisticated interpretation of statistics.* The government is poorly equipped to make decisions on this basis, and the public is ill prepared to accept them. . . .

We must invent new mechanisms, compatible with our democratic political traditions, that permit the generation of a national consensus behind a strategy whose validity extends well beyond the time horizon of elected officials [p. 852; italics added].

The interpreter of social data (whether evaluator or client) is likely to use common sense—that is to say, unexamined reasoning—to decide how broadly to word a conclusion or policy, or whether or not to take an action. The inference is in principle open to explicit analysis and debate, and applied social science will become more useful when such inference is made more explicit. Much of Model II is indefinite and open to disagreement. The more *UTOS* and **UTOS* differ, the more sentences the model requires (including sentences saying that certain differences do not matter). Each sentence has uncertainty, and the uncertainty of the conclusion goes up with the number of sentences. Studies can be designed to make many inferences less uncertain. That is the point of many of the Cook and Campbell recommendations and of recommendations that I shall develop. Hence, in what follows I shall speculate about how to express the uncertainty of a conclusion in numbers, once an argument is spelled out. This somewhat formal statement in Bayesian terms will serve two purposes: It will make clearer what is at stake in planning the original study, and it will amplify the concept of uncertainty—a concept important in theory of design. (Boruch and Gomez, 1979, offer another "small theory" for the same purpose.)

Calculations such as I discuss could be made in those rare cases where Model II is stated formally. A Monte Carlo study of an economic or engineering model, for example, can show which uncertainties make a large difference in conclusions from the model; this can suggest matters to investigate intensively. A person's choice among actions depends on the probabilities she attaches to various possible outcomes. As a simple example, consider a desirable outcome Y, which under existing circumstances is at level 5. If the decision maker is certain that the measure of Y will equal 10 following action A, action A will be appealing. "She is certain" translates into "She believes that, given action A, $Pr\{Y = 10\} = 1.00$." The probability that Y will have any other value is thought to be zero.

But social outcomes are uncertain. The decision maker's belief about the outcomes subsequent to action A can be expressed in probabilities such as Table 4 displays. These probabilities are like betting odds. On a bet that Y will be 13.5 or higher after action A, this decision maker would judge ten-to-one-against to be fair odds. A probability distribution

Table 4. Illustrative Array of Subjective Probabilities

Y	3	4	5	6	7	8	9
Pr {Y at this value}	.00	.01	.04	.05	.07	.10	.14
Cumulative probability	.00	.01	.05	.10	.17	.27	.41

Y (continued)	10	11	12	13	14	15	
Pr {Y at this value}	.18	.14	.10	.07	.05	.05	
Cumulative probability	.59	.73	.83	.90	.95	1.00	

is said to be "flat" over a wide range of Y if the $Pr\{. . .\}$ values are nearly uniform. The person has next to no basis for judging that one of those Y values is more likely than another. The distribution in Table 4 is not flat, but it indicates considerable uncertainty. One index of uncertainty is the distance that separates the 10th and 90th percentiles of the distribution. Here those bounds are 6.5 and 13.5; the range is 7 units. If the bounds were close together, uncertainty would be slight and we would speak of the distribution as "sharp." Other indices can be constructed; this simple one will be adequate here. The index is like an "80 percent confidence interval" except that it is based on subjective beliefs and not on sampling theory.

Prior probabilities reflect the person's beliefs before the investigation is undertaken; posterior probabilities are the beliefs she holds after examining the evidence. One year's posteriors are the next year's priors. In principle, a person can assert such probabilities about any outcome or set of outcomes, including verbal descriptions of alternate states of affairs. Sometimes probabilities are based on so much experience that they can be considered entirely empirical and objective; the player who throws a single die has good reason to assert that the priors on the outcome are flat. In social contexts priors are judgmental. The person who states what can be expected, for example, from a crackdown on speeders is judging from past experience and theory. Unless the available experience is directly to the point, she is wise not to speak as if the outcome is foreseeable (sharp priors).

Bayesian posteriors, in effect, combine prior probabilities with likelihoods determined from the evidence that the study produced. The relative weights depend on the sharpness of the two distributions. Strong evidence offsets flat priors; sharp priors outweigh weak evidence. Suppose that past experience gives strong reason to believe that, following action A, Y will be close to 10. Then an observed value of 8 will persuade us that 8 is the outcome to be expected in further samples only if the accuracy and representativeness of the evidence are beyond dispute. Two participants may have sharp but differing priors; if so, the conclusions they accept at the end of the investigation will probably differ. In other words, posterior beliefs will differ unless the evidence is powerful enough to override the priors.

In evaluation it is useful to think of community priors and posteriors, which are formed by pooling the probability distributions that describe individual beliefs. The evaluator, planning his experiment, aims to reduce the range of uncertainty in the community posteriors. There is a community distribution of priors regarding the question that *UTO* identifies. The evaluator hopes to offer evidence that, fed into Model I, will produce posteriors with a comparatively small range of uncertainty.

For the moment, suppose that inference only to *UTO* is intended. Assume that the mapping statements within Model I are believed by members of the community and that everyone agrees that the change from S to S^* is inconsequential. Then the sharpness of the posteriors depends on the strength of the evidence. Assume, now, that (1) *uto* is a sample drawn from *UTO* by a fixed plan for stratified random sampling; that (2) the mean of Y is taken as the index of the outcome; and that (3) Model I uses whatever assumptions reduce the error of estimate for Y (that is, it is a strong model). For each number in the Y range in turn, a likelihood can be calculated—a probability that the observed sample mean would occur, in a sample of the type drawn, if the population mean indeed equaled the target number. The sharper the distribution of likelihoods—near 1.00 for a few adjacent target values, near zero elsewhere—the smaller the posterior uncertainty.

A doubt about a mapping statement is expressed in a prior probability less than 1.00. This contributes to the uncertainty of the conclusion, unless the doubt is dispelled. In theory, one could set up an alternative Model I with a fresh set of mapping statements and derive a posterior distribution for it. If this produces the same conclusion as before, the doubt about the mapping carries less weight. For example, Monte Carlo studies have established that the sampling error of certain statistics remains much the same when the distribution of scores in the population departs from normality; an analysis assuming normality is therefore trusted when these statistics are used. Pooling results from all credible alternative models, with weights corresponding to their judged believability, would give a distribution that takes the doubts formally into account. No such analysis is feasible, however, if only because of the great number of mapping statements and of alternatives to them.

Impractical as a formal calculation with priors attached to mapping statements would be, the conception helps us see that the uncertainty of an internal inference is not adequately described by conventional confidence intervals or statistical calculations. These are no more than conclusions "in the model." To the extent that the mapping statements are implausible, the conclusion about the concrete *UTO* is more or less certain than the statistics indicate.

In Model II every sentence that states an implication of a difference is somewhat open to question. Therefore, a prediction about a **UTO* is ordinarily associated with far more uncertainty than a prediction about *UTO*. If, however, studies of several *UTO* can be put to use, a kind of triangulation becomes possible. An extrapolation consistent with several initial studies (not necessarily of the same question) can be less uncertain than the conclusion about any one of the *UTO*. The person designing any one study wishes it to reduce the uncertainty left by all the other sources of information.

6

✍ *Mathematical Extrapolations:*

Procedures and Uncertainties

This chapter looks at mathematical procedures for making external inferences. Some of these procedures have played a large role in the attempt to draw conclusions from studies with nonequivalent treatment groups, while others represent possibilities that have not received much attention from evaluators. All of them can be applied in making inferences about a U^* from data on U, and in fact most nonmathematical generalizations place tacit reliance on simple linear extrapolations such as these formulas embody.

The argument that follows is technical, and readers who are not specialists in quantitative analysis may be tempted to skip it. But I urge them to read it over lightly, as a minimum, since it will make them aware of pitfalls in commonplace evaluation procedures that they might otherwise accept without question. Moreover, at several points I come down to straightforward recommendations that can be un-

derstood even by those who do not work through the underlying argument. I have tried to distill from many sources the
insights most important for evaluators and professional interpreters of evaluations. To make the story as simple as possible, I have merely sketched the formal mathematics; readers
who want formal developments will find ample references to
sources in the chapter.

The adequacy of statistical adjustments and extrapolations has received much attention in the last decade—attention stimulated partly by disputes about the inferences made
from nonequivalent groups in the Westinghouse evaluation
of Head Start. It is to be said at the outset that most of the
news about the adequacy of all available approaches is discouraging. Whatever the refinements, all the methods depend on assumptions that are open to considerable question.
Not even the most elaborate analyses can be taken at face
value.

The extensive literature on quasi-experiments and approximations to experiments is concerned with inferring
what an experiment with equivalent treatment groups would
show. The same intent to adjust results for initial characteristics of the persons studied motivates writings on measurement of change in psychology and education, as well as
writings on the effects of selection in personnel psychology
and econometrics. Selection is also a concern in randomized
experiments, since deliberate selective admissions, self-selection, voluntary and involuntary withdrawal from programs,
and failure to respond on tests and questionnaires cause the
sample u to differ from the population of interest. In general,
when the final sample is not systematically representative of
the population that is of interest, the evidence obtained from
the sample may be a poor basis for making statements about
that population. Whether or not a formal adjustment is attempted, the interpreter has to judge how much the departure from representativeness affects conclusions.

Analysis of covariance was introduced not to adjust the
outcome difference but to increase the precision of statistical
inference in randomized experiments. The same calculations

later served to estimate the outcome difference when treatment groups were not equivalent. The computation was said to indicate what would have been found if equivalent groups had been treated. Gradually some methodologists came to recognize that this kind of analysis was as questionable as the older tinkering that picked "matched" experimental and control subjects after the data were in and then compared their final scores. The matching procedures had already been exposed as fallacious; it was seen that superficially similar cases actually differed systematically. Analogous biases and confusions began to be recognized in the popular regression adjustments (Lord, 1967).

The Campbell-Erlebacher (1970) charge of bias in the Head Start analysis was not the first criticism of covariance adjustments, but it focused the attention of evaluators on the possibility of bias. Head Start's control children were, initially, higher in ability than the children the program served. The adjustment attempted to estimate what the outcome would have been in a hypothetical control group whose initial scores averaged as low as those of the children served. Campbell and Erlebacher asserted that this kind of analysis necessarily underrates the treatment given to the group that is least able at the outset and that therefore the Head Start study unfairly discredited compensatory education. It has since been established, however, that bias can run in either direction.

Parts of the literature on adjustment methods were brought together and described by Reichardt (1979), and a wide range of analytic techniques have been reviewed by Anderson and associates (1980). Confining myself to basic issues, I shall look at simple linear models for data collected at two points in time. I shall formulate one central problem more simply than others have, while also reporting some new conclusions and drawing attention to procedures whose pertinence to evaluations has not generally been recognized. (My thinking has been aided by discussions with Reichardt, Weisberg and Bryk of Anderson's team, and several other specialists, particularly David Rogosa.)

For recent theory on multiwave or "panel" data, I suggest the following sources: McCain and McCleary (1979); Jöreskog and Sörbom (1979, especially chaps. 5, 6); Nesselroade and Baltes (1979); Bryk, Strenio, and Weisberg (1980). Bryk (1980, pp. 235–260) treats some approaches to analysis of change that I neglect.

Notes on Regression Equations

Three styles of adjustment are of interest here: subtracting out a pretest score, adjusting with the aid of a covariate, and reconstructing truncated distributions. The last two are based on regression equations, so I shall draw attention to some pitfalls in regression analysis before discussing adjustments.

Consequences of Sampling Error. Elementary textbooks on statistical analysis suggest that the inaccuracy of estimates of outcome scores can be described by attaching a confidence interval to the estimated Y score. This large-sample interval is described as a simple multiple of $\sqrt{1 - r_{XY}^2}$. This formula assumes that the regression equation is known accurately, but the regression equation calculated on a sample departs from the population equation. Because the slope of the population regression line differs from that in the sample, the average Y for persons at the same point on X is determined only approximately. Consequently, for units having predictor scores far from the sample mean, the uncertainty is much greater than indicated by the large-sample confidence interval for a Y score. Evaluators should be keenly aware of this when using a sample regression to estimate expected outcomes for individuals or groups (U^*) whose predictor scores are well above or below the mean of the sample.

Choice of Unit of Analysis. A major difficulty arises when evaluators study collective units, as when the Head Start study collected data on neighborhoods where there were experimental schools and classes, children being nested within classes. Psychologists and educators, accustomed to thinking of individuals rather than collectives, typically have poured individual scores into the computational machinery. But regression equations can also be obtained by computing from the pupils' class mean, school mean, or neighborhood mean; classes (or schools or neighborhoods) receive weight in proportion to their size.

Regressions at different levels of aggregation are unlikely to coincide (Cronbach, 1976; Roberts and Burstein, 1980). Effects that appear important when the analysis ignores group membership sometimes vanish when grouping is recognized (Cronbach and Webb, 1975). The opposite can also happen. These difficulties affect covariance adjustments, structural-regression analyses, and blocked analysis of variance. The model for individual-level analyses requires two mapping sentences that are rarely believable in evaluations: (1) that persons in neighborhoods, classes, and so on, do not differ systematically prior to treatment and (2) that the experiences of members of the same collective during the treatment period are no more similar than the experiences of members of different collectives. Each of the studies described in Chapter Two provided an example of violation of these assumptions.

An aggregate analysis is far more credible than an analysis that ignores collectives. I would ordinarily favor estimating the regressions at the highest level of aggregation where one suspects that relevant differences are associated with units, with smaller units treated as subordinate. Thus, in the Head Start study, I would favor analyses on neighborhood means, on schools within neighborhoods, on classes within schools, and on pupils within classes. The regression at the highest level would be calculated from the neighborhood means, weighted by the sizes of neighborhood populations rather than by sample sizes. At the next level, I would form deviation scores for all variables by subtracting the neighborhood mean from the school mean. The calculation would be run for all cases together, in a way that weights by school size. Other subordinate-level analyses use deviation scores similarly. Some caution is required, however. In an analysis of data on California schools, for example, giving Los Angeles its full numerical weight can mask a great deal of the variation among other school districts. Under those circumstances, it may be wise to repeat the analysis, omitting the outlier's data.

Some analysts take a dim view of high-level aggregation because a sample contains comparatively few high-level units. The statistical uncertainty attached to results may be huge, and then even large effects fall short of significance. But this does not bespeak a genuine loss of power. Rather, the significance levels reported from analysis that ignores collectives are spuriously high whenever the assumptions stated above are violated. (For more examples and a more complete explanation, see Cronbach, 1976.)

The advice to calculate a regression equation from means of aggregates does not rule out sensitive analysis of smaller units. For example, it is entirely appropriate to compare the responses of boys and girls to a particular kind of instruction. But the analysis would best be done within one class at a time; instead of pooling data, the investigator would compile class-by-class comparisons. This would make it possible to discover a sex difference in some classes and not in others—a difference that subsequent detective work might or might not be able to explain.

The presence of natural grouping has implications for the sampling plan. Statistical power is improved by selecting a greater number of large aggregates (such as communities or neighborhoods), because this approach requires comparatively thin sampling within units. Consider a study of social relationships among families in high-rise public housing units. Residents of a building probably develop a particular community style. That would make it advisable to collect data in a number of widely separated buildings, even at the price of reducing the amount of interviewing in any one building. An intensive anthropological study of every resident in one or a few buildings would be an equally reasonable undertaking, but it would be a poor basis for generalizing across buildings.

Role of Pretests

In an evaluative study, there are many reasons for measuring initial characteristics of persons and institutions. The information can be used first of all to make sure that the cases conform to the definition of U and perhaps to identify subsamples with particular characteristics. Second, the information can confirm that supposedly similar groups are actually similar. Third, the data enable one to ask whether the treatment affects all kinds of units similarly. Fourth, the data increase the precision of some statistical inferences. Beyond that, if the pretest is operationally similar to the posttest, the scores can provide a frame of reference for interpreting the distribution of posttest scores.

A pretest twinned to the posttest does not necessarily give the best initial information. Thus, in the Physics study, a pretest resembling the posttest would have made no sense because the incoming students had not yet studied physics. Ordinarily, initial measures should describe readiness for treatment; that is, they should describe factors likely to contribute to or condition success. When the subjects have already had plentiful opportunities to develop whatever characteristics the posttest will measure, then a similar instrument makes a good initial test. To pretest reading skills is sensible for a fourth-grade experiment on remedial reading. In grade 1, however, tests of perceptual discrimination and of vocabulary are better candidates.

There was a time when methodologists recommended that evaluators *not* give a pretest resembling the intended posttest. Let us take note of the worries that led to advice against pretesting. Measuring can itself have consequences. In a study of advertising, for example, a pretest on brand-name recognition may sensitize subjects so that they attend more closely to advertising presented later than they otherwise would. Similarly, a pretest on ability to interpret experiments alerts science teachers and their students to what they will be judged on at posttest time. If this directs their efforts in a desired direction, it makes the treatment more effective—

which is all to the good, as long as interpreters remember that the treatment consisted of pretest-plus-instruction. To ask about the outcome of the instruction *alone* is to ask about a *T**. To investigate pretest-plus-instruction is obviously suitable when the pretest is a natural part of the operating program. Pretests added for the sake of the evaluation are the suspect ones.

Campbell and his associates list the influence of the pretest as a threat to internal and external validity. The papers (Campbell, 1957; Campbell and Stanley, 1963) said rather forcefully that, when treatment-without-pretest is the treatment to be investigated, pretesting subjects in the evaluative study is inadvisable. The evaluator who proposed to give a pretest was advised to split the experimental sample and give one fraction no pretest; that would expose the effect pretesting had on the remainder. Recent advice has been milder. The investigator is told to judge afresh, in each particular study, whether the pretest is likely to have enough effect to confuse interpretation.

Campbell's comments (1969a, p. 355), made when he moderated his position, illustrate the broad methodological principle emphasized in Chapter Five:

> Too frequently we teach scientific method as though it were a dispensation from logic, prior to and external to science. [Earlier (Campbell, 1957)] I wrote as though it were a matter of obvious logic that if one has only experimented with pretested populations, one has no basis for generalizing to unpretested ones. This now seems to me to be quite wrong in emphasis. The authority came not from the logic but from the empirical plausibility, the probable lawlike character, of pretest interactions. Following logic alone, it was equally illogical to try to generalize to other groups . . . to other dates . . . or to other settings. . . . In this vast array of logical restrictions, this one was persuasive because of its empirical appeal. The hypothetical laws involved, as reviewed by Lana [1969], . . . do

not now seem at all as plausible as they seemed
then; and, as a result, we will no doubt see less emphasis upon experimental designs doing without
the pretest.

Because evaluators can make good use of information on initial characteristics, the burden of proof now rests on the designer who proposes not to collect such data on all units.
When one of the initial measures—a pretest—resembles the
posttest, that fact does not warrant analyzing the measure differently from other initial measures. I would look on this
measure as just one among several measures of initial characteristics that can enter a predictive equation.

Some persons ask the evaluator to report how much
the units change from the start of treatment to some later
point. I recommend against formulating evaluative questions
in terms of change, at least when measures are made at only
two points in time. The score formed by subtracting pretest
from posttest gives misleading impressions (Cronbach and
Furby, 1970). Regressions of posttest on pretest can play a
more valuable role in summaries than change scores. I can
see no warrant, however, for treating the pretest differently
from other initial measures in regression analyses.

A particularly suitable descriptive summary for many
evaluation data is a regression surface relating an outcome to
true initial status on a few relevant predictors. Such a surface
can be calculated for each treatment group separately, or by
forming deviation scores in each group and then pooling
groups. An important issue, requiring judgments more than
significance testing, is whether the numerical differences in
the three or more sets of regression coefficients are meaningful.

Estimates of coefficients for hypothetical error-free
predictors are obtained much as in other regression analyses,
after an estimate of true score variance is substituted for the
observed variance of each predictor. It is best to calculate
from a matrix of variances and covariances, not directly from
scores or from correlations. The covariances for true scores

are, under the usual assumptions about error of measurement, the same as covariances of observed scores. The variance of each predictor is reduced by subtracting the estimated variance of errors of measurement. Standard computer programs for regression analysis then apply.

Bias Arising from an Incomplete Covariate

Most that was written on adjustments in the aftermath of the Campbell and Erlebacher (1970) challenge to the Head Start analysis focused on treatment comparisons. When treatment groups are not equivalent, it is usual to adjust one or both treatment means on outcome Y by extrapolating with the aid of some initial measure W, a covariate. The regression of Y on W allows one to estimate the Y means for both treatments at the same value of W. The choice of covariate has a critical effect on the end result. It is simpler and more general to think about adjusting in one treatment at a time. The basic idea is that (within a treatment) the same process generates outcomes in populations U and U^*. Data are available for U, and extrapolation is made to U^*. I shall refer to a single covariate W, but W could be a composite variable. Also, for simplicity, I shall speak as if U rather than u had been observed. My conclusions, which extend readily to comparative studies, reach beyond those of previous papers. Moreover, they apply to regression systems such as are used in causal models, as well as to single adjustments.

The analyst starts with means and standard deviations for Y and W and with the Y-on-W regression coefficient for scores observed when population U was exposed to T. He substitutes into that equation the observed or postulated mean of W in U^* to obtain an expected mean of Y in U^*. This classical method extends the regression found in U into the range of U^*. If the regression equation does not fit U^*, the estimated mean of Y will be wrong. How large is the systematic error? And what determines its size and direction?

Pearson-Lawley Model and Its Derivatives. The algebra needed to evaluate the inference about U^* stems from the

work of Pearson (1903); Lawley (1943) simplified the formulation. Pearson and Lawley dealt with correlations, but the ex-
tension to regressions is obvious. The Pearson technique is
probably known to many readers, because psychologists use it
to adjust correlation coefficients for restriction of range. For
example, students in a first-year law school class are selected
on the basis of an aptitude test—the Law School Admission
Test (LSAT)—and other information related to their probable success. When their LSAT scores are correlated with their
first-year grade averages, the correlation is lower than it
would have been in a student body representative of all eligible applicants. The predictive power of the test is underrated
because the statistic gives it no credit for keeping out the poor
risks on whom no criterion data became available. The traditional formulas estimate what the validity coefficient would
be if all applicants were admitted, a U^*. (For the psychometric theory, see Lord and Novick, 1968, pp. 140–148. The
comparable theory for regressions in comparative evaluations was developed by Cochran and Rubin, 1973; Barnow
and Cain, 1977; and Cronbach and others, 1977. A formal
mathematical argument leading to the formula that I shall
discuss appears in Cronbach and Schaeffer, 1981.)

Two unobserved variables—P, the ideal covariate, and
D, the selection variable or discriminant—are central to the
model as I present it. P and D generate other variables in a
regression system. The bottom line is this: Bias in extrapolation arises from mismatch between the covariate and the
"complete" covariates P and D. Figure 4 suggests how the
variables are defined. A curved arrow indicates a correlation
between two variables measurable prior to treatment. A
straight arrow implies that one variable is observed before the
other and may correlate with it. Each arrow denotes a regression (for example, for P predicted from D) that is assumed to be linear. My arrows do not represent causal hypotheses. The variables E, E', and E'' are disturbances. Their
means conditional on D and on each other are set at zero;
variances of E and E' conditional on D are equal to their respective unconditional variances. It follows that selection on

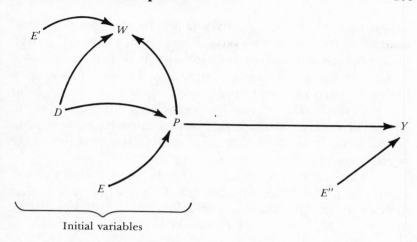

Figure 4. Relations among variables in the *P-D* model

D does not alter the linearity of the regressions represented by arrows and does not alter the corresponding regression coefficients.

The hypothetical ideal predictor P takes into account all the characteristics, measurable initially, that predict the outcome of T for the units in U or U^*. This perfect composite of aptitudes, attitudes, wealth, health, and so on, predicts Y as well as it can be predicted. The second variable is the ideal discriminant D. U differs from U^* in some respects. The investigator may have selected cases for U deliberately, or the differences may arise from uncontrolled and largely unknown sources. D is that combination of initial variables (all variables that *might* have been measured) that best distinguishes members of U from members of U^*.

General Regression Equation. In discussing traditional methods of extrapolation, I leave sampling fluctuations out of account and rule out a number of minor cases so that later statements can be straightforward. In particular, I assume that the means of W differ from U to U^*, that W has a non-zero correlation with P and D in U, and that P and D are positively but not perfectly correlated in U. Also, I assume that every component of D has variance within U and U^*. In a subgroup such that the mean of D is zero, the mean of Y is a, and (to simplify) the means of P and W are zero. Although most applications of Pearson's formula take U to be a subset of U^*, the theory does not assume this. U and U^* may span different parts of the D range, and U may include U^*. Most fundamentally, the regression coefficients corresponding to curved arrows in Figure 4 (β_{WP}, for example) are assumed to be the same in U and U^*. Moreover, it is assumed that these regressions are linear.

This leads to an equation for the regression in either population, where the subscript (p) identifies parameters that differ with the population. The following expression differs only in form from that of Lawley (1943):

$$\hat{Y} = a + \beta_{YP}\mu_{P(p)} + \beta_{YW(p)}(W - \mu_{W(p)}) \text{ or}$$

$$\hat{Y} = a + \beta_{YP}\beta_{PD}\mu_{D(p)}$$
$$+ \beta_{YP} \left\{ \frac{\beta_{PD}\beta_{WD}\sigma^2_{D(p)} + \beta_{PE}\beta_{WE}\sigma^2_E}{\beta^2_{WD}\sigma^2_{D(p)} + \beta^2_{WE}\sigma^2_E + \beta^2_{WE'}\sigma^2_{E'}} \right\} (W - \beta_{WD}\mu_{D(p)}).$$

For any one treatment and a particular covariate, the regression slope depends on σ_D. Two groups having equal σ_D and receiving the same treatment will have parallel Y-on-P and parallel Y-on-W regressions. To allow for a main effect of treatment in a two-treatment study, we may subscript a; then the "adjusted treatment effect" from analysis of the covariance of equivalent groups equals $a_1 - a_2$.

It will prove important later to recognize possibilities that traditional analysis of covariance rules out. P may change with the treatment, and β_{YP} may differ across treatments when P does not. (Where P changes, it is appropriate to employ a different W in each treatment.)

P *and* D *as Ideal Covariates.* From the assumption of linearity, coupled with the definition of D, a theorem follows. When any initial measure W is regressed on D, the equation linking W to D remains the same whether the calculation is made for U or U^*. Also, the between-groups regression line falls right atop both within-groups regressions. If D were known, the observed regression of Y on D in U would be the regression in U^*, and the investigator could estimate the expected Y at each point in the range of D within U^*. This extrapolation is not subject to systematic bias when the assumptions of the model are accepted. (Reichardt, 1979, pp. 102–105, has discussed sampling error, nonlinearity, and other sources of difficulty.)

Ordinarily D is unknown. It can be given a special interpretation in a comparative, controlled-assignment study with nonequivalent treatment groups. If the investigator records the selection rules that define U (and satisfies himself that any loss of cases from the sample can be considered random), he can write for each case an explicit D score that fully accounts for that unit's probability of entering U. An investigator who controlled assignment can observe the Y-on-D regression in U and obtain a satisfactory adjustment. In any one-treatment study that satisfies the assumptions, extrapolation based on the regression of Y on P or on any linear function of P gives an accurate adjustment. The Y-on-P regression is the same within and between populations. This is intellectually interesting; but since the investigator does not know the makeup of P and has not measured it, such an adjustment is an unattainable ideal.

Biases Generated by Operational Covariates. In typical extrapolation procedures, including analysis of covariance, the investigator chooses some W that he considers relevant and uses the Y-on-W regression in U as if it were the regression for U^*. Most of the time, his end result is incorrect. The Y-on-W regression equation in U will not be the same as the corresponding equation in U^* unless a very lucky choice of W was made. The error is systematic; that is, other investigators extrapolating to the same U^*, from other large samples of the same U and with the same covariate, will err in the same direction. The errors tend to be large when the range of W scores in U overlaps comparatively little with the range in U^* and when the standard deviations of W in U and U^* are far from equal. The direction and magnitude of the error can be estimated only if one is prepared to assume values for the regression coefficients entering the general equation, besides accepting the assumptions of the model. That is a tall order.

In special cases the regression calculated in U does provide trustworthy information about both the U^* mean and the regression equation. Most such cases are trivial. Some mathematical interest attaches to covariates having the special property that, among persons who have the same score on the covariate, P and D are uncorrelated. With such a covariate, selection on the basis of D cannot create a systematic difference in the Y scores of groups equated on W. Hence, the regression in U matches that in U^*, and the adjustment is unbiased. Many covariates might have this property, but they are impossible to identify. With the one exception of the study where assignment is controlled, extrapolation is to the population from which cases were assigned, and D is the covariate.

Numerical Examples. The following calculations will demonstrate the bias in estimated intercepts and slopes. Suppose that in U^* the means of W, D, and P are all zero and that the standard deviation of D is 1. To simplify further, set β_{YP} equal to 1, and a equal to zero. None of these specifications loses generality. But the following additional specifications are restrictive: $\beta_{PD} = .6$ in U and U^*; the mean and the standard deviation of D in U are 1 and .5, respectively; the standard deviation of E is .8, and β_{PE} is 1 (in U and in U^*). These specifications imply that the mean and the standard deviation of P are .6 and .85, respectively, in U and are 0 and 1 in U^*.

I formed five specimen covariates made up purely of P or D or both. That is, I set $\beta_{WE'}$ equal to zero. The covariates are listed in the first column of Table 5; the multipliers .56

Table 5. Comparison of Estimates Resulting with Various Covariates

Covariate W	Regression in U	Regression in U^*
D	$\hat{Y} = \;\;\;\;0.0 + \;\;.6(W)$	$\hat{Y} = 0 + \;\;.6(W)$
$.56(P + D)$	$\hat{Y} = -0.5 + 1.2(W)$	$\hat{Y} = 0 + \;\;.9(W)$
P	$\hat{Y} = \;\;\;\;0.0 + 1.0(W)$	$\hat{Y} = 0 + 1.0(W)$
$1.12(P - D)$	$\hat{Y} = \;\;\;\;.9 + \;\;.8(W)$	$\hat{Y} = 0 + \;\;.4(W)$
$-D$	$\hat{Y} = \;\;\;\;0.0 - \;\;.6(W)$	$\hat{Y} = 0 - \;\;.6(W)$

and 1.12 were chosen to make the standard deviation of each covariate in U^* equal to 1.

To see how the results in Table 5 are reached, consider the second row. I have specified:

$$P = .6D + E.$$
$$W = .56(P + D) = .90D + .56E.$$

Substituting parameters for U into the general equation, I get:

$$\hat{Y} = 0 + (1)(.6)(1)$$
$$+ 1\left\{\frac{(.6)\beta_{WD}(.25) + (1)\beta_{WE}(1)}{\beta_{WD}^2(.25) + \beta_{WE}^2(1)}\right\}[W - \beta_{WD}(1)].$$

Using .90 and .56 for the regression coefficients, I get:

$$\hat{Y} = .6 + 1.2(W - .9) = -.5 + 1.2W.$$

The regressions in U would be observed. The regressions in the third column of the table, which hold true in U^*, are what the investigator would like to infer. If the value of zero is entered for W (its mean in U^*), each equation properly reports that the mean of Y is zero in U^*. When W is set equal to zero in the equations of the second column, however, the estimates of the Y mean are $0, -.5, 0, .9,$ and 0, respectively. The estimate is correct only when a pure measure of P or D is the covariate. And only with such a covariate does the slope of the regression equation in U equal the slope in U^*. In the third column, the Y-on-W slope is greatest when $W = P$, as is implied by the definition of P. In the second column, the slope is greatest with a covariate intermediate between P and D.

The reader can form an integrated impression of the biases by realizing that the five covariates are an ordered series. The regression coefficients in each column, and the intercepts in the second column, trace out wave functions. The waves could be continued through values corresponding to $-.56(P + D)$, $-P$, $-1.12(P - D)$, returning to the starting point. A generally similar picture would have resulted had I started with other numerical values, as long as their signs remain the same and E' has no influence. The discrepancy between the two regression coefficients depends particularly on the discrepancy between the values of σ_D in U and U^*.

The influence of E' can most easily be brought into the picture by considering the limiting case where $W = E'$ (and E' has variance). Then the regression equation in U^* is

$$\hat{Y} = 0 + 0(W).$$

That is to say, Y is unrelated to W, and its mean is zero. But the equation in U is

$$\hat{Y} = .6 + 0(W).$$

If this equation is used to extrapolate, the mean of Y in U^* is erroneously reported to be equal to the mean in U; the covariate is irrelevant and fails to adjust.

Covariates that are partly relevant, such as $P + D + E'$ or $P + E'$, generate equations that fall between the equations given above and the equations in Table 5. Thus, with the covariate $.56(P + D + E')$, the estimated mean in U^* shifts from $-.5$ (second line of table) toward $+.6$ (equation given above) as the variance of E' increases from zero to a large value; the slope declines from 1.2 to zero. For one and only one variance, the U and U^* regressions are the same; but the investigator will never know when the covariate he chose has that happy property.

A Warning on Disattenuation. An elaborate literature has tried to take into account the measurement error that is included in the variable E'. Earlier I suggested one such procedure for describing regressions in the sample. Similar disattenuation procedures have been recommended as part of adjustment procedures, but *these* recommendations are unsound. (For reviews see Huitema, 1980, p. 311; Reichardt, 1979, p. 190.) Suppose for the moment that E' is wholly made up of measurement error. As indicated above, changing W from the fallible $.56(P + D + E')$ to the true $.56(P + D)$ would swing the error in the estimated Y mean from $-.5$ to $+.6$. But disattenuation cannot hit confidently on that intermediate value where bias vanishes.

If an investigator gifted with second sight knows that his W is a measure of P, plus error or other information unrelated to P and D, he can safely disattenuate—provided that he gets a good estimate of the magnitude of the unwanted elements. He can also do so if he knows that W is a measure of D with a known admixture of E'. Investigators who lack such second sight can make matters worse rather than better by even the best correction procedure of this type. Finally, several writers have recommended using the pretest-posttest correlation as a reliability coefficient in disattenuating. Huitema (1980, p. 312), in relaying this idea, correctly lists its assumptions, but he should have gone on to say that they are implausible whenever a treatment comes between pretest and posttest.

Extension to Comparative Studies

We move on to comparative studies. After examining some implications for studies with equivalent groups, I shall discuss certain quasi-experiments. In each section I shall assume that the comparison is between two very large treatment groups drawn from U. All the conclusions follow from the statements previously made regarding a single treatment.

Extrapolation from a True Experiment in U. The true experiment divides a sample of U at random, perhaps after blocking on one or more initial variables. The subgroups have the same distribution on whatever D differentiates U from U^*. There are two Y-on-W regressions in U, one for each treatment. Substituting the mean of W in U^*, for each treatment in turn, estimates the mean of Y in U^*. It is assumed that in U^* both treatment groups have the same mean and standard deviation on W but that these do not match the values in U.

Three cases are to be distinguished: (1) The same variable P is the best predictor of Y in each treatment, and the Y-on-P regression coefficients are equal; (2) the same variable P is the best predictor of Y in each treatment, and the Y-on-P regression coefficients differ; and (3) P_1 is the best predictor in T_1, and another variable P_2 is the best predictor in T_2.

In Case 1 the within-treatment regressions of Y on P in U do not differ in slope. The Y-on-W regressions will be parallel in U^*, because the only element in the regression coefficient that changes with the population is σ_D. This case is summarized in the upper row of Table 6. As the distance between the regressions in U^* is the same as the distance between the regressions in U, the treatment effect in U^* is the same as the expected value in samples from U. But even in this ideal situation, there is a difficulty. The change in μ_D from U to U^* implies that, within a treatment, the regression in U^* is distinct from that in U. This is true even if the regression slopes in U^* happen to coincide with the slopes in U. Consequently, the predicted mean in U^* for each treatment is likely to be wrong (though the error is the same in both treatments). The error is sometimes positive and sometimes negative, as in Table 5.

Table 6. Soundness of Inferences About Regressions in U^* from a True Experiment in U

Underlying Model	Are Y-on-W Regressions Parallel		Does Extrapolation Correctly Indicate Value in U* of		
	in U?	in U*?	Slopes?	Outcome Means?	Mean Difference?
1. Same P and β_{YP} in both treatments	Yes	Yes	No	No	Yes
2. Same P, different β_{YP}	No	No	No	No	No
3. P differs with the treatment	No	No	No	No	No

Note: The table entries give likely results with haphazardly chosen covariates. In certain exceptional cases, a "No" entry would change to "Yes," but only in trivial cases would this be recognizable.

Decision makers considering alternative programs want to know the difference in mean outcomes, but they also want to know how good the outcomes are. They want to know, for example, whether the probable outcome under an inexpensive T_1 is so low as to warrant adopting a more expensive T_2 that will accomplish more. Hence, the absolute levels of the means in U^* are important to estimate, but the regression in U does not give a proper estimate of them. The decision maker might also wish to interpret a Y-on-W regression coefficient in U^*; that coefficient will not match the coefficient in U unless σ_D is the same in both populations.

In Case 2 the Y-on-W regression coefficients differ from treatment to treatment. A within-treatment regression equation in U will have the same coefficient as that in U^* only if σ_D in U^* happens to match σ_D in U. Substituting into the U equation the mean of W in U^* will ordinarily not estimate correctly the mean of Y for a treatment, and the difference between the estimated means will not equal the treatment effect in U^*. Certain covariates do allow unbiased extrapolation; if the covariate W happens to be one of the rare choices that produces no bias, however, the investigator will not be able to recognize it as such.

In Case 3 the difficulties are precisely the same. The only novel consideration is that even in UTO the treatment difference ought to be described by means of a multiple-regression equation combining whatever predictors work best for the treatments considered separately. Errors in conclusions about U^* are like those in Case 2.

(Before going ahead, I should acknowledge the difficulty of establishing which case describes actual data. Because of sampling errors alone, within-treatment regression equations will combine data differently, and the coefficients for any single predictor will differ. I do not believe that the best plan is to assume Case 1 wherever possible and thus to accept the null hypothesis regarding interaction. Greater reliance on the modern cross-validation procedures of Mosteller and Tukey, 1977, is probably the best safeguard. I also note that the difficulties described are primarily significant for studies of social and educational interventions. Experiments in medicine are comparatively trustworthy because a drug dosage or a surgical procedure can be reproduced with little variation, and criteria for diagnosis of a specific disorder, if well developed, make it unlikely that unidentified variables will interact with the treatment.)

Comparative Studies with Controlled Assignment. If known and measured, D can be the basis for valid extrapolation in a one-group study. Therefore, using it as a covariate allows valid comparison of treatments in U when the treatment groups are not equivalent but are formed on the basis of D. Population U is divided into subpopulations U_1 and U_2 on the basis of an observed D; they receive, respectively, T_1 and T_2.

Cook and Campbell and others speak of the "regression-discontinuity design" (Reichardt, 1979, pp. 202–205), suggesting that a single sharp cut on the D scale defines who receives one treatment rather than the other. For example, a cutoff score on income can define eligibility for a social service. In principle, however, the investigator controlling assignment could assign an arbitrary probability of entering the experimental group to each level of D and still reach an unbiased result. It is not even necessary that the probabilities increase (or decrease) regularly with D (Rubin, 1977; Barnow, Cain, and Goldberger, 1980). The crucial assumption is linearity of the regression of Y on D, over the range of D in U_1 and U_2 combined.

It is possible—if the model underlying the general equation holds—to regard U_1 as U, to use the assignment variable as covariate, and to estimate what the mean of Y would be if T_1 were given to U_2 (which here is a kind of U^*). One can equally well estimate the mean for T_1 in any U^* whose distribution on D is specified, provided that D accounts fully for its difference from U. The same analysis, starting with U_2, leads to the mean for T_2 at any level of D and to a sound estimate of the treatment effect. This is true whether or not the within-treatment regressions are parallel.

This extrapolation is not the same as extrapolation from the true experiment, covered in the preceding section.

There the same D differentiated U^* from each of the experimental groups. Here D differentiates one segment of U from the other. To consider pointedly the problem of extrapolating to an "external" U^*, think of a U_1, U_2 discriminant (D_0) alongside a U^*, U_1 discriminant and a U^*, U_2 discriminant. The latter two discriminants are not known and cannot become covariates. The analysis of a controlled-assignment design with its D_0 as covariate gives no justification for a conclusion about a U^* that differs from U on variables other than D_0. What is said in the next section applies to this inference.

Extrapolation from Nonequivalent Groups. We turn now to comparative studies where formation of treatment groups was not determined by a score D or a random process. The within-treatment regression of Y on an arbitrary W in U^* will ordinarily differ in slope and intercept from that in U. Moreover, the difference between the regressions for the two treatments at any value of W will generally not match that in U. Crisscrossing biases usually enter the estimates of effects for the two treatments. When an attempt is made to estimate the treatment difference in U, no one can say whether the biases tend to cancel or to augment each other.

To be specific, suppose that the Harvard Project Physics (HPP) investigators had established the regression of a certain outcome on one or more initial variables for a representative sample of American physics teachers. Suppose also that they could now describe on those same initial variables the teachers around the country who, given free choice, decide to teach the HPP course in the year following the experiment. There is no dependable way to estimate what the mean achievement of students in this next set of classes will be— not even if confounding variables such as degree of commitment to Physical Science Study Committee (PSSC) physics are among the variables used in adjustment. Entering multivariate initial information descriptive of the new self-selected U^* into the regression equation obtained from u will give an estimate that is almost certainly incorrect. The direction of the systematic error will be unknown.

The one constructive statement that can be made is

that if treatment does not interact with W in U and if the treatment groups have equal standard deviations on W, it is likely that there is no interaction with W in U^*. But coincidental combinations of parameters can produce parallelism in U without parallelism in U^*. And if the regressions on W *are* parallel by coincidence, the regressions on covariates other than W are unlikely to be parallel.

Recommendations. This elaborate exposé of commonly used statistical methods can be boiled down to a few salient points. An investigator who limits himself to estimating a regression in U from a proper sample is on safe ground as long as he is mindful of sampling error and of the possibility that the regression may not be linear. This statement also applies to the comparative study in which assignment is controlled. If differences between groups are wholly due to sampling error, any covariate may be used in estimating the treatment means in population U, although one would ordinarily prefer whatever covariate gives the best prediction of Y in a particular treatment. If the assignment produces nonequivalent groups, the assignment variable must be the covariate, to ensure correct adjustment.

There is no secure way to extrapolate when u does not systematically represent the population of interest. Trouble is to be expected when a regression summarizing data on a single treatment or a comparison of treatments is extended to a new population. Trouble is also to be expected when a comparative study starts with controlled assignment but loses cases in a nonrandom manner. The one positive note: if an experiment used equivalent groups, if attrition was not systematic, *and* if the observed within-treatment regressions on the covariate were parallel, then the treatment effect in U^* can be estimated without systematic bias. Even then, an important safeguard against parallelism-by-coincidence is to repeat the analysis with another covariate.

Reports can be improved if data collection and statistical analysis are guided by the recently developed knowledge of mathematical difficulties. Most obviously, the extrapolation from U to U^* can be made several times with alternative covariates. The traditional approach has been to measure the initial variables expected to forecast Y, combining these into a best predictor (a weak approximation to P). That is still a sound plan, especially if one acknowledges that the relevant predictors may differ with the treatment. Beyond this, it would be desirable to "model the selection process," as the jargon has it. That is, one can assess variables expected to distinguish one treatment group from another, survivors from nonsurvivors, or U^* from U. The next step is to form an estimator of whatever D distinguishes a group supplying data from a U^* and to use that estimator as an alternative covariate. Unfortunately, however, even if the analysis with an estimator of P as covariate reaches the same conclusion about means in U^* as the analysis with an estimator of D as covariate, one cannot say that the result is dependable. It is entirely possible that both covariates are inadequate and their biases similar.

If nothing else, the findings developed here should put an end to the somewhat precious debates about whether randomization is more important than representativeness. It is now clear that the ideal random experiment gives incomplete information on a population other than the one represented, even when several stringent conditions—including the absence of substantive interactions—are satisfied. But conclusions can be firm when data are obtained on a systematic sample of the population of greatest interest. Ordinarily this can be accomplished only where that population is defined as a self-selected one (or where the dropout rate is the dependent variable!).

Reconstruction of Truncated Distributions

This final section briefly describes some recent work in econometrics. Econometricians are at present proposing a two-stage regression adjustment. Only a fraction of this work has reached publication, and opinions oscillate between optimism and pessimism as the methods are viewed from various angles. We are obviously seeing here an early stage in the evolution of a new breed of methods. Somewhere down the line, they may help many investigators to arrive at defensible adjustments in instances where the time-honored procedures are certain to fail. It is not yet possible to assess where the methods can be trusted and where they introduce new distortions. To alert the reader to developments in progress, however, I draw on informal communications from Arthur Goldberger, Zvi Griliches, James Heckman, Bengt Muthén, and David Rogosa.

The Pearson (1903) conceptions of a complete population and a selected population are the starting point for these corrections, and the model described earlier in this chapter is essentially that of the econometricians. They, however, entertain the possibility of selection on the basis of the outcome measure Y as well as on the basis of the initial variables.

Economists fit regression equations in which a dummy variable represents the treatment that a unit received and certain regression coefficients have an evaluative function. These purport to tell how much the outcome changes in response to the treatment. Coefficients are wanted for population U^*, but full information comes from a u that is not representative of U^*. In a study of the relation of earnings to education, for example, an investigator would find that some persons do not enter the labor market, or they drop out of training, or they do not respond to a survey. In these truncated data, distributions of predictor variables are known for u and U^*. The analyst estimates the regression in U^* by reconstituting moments of the U^* distribution. Barnow, Cain, and Goldberger (1980) reanalyzed the Head Start data in this manner, and Hausman and Wise (1976) made a similar reanalysis of the income maintenance data from New Jersey. These estimates of treatment effects differed from those that conventional analysis had produced.

One adjustment procedure rests on a theorem: If cases are selected on D, the partial-regression coefficient $\beta_{PW \cdot D}$ for any treatment will be the same in the parent population as in the select one. The work proceeds in two stages. Cases with complete data and cases with incomplete data are distinguished by a dummy variable V. A multiple-regression equation is formed for estimating V from observed variables. This estimate $\hat{V}$ for a person expresses the probability that such a person will provide full data. Assumptions are made regarding the joint distribution of certain variables that resemble those of my model. The average value of Y in the sample, among persons with the same P, departs from the average in U^*; the assumptions enable one to describe this distortion as a nonlinear function of $\hat{V}$, and this function makes an adjustment possible. When the distributional assumptions can be trusted, the method works whether or not $\hat{V}$ accounts perfectly for the truncation.

Heckman (1979) assumes normal distributions. The adjustment process appears to be delicate—small departures from normality have drastic consequences (Goldberger, 1980). A variation on the method (Olson, 1980) avoids the assumption of normality. The price of violating *its* assumptions remains to be examined. My own trials with made-up data and some mathematical analysis by Goldberger (personal communication, 1981) indicate that choice of variables to estimate V is also critical. The method can break down when the variables used to predict V do not include all those onto which regression coefficients of Y will be wanted. Whereas an incomplete set of variables introduces bias, using many predictors will make the results highly unstable because multicollinearity (redundancy) is then probable.

It follows from all that has been said in this chapter that the evaluator and his audience should distrust purely statistical extrapolations. Yet extrapolation is essential, and the evaluator should do what he can to facilitate it. One part of the solution is to rely heavily on substantive considerations in reaching conclusions about *UTOS. A useful device, I have suggested, is to employ two or more distinct covariates in turn. The main argument for such a practice is that experience with conflicting adjustments will make evaluators and their audiences properly skeptical of conclusions. The emerging corrections of the econometricians should be similarly useful in shaking confidence in results from conventional analyses.

I doubt that future improvements in adjustment machinery can overcome the difficulties that this chapter has discussed. Yet the great gains in insight during the 1970s encourage hope for further clarifications and for the invention of better machinery. In the past, statistical analysis has been largely separate from substantive analysis of the implications of social data; the need to bring the two into a close working relationship cannot be overemphasized.

7

⤺ Choosing Questions to Investigate

The evaluator asked to study a program is not a free agent in choosing questions to look into. A sponsor will support certain inquiries but not others. An informant is willing to supply some data but not others. The administrator in a research site will not accept all aspects of an experimental scheme. Nonetheless, the evaluator should at the outset entertain the widest possible range of questions.

The sponsor may accept proposals to broaden the inquiry beyond her original view of it. Or perhaps so many lines of inquiry are identified that everyone comes to see that no summative report attainable within the state of the art and available resources will be accepted as comprehensive and just. If so, the program—or its political environment—is not suitable for evaluation of that character; in Wholey's (1979) expression, the program lacks evaluability. It would be a service to convince the prospective sponsor that the evaluation as preconceived would lead to a dead end and that resources could be directed to a better purpose.

I shall speak of a divergent phase of planning, in which possible questions are listed, and a convergent phase, in which priorities are assigned. In practice, both activities go on at once. The agency proposing to sponsor an evaluation would be wise to do some divergent and convergent planning before it asks a contractor to work out an operational plan. Further thinking of both kinds will be required when the contractor sets to work. Exchanges and negotiations between the evaluator-designate and the sponsor will lead to a revised list of questions—a list to be amended further as field experience comes in. Since there will be investigations of related programs after the study in hand reaches completion, the divergent phase never ends.

Divergent Phase

The first step is opening one's mind to questions to be entertained at least briefly as prospects for investigation. This phase constitutes an evaluative act in itself, requiring collection of data, reasoned analysis, and judgment. Very little of this information and analysis is quantitative. The data come from informal conversations, casual observations, and review of extant records. Naturalistic and qualitative methods are particularly suited to this work because, attending to the perceptions of participants and interested parties, they enable the evaluator to identify hopes and fears that may not yet have surfaced as policy issues.

Sources of Questions. Many of the questions in an evaluation express uncertainties of members of the policy-shaping community; others arise because members hold firm but contradictory beliefs. In locating candidate questions, the evaluator ought to seek out a wide variety of informants. The ultimate omission of a question will then be a deliberate choice and not an inadvertent consequence of limited vision on the part of planners. Representatives of political groups, astute observers of political forces, practitioners and managers, and scholars who know the problem area will be useful informants.

The evaluator engages to produce something—information—that has value to consumers and for which they are willing to pay. Deciding what product to deliver is an economic decision; both sides of the supply-demand equation contribute to it. The sponsor, as procurer of information, should not have to take sole responsibility for specifying the product. In industry, suppliers perform a part of their economic function by offering options to customers. In a similar way, the sponsor of an evaluation should be a broker for the many interest communities. And, by anticipating the wishes of those who are in the market for social information, the evaluator assists the sponsor (thus increasing, in a quite legitimate manner, the demand for the evaluator's services).

The evaluator has certain advantages over the sponsor in locating questions. First of all, being relatively free of ties to present policies and operating agencies, he brings in a fresh set of biases. Second, although the sponsor probably is attuned to the political pressures of the moment, the evaluator may be in a better position to collect and appreciate the questions current in nonpolitical circles and in constituencies that have not yet coalesced into pressure groups. Third, from his knowledge of past research (not all of it evaluative), the evaluator can recognize the challenges and counterinterpretations to which a study is subject, and so can suggest needed controls. Fourth, the evaluator knows the state of *his* art and can tell the sponsor how adequately a question can be answered on a particular scale of expenditure. In the end, the sponsor will determine the political and administrative relevance of the questions that could be studied, but the sponsor should not have to make those decisions unaided.

The social services to be evaluated may be in place when the evaluator comes on the scene and thus may not be subject to modification for purposes of the evaluation. Then the evaluator should form a picture of the versions of the treatment that are in place, with a view to deciding which deserve study. He might study institutions with especially good

reputations or institutions in difficulty or institutions organized in an unusual manner. When the services in question
are open to manipulation, any number of innovations can be
listed as possibilities. The sponsor, aware of action alternatives that have vocal partisans and of pilot tests that have been
made, will suggest some candidates. Some practitioner is
likely to see faults in a proposed program and to suggest
modifications. A scholar may mention an alternative that has
not attracted political backing. At this time the door is, in
principle, wide open to any candidate.

Who Is Consulted? Scriven (1972) has advocated "goal-
free" evaluation. He warns that the evaluator who interacts
with the program developers, if only to learn what their goals
are, tends to become their confederate. The evaluator,
Scriven thinks, will become attentive to the positive effects
that the program is best adapted to achieve but will overlook
equally desirable effects that a rival program might aim to
produce. I agree that the evaluator should try to notice *all* the
ends toward which services in a given area might reasonably
aim, including the outcomes claimed for traditional programs and for competing innovative proposals. But I do not
advise the evaluator to avoid contact with program proponents.

The evaluator who does not talk to persons having
images of the program can only fantasize about what outcomes partisans hope for and skeptics fear, and how they expect these effects to develop. If the evaluator reports on the
outcomes that he saw as potentially significant but ignores
some outcome variable that the program's proponents considered important, his report can justifiably be attacked. The
evaluator who avoids collegial relationships with program
proponents escapes from certain forces that could bias him,
but equally strong biases flow from his own commitments and
preconceptions. The remedy seems to lie in communication
with persons whose biases diverge.

The evaluator should try to see the program through
the eyes of the various sectors of the decision-making community, including the professionals who would operate the

program if it is adopted and the citizens who are to be served
by it. What hopes and fears, regarding each of the alternative
interventions, are expressed by advocates of rival programs
and by those who advocate taking no action? What potential
good or harm do members of each minority community see
in the program plans? What effects do employers, psychiatrists, judges, or members of some other relevant elite suggest that an evaluator attend to? The reservations and enthu-
siasms of such diverse groups are bound to enter public
arguments about the program. It is appropriate to try to anticipate their arguments when the evaluation is planned.

The evaluator should also introduce values for which
there is no effective political voice. He can achieve this by lis-
tening to social critics and scholars and by playing the role of
critic himself. He should do his best, on the basis of his knowledge and social philosophy, to identify ways in which the program may damage its clients or affect institutions adversely.
One thinks of Moynihan's (1965) unpopular contention that
welfare programs should be judged in part by their effects on
the stability of the black family, and of the argument (Cook
and others, 1975) that "Sesame Street" does harm if, while
helping children from both well-off and poor families, its net
effect is to widen the gap between the two groups of children.
The critic should also keep an eye open for positive effects
that program advocates have not thought to claim.

To consult many sources is a divergent step. Sometimes
evaluators have used consultation chiefly to reduce the list of
questions, retaining those that interest all types of informants. But it is a mistake to use the sources only conver-
gently, as the study of planned variations of Follow Through
illustrates. Follow Through evaluators collected measures of
outcomes that informants had agreed on as significant. When
the study was completed, the educator backing a particular
variation could complain that the study had overlooked the
outcomes uniquely emphasized in that variation (House and
others, 1978). Assessing only the skills taught in all the program variations had biased the verdict, according to critics of
Follow Through, since programs that concentrated their

whole effort on those skills were bound to look superior when the scorekeepers confined attention to those few outcomes.

Similarly, critics of the National Assessment of Educational Progress have lamented that the use of consultation limited the list of outcomes measured. Laypersons, scholars in the fields of instruction, and school personnel were all consulted. But if some objective of concern to the community was not prominent in the school program, the evaluator's policy was to drop it from the list. For example, both lay informants and professional musicians favored assessing students' familiarity with jazz and contemporary music. However, because school personnel said that instruction gave little attention to those topics, the National Assessment ignored them (Greenbaum, Garet, and Solomon, 1977, pp. 54–56). Not to assess what the school neglects may have been politically necessary to maintain the cooperation of teachers and administrators. It obviously did make the assessment less complete, and it permitted Greenbaum, Garet, and Solomon to charge that consultation was not undertaken in good faith.

Questions on the original divergent list presumably refer to $U, T,$ and O significant to some participants in decision making or to artificial conditions that shed indirect light on a practical concern. (An example of the latter is the psychological measures in the INCAP study; they were distant from the policy makers' concern with everyday behavior but well suited to theoretical analysis.) The convergent process chooses some of these questions, after further specification, as the UTO or sub-UTO of the field study. The nonsurvivors remain as an illustrative list of $*UTO$ on which the research may be asked to shed light. The list is only partial, as new $*UTO$ will come to mind later.

Imagining Program Processes. A conception of the social problem and of a mechanism that could produce change is the source of possibilities for action. There are really two conceptions. The first considers how existing social conditions and the services already offered combine to produce an unsatisfactory result; the second envisions how the new service will produce a more satisfactory result. This second conception—Wholey (1979) calls it a "logic model"—identifies features of the treatment realization that are candidates for study, whether or not they can be directly controlled. This conception can be laid out as a chain of hoped-for events. For the Violence study described in Chapter Two, one part of the conception runs as follows:

Stage 1   Federal funds for developing local interventions are announced.

Stage 2   Certain schools apply for the funds; some of them are accepted.

Stage 3   Teams receive training and gain insights.

Stage 4   Teams in some schools establish procedures for hearing grievances.

Stage 5   Students in these schools feel an increased sense of control.

Stage 6   Hostility and fear diminish.

The chain can be elaborated by adding program variants at stage 1 and later. Working hypotheses can be introduced; for example, the evaluator can fill in the preconditions and posttraining attitudes that, he conjectures, would lead a school team to opt for a grievance procedure rather than for certain other forms of action. (For a more complete illustration of modeling a program and its events, see *Toward Reform*, pp. 254–261.)

   One obviously important feature of this kind of scenario is that it bounds the system in which action is thought to take place. The description of the Violence study suggests that the school is the unit treated and that schools respond as systems. Under that view, research questions would be framed in terms of schools, their collective staffs, and their student bodies. An alternative theory might see school violence as a community phenomenon. That would suggest studying schools in context—for example, collecting information on violence in neighboring schools and in community settings. Community teams might be considered as a form of treatment in place of school teams.

Sketching the branching tree of possible events, the investigator perceives additional questions. What are the probabilities at each branching point, and what conditions those probabilities? For example, what differentiates the schools that apply for the workshops from nonapplicants with similar histories of disruption? Does morale improve in every school where the grievance procedure is tried? Why not? Would training that "sells" the grievance procedure to the team work as well as a nondirective procedure that sets out options? The hypothesized process and the particular questions to be raised will differ with each program variant, planned or unplanned. As unanticipated variations are discovered, additional scenarios may be required.

Process questions go well beyond checking on prespecified program activities. Much is necessarily left unspecified, and much that was not anticipated occurs when plans are followed. When events do not take the course proponents had hoped for, evidence on intermediate variables indicates which expectations were ill-grounded. When the average outcome is satisfactory, evidence on intermediates indicates why some sites did especially well. Adaptations to be tried in the future and guidelines for implementation are based on such insights. In essence, to identify worthwhile intermediate variables is to envision how the program could fall short. The evaluator becomes for the moment a perverse thinker, a devil's advocate who brings to consciousness every conceivable miscarriage of plans or disappointment of hopes.

Intensity and Duration as Variables. The manipulation may inadvertently be too weak to override uncontrolled events. If the evaluator simply asks whether intervention of a particular kind has an effect, the negative report valid for the weak T may easily be overgeneralized into a rejection of stronger T^* of the same kind. One possibility is to try to determine what a treatment can do at its best. Typically, the first clinical trial of a new surgical procedure is a superrealization. A similar effort to arrange ideal conditions was seen in the bail bond experiment in Chapter Four. When informed persons are wondering whether a program along novel lines can possibly work, it makes sense to try an unrealistic supertreatment. Studies of the intensified treatment can then justify continuing or abandoning a line of development.

An evaluation intended to be the basis for operating policy, however, will study not a supertreatment but a politically viable, widely realizable version. A proposed treatment can be augmented—for example, by special teacher training or by adding a community participation feature. Or it can be degraded by eliminating this or that feature. The findings will add to understanding of the effect and indicate whether it is safe to dispense with a costly feature.

When the treatment consists of a monetary payment, payment rules can be conditioned in various ways on characteristics of individuals, families, or institutions. In Chapter Eight I shall describe how the first income maintenance experiment tried to visualize the "policy space"—that is, the full range of conceivable formulas—as a first step in choosing a few formulas for trial. The analysis showed that more would be learned by trying some formulas at the outer limits of political viability than by sticking to the rules most likely to be adopted. As experience developed, it was found that the range of possible formulas was far wider than had originally been thought, because even small details of the eligibility rules affected clients' responses. Each later study of these proposals therefore went through a painstaking process of considering which rules it would test. It became obvious that it was not possible to generalize about income plans; each set of rules created a different economy for the clients.

Note, here, the extent to which social planning was advanced by hard thinking during the planning of an evaluation. Each trial capitalized on earlier field experience, but possibilities that fell outside that experience were considered. Hollister (1979, p. 94) notes: "In some ways, lessons learned from rule definition may have had greater impact on the structure of income maintenance programs in the United States than the central experimental findings."

Duration of treatment (and of each phase of it) is an aspect of treatment intensity. Rothkopf (1978) criticizes the typical psychological experiment on instruction for giving a single test at the end of an arbitrary, often short period of instruction. To judge contrasting instructional techniques from scores collected on one date, says Rothkopf, is to assume that the learning curves are parallel or diverge steadily. A similar comment could be made about a one-time assessment of the effect of a welfare program on clients' self-respect and motivation to seek work: Treatment should in fact extend over a comparatively long period, with outcomes being measured at several times. The design might compare alternative durations for phases of a treatment.

Auditing Resource Distribution. Coleman (1975) advocates that, as part of planning, the evaluator spell out the expected flow of resources. An allocation of funds made centrally fills a trough; a bucket brigade has to move the resources to clients. A "social audit" of the resource chain is a significant—sometimes essential—kind of evaluation:

> In a social audit, resource inputs initiated by policy are traced from the point at which they are disbursed to the point at which they are experienced by the ultimate intended recipient of those resources. It is, then, those resources as experienced that are related to the outcomes in the research, rather than the resources as disbursed. For there are two possible causes of the ineffectiveness of resources: The resources as experienced may be ineffective in bringing about any change, or the resources as disbursed never reach the ultimate intended recipient and are instead lost somewhere on the path between point of initial disbursement and point of experience by the ultimate recipient. In re-

search that does not trace the resources along this path, it is impossible to distinguish these two causes of ineffectiveness, and the assumption is ordinarily made that resources as experienced are the same as resources as disbursed. But this may not be true at all. Consider a few examples in schools: A school board can spend identical amounts on textbooks in two different schools (or two school boards can spend identical amounts in two different systems), so that the inputs as disbursed by school boards are identical. But if texts depreciate more rapidly, through loss and lack of care, in one school or one system than the other, then the text as received by a given child (say the second year after a new text is issued) constitutes a lesser input of educational resources to him than if he were in the other school or the other system [Coleman, 1975, p. 37].

Anticipating Counterinterpretations. If, at the end of the evaluation, the program seems to have worked, the enthusiastic interpretation given by its proponents should nonetheless be challenged. Skepticism is an integral part of the scientific process. By anticipating reactions to the whole body of evidence—reactions of a program advocate, along with those of an opponent—the evaluator can search for data that will speak to the issues evenhandedly. When planning a study, the evaluator should anticipate the various possible outcomes of any subinquiry, and also the competing interpretations that could be given to each outcome. These rival hypotheses suggest research questions. Speaking of the comparative study that reports average outcomes at the end of treatment, Cook and Campbell (1976, 1979) draw attention to the long list of counterinterpretations logically available to the skeptic; some of these will be examined later in this chapter. In almost any evaluation, the Cook-Campbell list would supply questions pertinent to several links in the chain of reasoning.

For rival substantive conceptions of the social problem and the services offered, no master list can be given. It will be recalled from the Nutrition study in Chapter Two that added calories provided a better explanation of the INCAP findings than did added protein, the manipulation under test. Important counterinterpretations may be specific to particular variables. For example, the early evaluations of compensatory education used IQ as the dependent variable, and some modest gains in average IQ between pretest and posttest were found. But, according to psychological research reported previous to these evaluations, simple habituation to test taking could account for the gains. To the child entering an educational setting for the first time, seatwork tasks are a new experience. Psychologists noted long ago that when school beginners are retested after a few weeks of experience with unfamiliar adults who ask questions and set tasks, they score better than they did initially. This is true even when the intervening activities do nothing directly to develop reasoning processes and language skills.

Pretesting the control group as well as the experimental group guards against crediting the treatment with gains that arise from whatever practice the initial test affords, but that suggestion misses the point. The counterhypothesis is not that the compensatory program has no effect but rather that much of the effect is achieved in the first few weeks, by learnings peripheral to the main curriculum. This proposition challenges the developers' image of the intervention and stimulates thought about efficient short-term treatments. If at the divergent stage of planning the evaluators of compensatory education had asked what counterarguments could challenge a positive finding regarding IQ change, the truism about test-taking practice would probably have come to mind. They might then have considered measuring some children after their initial weeks of exposure to school and before any large fraction of the compensatory curriculum had been completed.

Outcomes. Goals stated for the intervention are a significant source of questions for the divergent phase; but goal attainment has received more emphasis in evaluation than it should (*Toward Reform,* pp. 129, 169). Some observers say that legislators and policy makers do not expect to achieve the goals that decorate their proposals; they act so as to be perceived as "doing something" and to reduce complaints about a problem. Their rhetoric may refer to goals too distant or effects too abstract to be investigated. Indeed, proponents of a program are often wise not to make all their goals specific and public; publicizing an aim may mobilize political opposition to it (Schultze, 1968, pp. 47–48; Donnison and others, 1975, p. 297). Even a full and unambiguous list of goals is incomplete as a source of questions, however, since it gives no attention to unwanted outcomes. A properly devilish evaluator will direct attention to side effects and opportunity costs.

In regard to continuous outcome variables, it is usually sensible to identify one pole of the scale as positive and to applaud when scores move in that direction. To ask whether a program has achieved its goals in that respect, however, implies a discontinuity of value along the scale; some one level is taken as acceptable, and performance below that level is called deficient. In rare instances such discontinuities are meaningful. For example, in industry there is some minimum speed below which a worker cannot function on an assembly line; as a goal for training, nothing less will do. In education, however, increments of progress are welcome no matter where the student is on the scale. No distinct point represents minimal adequacy. Setting a quantitative goal thus becomes an act of gamesmanship; planners who promise too little lose customers, and those who claim too much expose the program to a charge of failure. Pressure to state quantitative targets leads to evasions ("students will show gains in self-confidence") or to arbitrary and ill-considered specifics ("students will gain twelve months in reading level on a standardized test"). At the time the study is planned, the only reasonable question is "What outcomes should we attend to?" Whether the level reached is satisfactory will be judged through political negotiation after the assessment.

Although the evaluation staff ought to press for clear

statements about the outcome variables that program planners have in mind, trying to collect descriptions in operational or "behavioral" form is unimportant and can be counterproductive. Pressure to speak in a particular style annoys
the informant and reduces the yield. When pressed to give
operational definitions, respondents will fail to mention variables that are hard to define. Affective outcomes, and variables on which the desirable result differs over persons or
over sites, are especially likely to drop from sight.

In the educational discourse of the last decade, the
meaning of the term *behavioral objectives* has been narrowed; it
now looks at instruction through behaviorist spectacles, and
that works against full recognition of what instruction based
on other views can accomplish. When Tyler (1950) introduced the concept, he did not call for specifying test stimuli
and desired responses in advance. Many different school (or
life) activities could promote a desired development; the goal
was often to prepare the student to cope with situations that
cannot be specifically foreseen. For example, if an educator
claimed that her program would "build character," Tyler's
response would be a disarming invitation to elaborate: "Just
so I have that clear, would you give me an example of what a
youngster might do that would indicate that she has developed as you would like?" The incidents so elicited provided
referential meaning for a vague phrase, and the evaluator
was guided to make a relevant observation. But neither the
situation the student was being prepared for nor the "correct" response was prespecified.

Those who impose a behaviorist form on instructional
objectives—"Students will learn to give response Y to prespecified stimulus X"—restrict the range of outcomes investigated. A few, but only a few, instructional programs set out
to train a student to make standard responses to standard
tasks. It is difficult, if not impossible, to describe improved
judgment, sensitivity, and self-understanding in behaviorist
terms. E. L. Thorndike's followers may have gone too far
when they told the social scientist, "If anything exists, it can

be measured." The neobehaviorist in evaluation certainly goes too far when he suggests that what he does not measure does not exist.

The divergent list of outcomes ought to stretch far into the future, including those observable only after the current evaluation has been completed and reported. As I have already remarked, long-run differences between treatments are unlikely to match those seen on the immediate posttest. As in the Head Start data, effects of special training can erode as time passes. And, the other way around, the trainee may build on the strengths that the program gave her; thus, long-term results may be more impressive than immediate ones. Knowing what remote outcomes would be of interest, the planner may be able to construct a chain of reasoning that identifies proximate indicators. Nascent change can perhaps be detected before the evaluation has run its course. Furthermore, planners can pave the way for follow-up even if the initial budget is to be spent within a short period.

The political community has to act without waiting for a report on ultimate outcomes. Just how long the investigation should be extended (with or without interim reports) is an important consideration in the convergent phase of design. Since it takes the long perspective, the divergent phase helps everyone to realize the degree to which the research plan stops short. The evaluator who knows what he has not investigated is more likely to talk sense to clients.

Some evaluations mistakenly adopt a black-box, input-output analysis that tests a program over its longest possible reach and relegates evidence on intermediates to an appendix. Testing the effect of a program on a distant variable that is subject to dozens of other influences invites a negative report (Cook and others, 1975, p. 54). Can one reasonably expect a high school course on family life to have a perceptible effect on the ultimate divorce rate of its students? The path to such a remote effect would have many way stations. A person's acts and feelings at each point reflect the past, but at each point new influences intrude and attenuate the effect of the initial intervention. The connection of the intervention to the remote outcome is likely to be exceedingly weak. No one believes that services have no consequences, but over a long period of time the signal from any one cause is swamped by all the other signals.

A series of short-reach evaluations, each looking at a section of the path, can indicate that much of the thinking behind a program is sound and can identify where extraneous variables count heavily. Such testing can be expected to give more indications of program success, to add to an understanding of the problem, and to provide guidance for improving the intervention. Even if it is decided that the intervention that was tested should be discarded, positive and negative findings about segments of the activity suggest what to try next. From this point of view, Harvard Project Physics (HPP) set off in the right direction when it asked how each teacher conducted the experimental course and what attitudes each class developed. Teachers had been urged to organize activities as they saw fit, and treatment realizations were diverse. Unfortunately, these data were shunted off into the basic research sector of the project, and the evaluative report attended only to the posttest means that came out of the black box labeled "HPP classes."

Programs are usually thought of as providing persons, families, or communities with resources that will make them happier or more effective sometime in the future. Writers on evaluation have been duly skeptical when "goals" refer to activities rather than outcomes, as in "Each student will read three of the books on the following list." It is currently being said, however, that evaluators should give programs credit for the immediate benefits that their activities confer, without insisting that the programs show down-the-road consequences. A report on programs for young children (Travers and Light, 1982) urges that daycare arrangements be judged on the "quality of life" that they provide for children, as well as on their contribution to the children's later self-reliance and abilities. Whatever a phrase such as "quality of life" may mean, enriching a child's life today is certainly a social good. The force of the point is evident in a negative example. No evaluator would turn in a positive report on a school with admirable academic results if the school treats its pupils cruelly.

Convergent Phase

The preceding section spoke as if the ideal were to make the evaluation complete, but that cannot be done. There are at least three reasons for reducing the range of variables treated systematically in an evaluation. First, there will always be a budget limit. Second, as a study becomes increasingly complicated, it becomes harder and harder to manage. The mass of information becomes too great for the evaluator to digest, and much is lost from sight. Third and possibly most important, the attention span of the audience is limited. Very few persons want to know all there is to know about a program. Administrators, legislators, and opinion leaders listen on the run.

The divergent phase identifies what could *possibly* be worth investigating. Here the investigator aims for maximum bandwidth. In the convergent phase, on the contrary, he decides what incompleteness is most acceptable. He reduces bandwidth by culling the list of possibilities. As candidates come to the investigator's attention, he drops some without much consideration, judging them to be impractical to investigate or unimportant. Others, he judges, can be examined incidentally, without special plans. The review of the remaining questions is more systematic in the description below than it can be in practice. My intention, of course, is to show the principles behind the selection among questions.

Four characteristics considered together determine how resources will be committed. The planner is more likely to invest in study of a particular question when

- there is great prior uncertainty about the answer,
- the study promises great reduction of uncertainty,

- the inquiry costs comparatively little, and
- the information would have a high degree of leverage on policy choices or operating decisions.

Each quality is a matter of degree; in principle, the four qualities could be combined (but not additively) into a cost-benefit index. Indeed, Thompson (1975) offers a mathematical model for evaluating the contribution of information to prospective program decisions and thus for determining which investigation, if any, to mount. In order to reach this formal statement, Thompson has to assume a closed set of action alternatives. Also, he sees choice among investigations as a matter to be thought through in advance by the sponsor. I see these decisions as continuing throughout the evaluation, as a shared function of evaluator and sponsor.

I shall devote at least one subsection to each quality except cost, about which little need be said. Although that rubric refers particularly to costs in dollars and in the time of evaluation staff, program staff, and informants, it also includes the stresses that come with intrusive or threatening inquiries. Cost is a generalized label for factors that may make a probe or procedure infeasible or inadvisable.

Leverage. Leverage refers to the influence that reducing a particular uncertainty has on decisions. After an evaluation is completed, leverage is directly visible in the response of the community to the evidence. In planning an evaluation, one can only judge what leverage information bearing on a particular issue will have. The planner is to ask: "How much influence is each of the conceivable answers to this research question expected to have?" That requires reflection on the politics surrounding the program; for example, a matter that receives appreciable attention from the whole community has great leverage. A matter also has leverage if some partisan bloc cares about it or if it could sway a powerful uncommitted group. But leverage is not to be identified with political controversy alone. Information that clarifies why a proposed program does or does not work well can be expected to affect the evolution of this program and alternative programs. An issue influencing decisions in the large has more leverage than an issue whose resolution would affect only details.

Not all decisions to which an evaluation might logically apply are open to influence. A program may have so much political backing that not even evidence of its total ineffectiveness would bring funding to a halt. In that case, even logically relevant information would have no leverage. Moreover, leverage is likely to be directional. Answers that point in one direction may change votes, while answers pointing the other way may have little effect.

To illustrate political analysis, I take up the Laetrile controversy. Succumbing to overwhelming political pressure, members of the cancer research Establishment agreed to a clinical trial of Laetrile in the mid-1970s. The medical and research communities had judged the substance lacking in therapeutic value, but a variety of motivations and sympathies forged a coalition of outsiders who distrusted this judgment. Laws authorizing sale of Laetrile were passed in a number of states, and the coalition pressed for favorable federal action. The coalition stressed that Laetrile did no physical harm, and that fact was not challenged at the time. The Medical Establishment may have decided to conduct clinical trials as a way of showing that no conspiracy against unconventional therapies exists. That is a reasonable political use of evaluation—but is it a profitable means of reducing contention? Looking at matters as they stood when the evaluation was proposed: Would a well-designed clinical trial be expected to alter the trend of political action and medical practice?

A positive finding would surely have leverage. The medical profession is committed to taking responsible research at face value. If scientific critics could find no fault in the conduct of the experiment, professional values would impel skeptics to give ground. Opposition to legalizing Laetrile would be enfeebled. Note, however, the supposition that the study was a sound one. If the design left a loophole for critics, the medical leaders who distrusted Laetrile would amplify the sour notes. If there were no placebo group, for example, medical leaders would probably attribute positive reports on remission of symptoms to the power of suggestion. Impeccable positive evidence on Laetrile, then, would have leverage on medical decisions, but less excellent positive evidence would have little or none.

What about a negative finding? Those deciding to mount the evaluation could foresee that the Laetrile coalition would do its best to discredit the study if its findings were negative. True believers can always find a way. In the event, when the first series of treated cases seemed not to benefit, spokespersons for Laetrile instantly rejected the finding. Their counterargument was that amygdalin, the chief ingredient in Laetrile, had been tested in a purified form; the putative benefits of the impurities in Laetrile produced from apricot pits had therefore been eliminated. (T^* versus T, once again!) The stubbornness of the Laetrile advocates is increased by the nature of their options. As long as it is not established that Laetrile does direct damage, the advocate is able to appeal to legislators: "If a placebo makes people more comfortable, why should they be denied it?"

An evaluator, of course, could point to the risk that Laetrile will displace sounder treatments. Very likely, however, that concept is too subtle to be communicated in the usual way to legislators and the public. The information could have leverage; one can imagine televising pathetic case histories of patients whose faith in apricot pits caused them to shun approved treatments until the time when they could be helped had passed. (Perhaps the evaluator should ferret out such cases. That kind of inquiry would lack the niceties of the controlled trial, but it would have leverage.) If the Laetrile example is representative, strong positive evidence can convince unbelievers, but negative evidence is unlikely to discourage enthusiasts. Millennialist cults do not collapse when the world fails to end on the date they have proclaimed (Festinger, Riecken, and Schachter, 1956).

It is in examining leverage that the evaluator explicitly considers the values of participants, and nothing on the divergent list of questions deserves consideration if the findings are not value laden for at least some members of the policy-shaping community. Things that would merely "be nice to know" are not good investments of inquiry. At the same time, it is not for the evaluator to settle on the social policy he prefers and then collect evidence whose leverage acts in that direction. The agency that commissions an evaluation sometimes does want the evaluation to support its intended course of action. As honest broker, the evaluator ought to give the agency a chance to move community sentiment in that direction. He should also bring out any evidence that could turn the policy in some other direction, as Cook and his associates did with "Sesame Street" (Cook and others, 1975). This may require looking under stones that the agency would prefer to leave unturned.

The evaluator, by his choice of questions, should open the door to neglected values. He should make a special effort to bring in the questions and interests of groups that are comparatively powerless, notably the disadvantaged (Coleman, 1980; House, 1980). Persons in high positions inevitably have blind spots. Impartiality requires seeing the problem whole. But insistence on evenhandedness—a commitment spelled out under "The Evaluator as Teacher" in Chapter One—is itself value laden. A Marxist, a technocrat, or even a liberal can object to the evaluator's implicitly accepting the political system (Green, 1971; Wiles, 1971; House and Mathison, 1981). Historically, program evaluation has been linked to gradual reform *within* the system; evaluation and revolution are improbable bedfellows (*Toward Reform,* p. 159).

How far the evaluator will be allowed to pursue evidence that might speak against the policy favored by a sponsoring agency will vary from study to study. In an ideal world, outside evaluators would be financially independent, able to resign from a commission when a sponsor insists on a slanted investigation or report. The inside evaluator is necessarily in a different position, but even he will find support for a balanced evaluation when a manager believes that she can control distribution of the findings. Managers dislike bad news, but they are usually not foolish enough to consider ignorance the best policy.

Prior Uncertainty. Other things being equal, attention

should go to the questions about which uncertainty is greatest; that is, when two questions seem to have equal leverage and to be equally open to investigation, greater resources should go to the question for which the community priors are flatter. The evaluator's casual judgment, after he listens to political participants, will serve well enough to assess uncertainties. As he discusses the emerging plan with the sponsor and with advocates of various actions, he will confirm or amend his initial judgment. Surveying community priors formally would be prohibitively expensive; moreover, priors expressed in Year 1 can shift before the evaluation is complete.

I speak in terms of "uncertainties" since a highly credible assertion or a highly implausible one is not a prime target for investigation. Not much will be invested in demonstrating what everyone confidently believes or in testing social programs in which only the inventor has faith. After saying this, however, Cook and Campbell (1976, p. 230) add a qualifying remark: "Theory testers place great emphasis on testing theoretical predictions that seem so implausible that neither common sense nor other theories would make the same prediction." This is true; a finding that confirms a statement with low prior credibility has great information value. But this remark does not contradict the previous statement. A scientist does not mount an expensive investigation of a conjecture until persuaded that the "implausible" could account for anomalous observations made earlier and so has to be given some credence, or until it has been shown that what is contrary to experience is distinctly possible. An example is found in the first expedition made to observe the bending of light rays during an eclipse—a bending predicted from Einstein's mathematical argument.

Even universally held beliefs about society and human services may be ill grounded; hence, even "certainties" must be open to question. The force of the statement that resources should address uncertainties is preserved by introducing the *evaluator's* priors. It would be foolish to set up research to challenge what he and the community believe to be true. It is when he has grounds for skepticism that he challenges a belief. In this spirit, I earlier advised the evaluator to anticipate at the divergent stage the ways in which program processes are most likely to go wrong.

Credibility and leverage obviously work hand in hand. In the Laetrile study, there would be distinct value in a placebo control—or, more happily, in use of some accepted treatment X that would pit X-plus-placebo against X-plus-Laetrile—since the power of suggestion could account for relief from pain and even for remission of symptoms objectively assessed. In Harvard Project Physics (HPP), to use another example, the mixed control group provided a check on the plausible hypothesis that other courses would *on average* have effects equal to those of HPP. It did little to guard against counterhypotheses that had great leverage for some educators. When HPP results surpassed the mean of a group that embraced classes of types A, B, and C, the person who had faith in course A could easily believe that the control mean was held down by the admixture of results from B and C.

Credibility of Counterinterpretations. In the divergent phase, counterinterpretations are sought out. Whether one of them should influence the shape of the investigation depends on its credibility. If a vociferous critic would find it difficult to persuade members of the community that a particular counterexplanation is valid, guarding against that threat would be a waste of resources. (In checking on a basic training program for airplane pilots, it would be pointless to test an uninstructed control group; no one believes that flying skills come with maturation. But maturation and accretion of experience do bring change of character; in an evaluation of character education, then, collection of maturational norms is likely to remain in the research plan.)

Consumers of the evaluation of a new program to develop reading comprehension may accept published test norms as an adequate way to assess "maturational" effects. Alternatively, they may take, as their baseline, past experience in the school system where the experimental T is tried. In that case, the conclusion rests in part on the statement—

which may be plausible enough—that the population of the school system and the quality of the teaching staff have not changed appreciably from year to year. In instances where the school has changed, or where baseline experience is limited, or where different sectors of the community hold different priors, fresh control data will reduce dispute. If the published norms are out of date, similar questions will arise about them. Greater uncertainty makes control data a better investment.

In the famous "breathalyser" study, records of road casualties had been accumulated for two years prior to the trial. Ross (1973) contrasted these with records during the first three years of the trial (see Cook and Campbell, 1979, p. 219). The finding of a notable short-term decrease in traffic injuries was open to the counterinterpretation that coincident events had produced it. Because the audience had sharp priors against such a coincidence, however, the interrupted time-series design was usable. Although it guarded against the coincident-event interpretation less thoroughly than concurrent casualty data from regions with no breathalyser program would have, there was no call for investment in such data.

We must now think further about verifying that whatever was done to experimental subjects "has made a difference" within the specified *UOS*. Others have said that the designer of research ought to be especially concerned with ensuring the internal validity of his conclusion. The challenges that matter, however, are to the explanation of an outcome; they are questions about *what* made the difference. As I see it, there is no reason to treat as a special category the hypothesis that the intervention created the difference. Rather, a question on that point is to be judged with respect to leverage, prior uncertainty, cost, and information yield, just as are questions about treatment variations. Testing a causal hypothesis competes for resources with proposals to enlarge or diversify the sample of sites, to represent a variable by several measuring operations, and so on.

If the design collects data on just one treatment and reports a desired outcome, the skeptic does her job by challenging the evaluation in the following ways:

1. "How do you know that this change would not have come to pass in this US over this time period if the preexisting treatment had continued unmodified?" This is the Cook and Campbell (1979) "history" counterhypothesis.
2. "How do you know that this change would not have come to pass spontaneously, because of changes already under way in the population or setting?" The "maturation" counterhypothesis is one version of this.
3. "How do you know that the change was in the U and not in the o?" For example, perhaps the scorer expected the treatment to produce good scores and gave good marks to the experimental cases. This falls under the "instrumentation" counterhypothesis.
4. "Would the change have occurred if you had given the pretest and posttest without the ostensible experimental treatment?" This is the "testing" threat of Cook and Campbell (1979).
5. "Would the same effect be found in this UOS if t were replaced by a neutral treatment disguised as the intervention?"

The force of each question can be reduced by suitable controls. A planner will be wise to reserve expensive controls for the challenges that the audience is most likely to take seriously.

Placebos, which seem to guard against all these counterhypotheses, have little relevance to educational and social evaluations. Student and teacher know what instruction is going on. A science fiction writer might have fun designing a "blank dose of instruction" (Scriven, 1967, p. 69), but to administer such instruction for more than a few hours would be unethical. It is to be hoped that teachers, if not students, would recognize the placebo as the fake it is. And if suggestion brings improved learning, no one will complain.

The reasonable question is not "Is there a difference?"

but "Which of the costlier features of the original T can be stripped off without reducing the benefits too much?"

I return to the subject of "guarding against threats." As long as the original t represents the one experimental treatment, each of the five questions challenges *external* validity. Each asks about the outcome in a specified hypothetical alternative treatment. Nonintervention (question 1 or 2) is a T^*; a pretest-only treatment (4) is a T^*; a blank dose (3 or 5) is a T^*. Other counterhypotheses such as "selection bias" keep T the same but inquire about a U^*. During the divergent phase of evaluation planning, every one of the threats implies the possible usefulness of investigating one or another UTO_2 alongside the basic program.

Each control treatment expected to give null or baseline results has a status like that of a variant experimental treatment from which positive results are expected. Among all the comparison T that one might list, only a few can be represented in the design. The Transitional Aid Research Project (TARP), to be described at the end of Chapter Eight, decided to divide resources over three forms of the experimental treatment and three essentially null treatments. Thus, it chose one set of contrasts rather than another.

Information Yield. Information reduces the range of uncertainty; and, other things being equal, the more numerous or more precise the observations, the greater the yield of information. The more persuasive the inference from observations on *uto* to a particular answer, the greater is the study's information yield on that subject. Reproducibility—hence reduction of uncertainty—can almost always be increased by investing more effort in a study or substudy. In what follows, I shall discuss yield on the assumption that resources for a study have been fixed.

The information yield regarding every uncertainty that has leverage is to be considered in comparing proposed designs. Precision of one central answer is often seen as all-important, because statistical power calculations are made for one hypothesis or relationship at a time. Small reductions of uncertainty regarding many variables cumulate, however, and the total information yield can exceed that from precise information on one variable. Hence, though the concept of power is fundamental to design, it must be interpreted with an eye to the net reduction of uncertainty, summed over all the inferences that the policy-shaping community cares about. And, in judging information yield, one must consider the credibility of all the steps in the inference, not sampling errors alone.

The traditional analysis aims to reject the hypothesis that a parameter has value a when in truth it has a specified other value b. In the usual investigation of a null hypothesis about a mean, for example, the power of the investigation lies in the likelihood that it will deny that the mean is zero when the actual value is c. A powerful design will reject the null hypothesis in the majority of samples even when c is assigned a comparatively small value. By this definition, power is inversely related to the posterior uncertainty of the internal inference (referred to in Chapter Five as "the conclusion in the model"). Traditional power calculations assess uncertainty as if priors are flat and the proposed investigation is the sole source of information. If priors regarding a hypothesis are sharp, there can be little reduction in uncertainty, and the investigation will be less informative than conventional calculations indicate.

Inference When Statistical Power Is Low. Large investigations may lack statistical power. The expensive Nutrition study discussed in Chapter Two could afford to include only four villages and thus had negligible statistical power for treatment comparisons. But the study could determine, for each village sample in turn, the regression of dependent variables on caloric intake. As the study evolved, number of calories (treatment delivered) came to be considered more important than the better-controlled contrast between *fresco* villages and *atole* villages. If the four regression equations agreed closely, one would have some confidence that the relation applies to villages in Guatemala generally; in contrast, change from village to village would imply great statistical uncertainty. The strength of the study lies in the interconnec-

tion of the numerous facts collected and the acceptability of
the assumption that processes found in one community will
be found in many others. An intervention followed by a correlational analysis in just one village would have had that
plausibility.

Trying to establish statistical significance can throw an
evaluator completely off the tracks. The report of Follow
Through Planned Variations provides a conspicuous example. The evaluators intended to compare twenty-two treatments. A treatment was applied to a site or project containing
one or more schools; each site provided evidence on one
treatment and on a control group that received no special
treatment. There were only 178 sites to begin with—an average of 8 per treatment—and not all those survived to provide
data. It would have been appropriate to carry out calculations
on the set of site means. Because the number of sites was
small and the variation among sites was great, the evaluators
knew that sizable differences would not reach statistical significance if sites were the unit of analysis. *Therefore,* in order
to have "significance" to report, the analysts retreated to
using children as the unit (pooling classes and schools within
each site; see Stebbins and others, 1977, p. 67). This provided
hundreds of "cases" per site and generated many allegedly
significant results. But the p values are falsely high (as the analysts acknowledged). The regressions calculated from individual scores tell a different story than regressions fitting
school or site means would. The latter regressions, manifestly
based on few data points, are unconvincing. The more impressive but spurious N of individual-level analysis comes
from the same thin sample.

Follow Through investigators (Cline and others, 1974)
once made roughly parallel analyses with (respectively) site,
class, and student as the unit. This procedure avoided the
risk, present in an analysis limited to any one unit, that a critic
would argue for another choice of unit and mutter darkly
that his preferred analysis would probably reverse the conclusions. Offering three analyses disarms such potential ad-

versaries in advance—*if* all three lead to the same conclusion. In the parallel analysis of Follow Through, they did not.

Contradictory analyses throw the policy-shaping community into confusion—a confusion that very likely expresses proper uncertainty. Sometimes several conflicting models, or weaker and stronger versions of a particular assumption, will all seem plausible. Uncertainty about an assumption renders a conclusion uncertain. Evaluators should employ "alternative methods of error-prone inference," in the words quoted earlier from Gilbert, Mosteller, and Tukey (1976, p. 369). When two analyses with contradictory assumptions lead to much the same conclusion, the analyses together deserve more trust than either deserves by itself.

In judging how much a study will reduce uncertainty, the investigator should consider carefully the plausibility of the available models. Partisans ought to put forward conflicting sets of assumptions, and the analyst ought to use whatever sharply contrasting models fall within the limits of reason. These activities bound the range of tenable answers instead of presenting an estimate as conclusive. *Genuine* posterior uncertainty is highlighted by alternative analyses with well-considered models.

Inferences from breakdowns of the data are comparatively weak because samples become small. In Harvard Project Physics (HPP), only six out of nineteen control teachers taught the Physical Science Study Committee (PSSC) course, so the power of any comparison between HPP and PSSC was low. But the small batch of data would be useful in showing that HPP results were (or were not) wildly out of line with PSSC results. If more exact comparison would influence decisions, the designer could increase the power of one comparison or another. Perhaps he should have fewer experimental and more control classes. Perhaps he should choose control classes that are all traditional, or all PSSC, or ten of one and nine of the other. Each such choice shifts posterior uncertainty from one subgroup mean to the other. In comparison of treatments across able classes, below-average classes, or classes with supportive teachers, the sample in each cell becomes small and power is low.

Analyses based on fractions of the data are justified. Exploration of detail costs almost nothing extra, and it does give leads. The community has no other inexpensive way to learn about variables that alter the size of effects. "Nonsignificant" findings can be highly believable. Subsequent chapters will develop the view that qualitative data are especially needed when treatments and responses to them are expected to be heterogeneous.

Uncertainty of External Inferences. When the answer does not generalize beyond *UTOS,* information yield corresponds to reproducibility. An inference to a question not directly investigated depends heavily on uncertain extrapolation. When a question has great leverage and prior uncertainty, one would like to investigate it directly; but the strictly relevant study may be impractical or costly. The planner will choose between the direct inquiry and alternative studies that offer to reduce uncertainty less directly.

Sometimes the best imaginable indirect inquiry has so loose a connection to the **UTOS* of greatest leverage that the information yield on *UTOS* counts for nothing. Changes from *T* to the anticipated *T** may be so great as to make study of *T* a poor approximation. This is especially a problem when one examines a policy that will operate on a wide scale. No study of Prohibition when the laws were being passed on the local level could have anticipated the effect of the Eighteenth Amendment on organized crime and the citizen's respect for law. No test of the birth-control pill on a community could have anticipated its society-wide effects on the role of women in work, politics, and the home. Whether the income maintenance study gave highly relevant evidence of work-seeking behavior has been questioned; it was said that those receiving payments were less likely to break off their connections with the world of work when they knew that payments would stop after three years. Nor would payments to a fraction of the community plant the seed of a new community work ethic as a large-scale program might (Hollister, 1979). This is not to deny the utility of partial information, but it reminds us to ask whether a tryout far removed from operational realities is worth its cost.

Convergence on a Mix of Questions

The evaluator, working within fixed resources, reduces the initial list of questions to a manageable subset; then he budgets resources unequally over the survivors (holding back some reserves). Not many questions drop entirely out of consciousness. Where the priors are sharp, it is sensible to pick up inexpensive information. Recording incidental observations costs almost nothing, while it costs somewhat more to cull data from records produced by normal operations and still more to collect fresh data. To manipulate conditions in the field is costly, so the number of treatment categories has to be held down. A decision to put certain T into place and not others is nearly irreversible; therefore, the initial choice among T is critical for a manipulative study. The hazard is reduced by installing one or more treatments on a modest scale and then deciding after some months of observation whether to install those same T in further sites or to try a modification of them.

Which process variables to emphasize can be judged sequentially. Suppose that the plan calls for 200 minutes of instructional activity of a certain kind during each week. How much effort does the evaluator make to verify that each child actually had that amount of instruction? If delivery-as-planned is a good bet, a cheap investigation will suffice. It may be enough to ask each teacher to report any major shortfall and the reason for it. If the question has leverage, however, and the evaluator comes to doubt that delivery was adequate, he may go so far as a day-by-day documentation of the schedule for each student. Something similar is to be said about outcome variables; effort gradually comes to focus on variables that early data indicate to be problematic.

A crude priority scale can be suggested for deploying investigative effort.

1. A question with high leverage and high prior uncertainty merits close attention. Without investment in each such question, somewhere in the sequence of investigations, the other findings of the evaluators may have little influence.
2. If leverage is low but not negligible, a question with high prior uncertainty deserves some investment.
3. If leverage is high and prior uncertainty low, low-cost information should be collected. If it confirms the sharp priors, it will help to muzzle the kind of critic who, at the end, raises doubts for the sake of doubting. If the modest inquiry suggests that the priors were wrong, the question rises to the topmost category.
4. If leverage is low and uncertainty is low, the investigator should do no more than keep open the channels for incidental information.

Among questions with leverage, the first basis for assigning priority is prior uncertainty. Then one moves on to balance posterior uncertainty against cost, while continuing to give preference to the high-leverage options. Judgment is to be made in the light of a tentative sampling plan and a probable analytic procedure.

A first step is to propose one or more overall designs to cover questions in the topmost category. The structure suggested—for example, so many classes with this treatment, so many with that, all followed up for twenty-four months—will almost certainly collapse of its own weight. When rough calculations of posterior uncertainty are made, it will be painfully evident that the list was overambitious and that the plan disperses resources too widely. Priorities have to be cut to fit the purse.

Successive screenings will restrict the domains of units, treatment alternatives, and observing operations; the discarded possibilities will become *UTO. The evaluator hopes that bits and pieces of the data will provide reasonable bases for an external inference regarding some of them. Other questions will be too costly to investigate adequately or will have too little leverage to command investigative resources.

The planner ought to consider the plausibility of the arguments that the data will lead to. Thus, Harvard Project Physics judged that a sample drawn from New England physics teachers and students would not be accepted as relevant by educators in other parts of the country. For the sake of a nationwide U, they gave up the possibility of firsthand acquaintance with the sites. Similarly, to make the inference more straightforward, the New Jersey investigators in the income maintenance study included mid-range treatments similar to T^*, even though the optimum plan could have been established more efficiently (by relying on assumptions) from outlying data points.

While convergence requires a cut in bandwidth—that is, in the number of questions addressed—it should not continue unchecked. Members of the planning group should press the claims of questions and variables from which investigative resources are being withdrawn. There will be no clearly "right" resolution to the conflicting claims, but a hard-fought compromise is likely to be a good one.

It is helpful to break evaluations into comparatively small studies with varying starting dates and durations, and with different central questions (*Toward Reform,* pp. 221–223; Berryman and Glennan, 1980). The massive study that moves as rapidly as possible to a "definitive" report is inappropriate, given the shifting political alignments and the usually complex subject matter of evaluations. Evaluation has the function of monitoring changing phenomena as they are influenced by evolving social machinery. Every design—even a massive true experiment—yields information that is limited and incomplete within the panorama of relevant uncertainties. Hard though it is to communicate the uncertainty of inferences, evaluators must keep up a flow of steadily improving interpretation that, if comprehended, will affect decisions.

My rationale for allocating resources is in substantial accord with the position Wholey (1979) has developed, despite the fact that he and his Urban Institute colleagues have an orientation quite different from that of my circle. Wholey,

who has been an officeholder as well as an evaluator, would
tailor evaluations to the concerns of specific officials; and he
has correspondingly little interest in the conceptual uses of
evaluation. Wholey sets out to answer questions in the minds
of program managers. He thinks in terms of a context of
command, but a broader perspective could be introduced.
His techniques thus define a direction in which evaluations in
a context of accommodation could profitably move.

Wholey recommends "sequential purchase of information." The first stage, "evaluability assessment," surveys the
potential benefits of extended inquiry into the program. Is a
sensible program actually being carried out? Are objectives
well defined and objectively measurable? Can the planner
foresee specific ways in which evaluation findings would open
the way to program improvement? Wholey recommends
highly divergent thinking in this phase. He says, for instance,
that the program should not be given too specific a definition
at the outset: "Federal managers have a tendency to draw a
box around a piece of the program and say, 'Evaluate this.' In
most cases, the better course will be to include all of the related activities in the program to be evaluated" (1979, p. 52).
Wholey's process is more extensive and more empirical than
is usual in evaluation planning.

Assuming that the first analysis whets appetite for
deeper study, Wholey would go on to performance monitoring or "rapid feedback evaluation" or both. The former is familiar: It requires establishment of an information system
that will keep track of facts and figures that seem important
and that are thought likely to go out of tolerance if not
watched. Rapid feedback involves a survey of the adequacy of
the program and of the uncertainties of the available information on it. Wholey uses the planning process itself to bring
facts promptly to the attention of management. Beyond that,
he surveys proposals for evaluation design that come down to
operational brass tacks on focal questions, measurement
methods, sample sizes, analyses, and posterior uncertainties.
This survey indicates the promise and cost of a longer evaluative study. Until it is complete, Wholey holds open the ques-

tion of whether a major evaluation is really wanted and what its focus should be.

Wholey implies that the major evaluation will often be shelved because objectives are vaguely defined, or causal hypotheses about program events and consequent outcomes are indefinite, or management is not eager to obtain and use findings. *Toward Reform,* in contrast, sees evaluation as a learning process rather than as a managerial technique. From this perspective, there is value in substantial studies of broad-aim programs for which theory is indefinite and lines of possible action are poorly defined. Wholey would follow through with an experiment or quasi-experiment if its design will "provide conclusive [!] evidence about the effects of a program" (1979, p. 167). He would do this for specific, focused questions that have high leverage and great uncertainty. Wholey would ordinarily recommend against such a study unless the findings would strongly influence a choice between action alternatives that are already clearly envisioned. Wholey reserves the strong evaluation design for an uncertainty that has come to a head, just as costly confirmatory techniques are reserved for the well-ripened hypothesis in basic science.

Wherever the public has delegated substantial responsibility to the manager to achieve agreed-on ends, the procedural alternatives that concern the manager are a profitable target of controlled research. Otherwise, evaluation in the service of managers is open to question. House (1980, p. 155) makes these pertinent comments (without reference to Wholey): "Reproducible results may be reprehensible from a democratic or moral point of view. . . . It may be that the government official, anticipating a severe challenge to his authoritative decision making, strongly urges the evaluator to employ his 'hardest,' most scientistic methods to bolster the government's authority."

The remedy, House says, is to bring all those affected by the program into the planning, even to the point of asking representatives of client groups to countersign the formal charge to the evaluator. I doubt that this device would bind the parties to respect the evaluation when it is complete, so I put the stress on the evaluator's acquainting himself with the perceptions of these parties rather than on a contract mechanism. Still, House (1980, p. 78) makes a valuable point that supplements Wholey's concept of evaluability: If the policy-shaping community (which includes clients and taxpayers) does not, from the beginning, accept the questions that the evaluation will answer as the significant ones, the evaluation is unlikely to serve the long-term ends of the policy official who ordered it.

8

✍ Controls That Promote Reproducibility

I undertake now to place in perspective the devices that can heighten the reproducibility (internal validity) of evaluations. Design of investigations is usually discussed within the Fisherian tradition of treatment contrasts, with assignment of units to treatments being emphasized as the chief feature of design. But many additional means of strengthening internal inferences are to be recognized. This chapter will speak about design as if external inference were of no concern, all resources going to the study of one *UTO* and prespecified sub-*UTO* within it. In other words, I shall concentrate on the targeted study in which the investigator has fixed on a *UTO* and wants to conduct as conclusive an inquiry as possible.

In seeking reproducibility, one does not introduce all possible controls. Each control has its price in supervisory time and subject time, or perhaps in time needed to prepare instruments or to build a roster of persons or sites from which to sample. One virtue is achieved by sacrificing another; for example, lengthening a questionnaire reduces the likelihood that subjects will respond thoughtfully. Even a targeted study embodies substudies, and a control that makes one substudy more reproducible withdraws resources from another. As is true throughout the convergent phase of selecting questions, the planner works by successive approximations to distribute effort.

Field operations are never perfectly consistent with a plan. The breakdown of one control reduces the payoff from related controls. Thus, if refusals to accept an assignment are frequent, even a highly refined assignment plan will guarantee little net control. Tightening a few links in an otherwise loose argument does next to nothing to relieve net uncertainty. An iron chain of logic, in which specifications are followed by operations in perfect accord with those specifications and then by invulnerable inferences back to *UTO,* is an unattainable ideal in a field study. The rubber bands of plausible inference will always supply some of the needed links.

Three kinds of controls will be discussed:

- Clear specification of plans and acts that generate or harvest data and develop a conclusion from them.
- Controls on sampling or realization of program events and evaluative operations.
- Restriction of inquiry and inference to a comparatively narrow, homogeneous *UTO*.

Each control contributes to reproducibility in one or more of the following ways:

- Identifying the target to which the conclusion applies. By making explicit the definition of *UTO* and the procedures for selecting cases, arranging treatments, observing, and analyzing data, the investigator makes it more likely that he will be able to repeat what he has done. Documenting the plan and the actual operations makes it possible for others to replicate or, when replication is not in prospect, gives a reader confidence that a conclusion is replicable.

- Tying *uto* more strongly to *UTO*. The size and quality of the sample of units, the steps taken to establish or identify instances of the intended T, the validity of the o, and the credibility of Model I—all strengthen the inference to *UTO*.

- Narrowing *UTO*. Standardizing treatments and measurements and specifying a more homogeneous population make it easier for independent studies to reach the same result as the original inquiry did.

These functions are intimately related. For example, standardization enhances reproducibility when the restriction is made explicit; at the same time a decision not to narrow the domain makes more extensive sampling advisable.

Recall the three levels of reproducibility discussed in Chapter Four. The first has to do with the degree to which the investigator standardizes and otherwise strengthens procedures, so that *he* can expect to get consistent results from study to study. The second has to do (in addition) with the clarity and completeness with which the procedures are communicated—a clarity and completeness that would enable investigators working independently to obtain results consistent with those of the original investigator. The third envisions that investigators start with a question that is not in strictly operational form and choose procedures independently. The targeted studies considered in this chapter assume that a question has been put in definite language; the tactics to be discussed in Chapter Nine are those that heighten reproducibility$_3$.

Targeted studies abound in pure science. The scientist who aims to nail down a definite answer to a basic research question—once it has been sharply defined—can generally achieve high reproducibility. Previous research has identified the variables that make no difference and need not be controlled, and it has also established standard procedures for holding other variables constant. Exploratory studies have focused the scientist's attention on appropriately sensitive observing operations and have indicated a particular species or substance likely to give a strong indication of the effect under investigation. That makes a highly controlled study feasible.

Targeted evaluations of social programs are rare (and many studies that begin with a sharp focus become diffuse in the execution). For illustrative purposes I shall refer to a hypothetical evaluation of an in-service training plan for surgeons. To encourage practitioners to bring their knowledge up to date, a national board mandates periodic recertification on the basis of an examination. The professional organization of surgeons provides a preliminary test to guide members in their preparation. Constructed independently of the board examination, this study test is mailed to surgeons who request it. A surgeon's test paper is scored and returned with an explanation for each item. The evaluator's question is whether the preliminary test, together with the explanations provided, raises the rate of success on the board examination. The program I describe does exist; but, so far as I know, evaluation of it has been impressionistic and based only on comments volunteered by those who used the study test. This fiction of a systematic evaluation of the surgery examination is the survivor of several efforts to generate for this chapter an example of an investigation where extrapolation is unlikely to be wanted.

What features would make a targeted study suitable for the surgeons? The constituency for the program is a group of professionals who share the same need and through their association supply the program's resources; the values and assumptions of outsiders are irrelevant. Moreover, the program is pointed toward a defined goal—recertification—and the conservative board mechanism is unlikely to change markedly. The program offers a packaged product, and it is expected that each practice examination in later years will be constructed similarly. The working hypothesis is that the program is fixed, though dissatisfaction with it could return the decision makers to an exploratory mood that would call for less targeted trial and error. (If the surgeons were to address a larger question—"What service to members will most improve the quality of their surgical practice?"—evaluation would be more difficult and the relevant investigations unbounded.) Two other examples will receive substantial attention: the income maintenance experiment in New Jersey and the Transitional Aid Research Project (TARP), which involved a system of payments to aid released prisoners in reestablishing themselves in society. These studies had strong designs, but external inference played a large part in their use.

Specification of *UTO*

The targeted investigation terminates in a statement about *UTOS* that characterizes the domain of relevant observations that could have been made. Observations are to represent that domain. If the specification of *UTO* leads everyone to the same understanding as to what is (or was) to be under investigation, the specification is excellent and the prospect of reproducibility is good. Insofar as the planners who selected *UTO* provide a sketchy or indefinite description of the target, however, the investigator has to make further decisions about what to observe.

It is natural to think of specification as completed before a study begins, but such specification is preliminary and incomplete. In Harvard Project Physics (HPP), for example, the *U* was confined to teachers who agreed to let the flip of a coin determine whether or not they would teach HPP. This is an operational definition of the HPP *U*; its characteristics were known only after the fact. The experimental *T* and the observing operations *O* inevitably are modified during pilot work or the main fieldwork, so some part of their specifications is also put down after the fact.

Admissible Units. Social scientists are accustomed to defining the bounds of the population to which generalization is made, but specification of *U* has many subtleties (starting with a judgment as to whether the unit is to be a person, an institution, or a collective). In the study of surgeons, the most relevant population is presumably the members of the profession who request the materials and later take the board examination. But there could be interest in a broader group; for instance, a first question might be "Who requests the materials?"

Treatment Categories. The specification of T may be elaborate or succinct. Grossness of specification does not necessarily preclude a reproducible study. Setting out to evaluate the U.S. Postal Service, one might define the treatment as whatever home delivery service is rendered to any patron within the contiguous United States during a certain month. Diverse though those services are, independent investigators drawing suitable samples could report on the same target.

The specification may call not for a uniform treatment but for one that depends on characteristics of the unit or on responses that occur as treatment proceeds. Logic does not require specifying the contingencies or branching rules. The policy of HPP was that the teacher would use judgment in selecting instructional procedures, and this very *policy* of encouraging variation was an important part of the specification.

In the nonmanipulative study, the specification bounds the class of admissible treatment realizations. It says what kinds of realizations are to be accepted as within the scope of the study. If realizations can be divided into types, each of those types will be bounded by additional specifications. Specification of T in the manipulative study takes another form. The specification for the manipulation tells what operating personnel are to do and how they will be induced to perform those actions. A crucial distinction is to be made between the experimenter's manipulation (or that of an official who "gives the word") and the treatment operations themselves. Communications will go out from headquarters to tell operators on site what they are to do. That is what sets T in motion, and it is what the replicator will imitate if the study is to be reproduced. But the specification of the manipulative communication is not the same as the communication realized, because the plan will not be fully detailed and because there will be slippage in transmission. The specification frames the deliberate part of the message.

The manipulation may try to mold treatment realizations in every important respect, as in a laboratory psychologist's instructions to assistant experimenters who will be running rats through mazes in separate rooms. At the opposite extreme, the manipulation may be no more than a mailed announcement that schools with certain characteristics are eligible for a stated number of dollars to support racial integration of their student bodies; their only obligation is to turn in financial reports and to allow the evaluator to ask his questions in due time. Obviously, the greater the detail and the fewer the options allowed the program operators, the greater the reproducibility (other things being equal).

To constrain T too forcibly may reduce the relevance of the investigation. If the domain for inquiry is conceived in somewhat broad terms, the designer who overspecifies sets up a reproducible study of the wrong question. The specified manipulation should pin down no more and no less than properly enters the *definition* of the intervention to be tested. Novice planners sometimes specify innovative treatments with care but give little thought to specifying null or baseline treatments. There may be many ways to define such treatments, as I have illustrated earlier.

How Units Are Distributed over Treatments. With two or more treatment categories, a U,T correlation in UTO is to be specified. (I take up later a comparable question about the sample.) The ecological correlation—that is, whatever linkage of units and treatment realizations is normal in the setting—defines one possible UT. The study investigates the outcome of T_1 when prevailing forces of distribution and self-selection operate to draw in and retain units (the study of surgeons is of this type). This means that UT is defined in part by all other services that compete in any way for the patronage of these clients. Change the alternatives present in the setting (as happened in the federal income maintenance study when New Jersey adopted a new welfare program), and the ecological correlation changes.

The investigator may want to know what the outcome would be if all admissible units were to receive a treatment. In a comparative study, only controlled assignment allows an internal inference to the intended UT. Specifying how units are recruited and persuaded to accept assignment then becomes important, as this may have a causal influence. Fetterman (1981) comments on a comparative study in which minority welfare recipients were strongly encouraged to apply for job training, and members of a no-treatment control group were then randomly selected from the recruits. He offers some evidence that the disappointed hopes thus created generated alienation among the controls. It would have made better sense to examine a control community (or several) where everyone received the null treatment because the community offered no alternative. Making both experimental and control treatments available in the same community changed "no treatment" into an aversive treatment. To speak formally: The UTO of interest was one with a zero U,T correlation over communities and with uniform treatment availability within a community.

Observing Operations. Inference can be strict only if every pretest, intermediate measure, and posttest is specified. Information on the actual operation is not enough when inference is to a class of observations. Until the class is identified, the report is an uninterpreted record, and no issue of reproducibility arises. Even with so narrow a concern as the success of surgeons in winning recertification, the realized operations—a particular set of items for the official examination, a particular date of testing, review by a particular board —constitute only one of many admissible sets of operations. Assessment on another day with other items, reviewed by a board having other members, would also serve the purpose. A surgeon would not earn identical scores on the two measurements. If her performance is marginal enough to require a board judgment, independent judgments on the same record might reach different verdicts.

Defining the O for a particular variable (or for variables observed together) amounts to bounding the class of procedures considered acceptable for the purpose of the inquiry. It is obviously appropriate to mention occasions, situations, and observers. Each of these has many aspects. For example, the study may call for observations of the style of teachers' remarks to pupils. A full plan will specify occasions for observation in terms of a time span, divisions of the span (class hours? single remarks of teacher?), and admissible times within the span (when class is in session? only during discussions?). Situations may be selected out of the ongoing affairs of the unit; thus, attention may be confined to English lessons or to occasions when a student asks a question of the teacher. (Whether this is said to define the occasion or the situation is of no importance.)

Sometimes an artificial situation, such as a test instrument, is to be specified. The class of admissible instruments would be defined by content specifications, format specifications (for example, free response on thirty items), and specifications for administration (twenty-minute time limit and group administration). Finally, the plan would identify the domain of observers for any operation; that is, the kinds of persons admissible to each role (presenting questions or tasks, recording events or responses, scoring or coding, and so on).

The plan may or may not call for the same data on all units in the study; that decision, however, ought to be a deliberate one. It may make no sense to collect certain data within one treatment. One probably would ask surgeons taking the preparatory test how useful they found it; one would not ask the controls. In a study of instruction, a treatment group can reasonably be tested on the content *it* studied, but it may be pointless to give that test to groups that studied something else.

Analytic Operations. Reproducibility is wanted for analytic operations as much as for field operations, but only as an exercise would an investigator specify all these operations in advance. Such an exercise would be useful, giving assurance that at least one way of handling the data has been envisioned. But data rarely take the shape foreseen in advance; they are more unruly and more complicated than standard analytic schemes allow for. Hence, a sophisticated analyst fits the analysis to the data (Tukey, 1977a) and can specify the operations only when the job is done.

How to handle missing data, for example, cannot be decided until a preliminary compilation has shown the number of losses and their patterning. That compilation will suggest whether to discard incomplete cases and seriously incomplete cells of the research design, whether to use different sets of cases in different analyses, or whether to fill scattered gaps with best estimates. Another kind of judgment during analysis is whether to combine all units in one statistic or to report on subgroupings that responded similarly; measurements may likewise be analyzed one by one, or several of them may be lumped together in one indicator.

Controversy about the findings of evaluators is likely, and it is proper for others to rework their data. To permit this, evaluators establish data banks; the banked data, however, will be worth little without the rules for scoring, coding, and aggregation that produced them (Boruch, Wortman, and Cordray, 1981). A complete posterior account of a study will describe the steps from observation protocols to conclusions: scoring rules for converting statements of informants into tallies or numerical scores, rules for assembling composite scores and statistics, and inference procedures for transforming statements about *uto* into statements about *UTO*. Choosing these procedures amounts to adopting mapping statements or assumptions.

Insofar as data reduction and analysis are rule bound, reproducibility$_2$ of the analysis is virtually assured; only carelessness can spoil the replication. The investigator who spells out the rules for judgments increases reproducibility, but it may be difficult to specify the *principles* to be followed, for example, in handling missing data. Sensitive principles will allow for actions that vary from replication to replication, according to the patterning of the data.

The greater role of judgment in qualitative research makes reproducibility much harder to achieve there than in quantitative research. One of the virtues of the qualitative study, however, is its lack of constraint, its openness to whatever events catch the observer's or interpreter's eye. Since not even the questions to be answered are prespecified in qualitative research, it is not likely that independent investigators observing the same series of incidents will come to the same conclusions. But I shall argue later in the chapter that interpretations can be reproducible even when the data are not.

Rules for Sampling and Assignment

The specification of *UTO* is, in principle, a sampling frame. In a strictly controlled study, the *u*, *t*, and *o* are derived from *UTO* by formal sampling; systematic representative sampling promotes reproducibility. Studies often settle for samples of convenience, yet the internal inference is made as if sampling of units had been strict. This is legitimate and reproducible if units in *U* are homogeneous; otherwise, the inference is open to challenge. Sampling and assignment are closely linked and may be carried out simultaneously. Sampling in two or more stages is often advisable. In the Violence study discussed in Chapter Two, schools in separated communities were taken to be independent. The schools were assigned to treatments, and questionnaires were given to a sample of students in each of the chosen schools. My remarks about sampling plans apply to all stages of sampling.

A proportional sampling scheme sorts elements in *U* into categories and assigns a sampling fraction to each cell; sampling within cells is random. (The simple random sample is one variety of proportional sample.) Other things being equal, a change in design that reduces the sampling error of an estimate increases reproducibility. A narrow confidence interval implies that the next investigator will reach nearly the same point estimate as the original investigator did, provided that they sample similarly from the same population. With other aspects of the sampling plan held constant, the variance of estimates of a mean is cut in half by doubling the number of independent units. In many uses uncertainty is better expressed by the standard deviation than by the variance; by that index improvement is roughly proportional to the square root of cost. So returns taper off as sample size increases.

Stratifying cases before sampling reduces sampling error. Few stratifying variables can be used, as cells multiply rapidly. A common compromise is to combine background variables into a single index that is presumed (on the basis of past experience) to forecast outcome. In an evaluation such as the Violence study, demographic variables and frequency of disturbances in the recent past could be combined in an index of social disorganization. Index values could be determined for schools before the sample was drawn; the scale of the index would be sliced into perhaps four segments, and the desired number of schools drawn from each segment.

Nonuniform Sampling Fractions. By varying sample size from cell to cell, one can recognize uncertainty, cost, or leverage. If the sampling fraction for each cell is recorded, the data from *uto* can be weighted to simulate representative data from *UTO,* no matter how uneven the sampling density. For example, questions about an innovative treatment are likely to have weaker priors and greater leverage than information about a familiar treatment, and this situation justifies a larger sample for T_E. Heavy sampling may be confined to particular cells of the design. Since, for example, boys are more likely than girls to fail in beginning reading, an investigator could reasonably study more boys than girls in any part of the design that calls for costly individualized procedures.

In the hypothetical Violence study, it might be known or suspected that violence-prone schools tend to vary considerably in amount of violence from month to month or from year to year as a consequence of local crises, whereas affairs are more stable in other schools. Under that assumption, the designer should stipulate a comparatively large sampling fraction for schools in the high-disturbance end of the sample, to reduce the variance of the weighted overall mean. A side benefit would be that case histories are likely to be most illuminating in the schools where events are least predictable. A mundane reason for varying sampling fractions is that nonresponse and dropout rates vary. If it is anticipated that data will be more seriously incomplete in violence-prone schools, the sampling fraction in that category should enlist more cases than are required for the final analysis.

With more than one treatment, rigor requires proportional sampling within the U for each treatment. Even when U is to be the same for T_1 and T_2, it is not mandatory that the sampling plans for U_1 and U_2 be similar. If outcomes in T_1 are expected to vary markedly from unit to unit, considerable variety of u would probably be wanted in the sample for T_1 in order to shed light on the reasons for variation in response. If units are believed to respond rather uniformly to T_2, a simpler sampling plan should serve for it.

The proposal to vary sampling fractions will come as a surprise to persons taught that a "true experiment" requires equivalent samples. In the reading example just given, the assignment set up a correlation between sex and treatment. It is easy to estimate from these data what the mean difference between treatments would be in a population where sex and treatment are uncorrelated; if independence of individual subjects can be assumed, simple weighting does the trick. The design with equivalent samples is the option to be chosen when the investigator can foresee no advantage, in either cost or benefit, from comparatively heavy (or light) sampling of any sub-UT.

The usual elementary textbook on sampling or experimental design devotes nearly all its space to symmetric plans with uniform sampling fractions. That is appropriate for an introduction. For a beginner to understand the theory, a teacher of statistics has to emphasize the abstract logic and minimize the art. Moreover, laboratory investigators lose little when they settle for symmetric designs. The expected costs and benefits associated with each cell are much the same, especially after pilot work has been completed. In a field study, however, within-cell variance is not likely to be uniform, differential loss of subjects will probably occur, cells will not be of equal interest or cost, and each case will add appreciable marginal cost. Designing a sample for an evaluation does not lend itself to textbook treatment because choosing cell sizes requires judgments based on the substance and political context of the evaluation. This is particularly well illustrated in the design for the New Jersey experiment on income maintenance, in which the nature of the issues and the expertise of the economists who designed the study allowed a degree of quantitative refinement that is rarely possible in social experimentation.

Income Maintenance Study. According to the New Jersey plan, a "negative income tax" would support families whose earnings fell below a specified level; benefits would be reduced in proportion to any increase in earnings. The evaluators presumed that Congress would expect many beneficiaries of the plan to leave the job market and would not approve the plan if that effect were strong. On that presumption, it was the evaluators' task to find the payment rules that would create the least "work disincentive" and to assess its strength. The planners therefore designed the experiment to answer one high-leverage question.

A payment formula could be specified in terms of two quantities: g, the floor guaranteed for income (earnings plus benefits), and r, the rate at which benefits were cut back as earnings rose. A policy space representing the admissible range of g and r was defined; any point in that space defined a possible rule for operating the program. The final plan identified nine formulas as treatments to be tried out and specified how many families (drawn at random from a specific income stratum at a specific site) were to be invited to enroll for a particular g, r combination. The treatments were located after the region of the policy space considered most likely to include the optimum treatment was marked off. Six points defining treatment rules were spotted around the edge of that area, and two more were placed in the middle. The ninth point was a control condition: no benefit, no tax. The study was not conceived as a pick-a-winner race among nine horses; rather, a surface was to describe a response (work seeking) as a continuous function of g and r.

The final design emerged only after several phases of armchair analysis and fieldwork (summarized by Rossi and

Lyall, 1976). Decisions rested on such considerations as the following: Since applying the treatment to experimental cases with g high and r low was expensive, the sample size of cases in those cells was kept modest. It made sense, however, to put many cases into the 0, 0 cell. Those subjects had little reason to cooperate with the experiment, heavy attrition was expected, and extra cases would cost little. The experiment was redesigned after the sample had been drawn for the first site and treatment operations had begun, since willingness to participate, attrition, and the scarcity of white families in the first site had been observed.

On the basis of such economic theory as existed, a guess had been made prior to the first sampling as to the curvature of the regression surface and the location of its maximum. After more was learned from the first sample, an elaborate mathematical analysis was used to evaluate different distributions of cases over treatments (assuming a fixed budget), to find the mix of sample sizes that would make estimates most precise. The early data showed that the uncertainty of the outcome mean in a cell depended on its g, r values and on how far below g a family's income normally fell. The mathematics showed that placing cases in treatments at the outer edges of the policy space would lead to more precise (reproducible$_3$) estimates of the surface than locating cases at the g, r value associated with the presumed optimal treatment.

The result of the calculation did not dictate the final design. It was felt that lay policy makers would be more persuaded by direct observations near the optimum than by indirect estimates reached by inserting data on peripheral cases into a mathematical model. Consequently, the design was altered to collect more evidence on formulas that seemed likely to appeal to Congress. This example shows how sophisticated a design can be, and how considerations of prior uncertainty, leverage, power, and cost all enter the picture—even late in the planning.

Such formal approaches, however, can be applied only in a study with a narrow target. And, by accepting that kind of target, the planners of the study weakened their political influence. The evaluative evidence could have had over-whelming leverage *against* the program if work seeking had declined under all defensible payment schedules. As political discussion moved forward, the positive finding that there was little change in work seeking did not seem to interest Congress much. Critics later suggested that the evaluation had been too narrow (Rossi and Lyall, 1976, p. 176). The legislators wanted to know the probable cost of a national program, and the design was not appropriate for this purpose. As Rossi and Lyall read the history, the national cost estimate was the underlying interest that the sponsor had from the outset, so concentration on the response surface diverted the study from its proper function. It is also true that family stability, a variable that the original study learned about only incidentally, loomed large in later policy discussion.

The reviewers find other faults with this study of work response. Rossi and Lyall note that race was not directly used in constructing the sampling frame, so the study gave a poor reading on an apparent interaction between treatment and race. Families headed by females are of policy interest; yet, to reduce variability, the study was focused on males. Concentrating the study in a few communities made findings peculiarly sensitive to local labor markets; the communities were the units of the study, and the small sample made for poor reproducibility$_2$.

As time went on, several additional income maintenance studies were put in place. But even with the benefit of hindsight, no one was able to invent a design that escaped all criticism. Reviewing these studies, Hollister (1979) gives a list of the advantages and disadvantages of experimental control that is generally consistent with arguments I have been making. The whole series of studies showed a steady broadening of sophistication, but not a convergence on a definite answer to the evaluative question. The studies became increasingly complex with each round of learning.

Realizing the Sampling Plan. Slippage can occur when a sampling plan goes into operation. For example, innumerable anecdotes make the point that haphazard choice is not random choice. Moreover, while documenting that a random procedure was indeed carried out enhances credibility, such documentation has not been common in evaluation. It will become more important, however, if the General Accounting Office and similar agencies follow through on the idea of auditing evaluations. The auditor can properly ask. "Were these the cities originally drawn?" Or "Why were data not collected from that particular unit, even though it was drawn for the sample?"

A real sample is unlikely to follow a plan perfectly, if only because not everyone approached agrees to cooperate and not every unit entering a study supplies final data. Although Harvard Project Physics (HPP) could not enlist all the teachers drawn from the national roster, the investigators did check on availability before making assignments to treatments. If they had assigned teachers and *then* asked a random fraction of them whether they were willing to change to HPP in the following year, their HPP sample would have been far less similar to the control sample than it in fact was.

Some controls make the *uto* supplying data conform better to the sampling plan than do others. The New Jersey study paid respondents on the spot for each of the interviews, trying to adjust the payment so that it would motivate continuance in the program without becoming a significant "treatment" in itself. In a similar vein, parents in Mexico who provided information on their children's response to "Plaza Sésamo" received tickets for a lottery. One may go too far in pressing for data. Callbacks to nonrespondents reduce bias, but it may be better to let a reluctant respondent go than to count the perfunctory responses that she gives to get rid of the questioner. Departures from the ideal can be documented. If it proves impractical to trace the families in the income maintenance study who leave town, facts about those families can nonetheless be kept in the file. Later the analyst must ask how loss of cases affected the data and especially whether the losses were similar over treatment groups. The "missing cases" play a significant role in the statistical workup, especially if econometric corrections for truncated distributions are attempted.

Operationalizing the Treatment

I shall first discuss wholly manipulated treatments before turning to studies where the treatment was installed independent of the evaluation.

Manipulated Treatment. Decisions made by the planner in installing the treatment may, in effect, redefine the manipulated variable. The manipulator is not investigating the question originally stated if he goes beyond the specified manipulative procedures in an attempt to make the t match T. A subtle distinction is to be made, however, between the central manipulator—the experimenter or the agency he works through—and the program operator who responds to the manipulation. If the latter's actions control the treatment more narrowly than was specified, this is simply evidence of what can happen within the plan as outlined.

Consider, for instance, a plan that calls for the state department of education to mail guidelines to participating schools. That is the manipulation agreed on by the evaluator and the sponsor. Now suppose that state officials visit schools as the activity gets under way, seeking to promote compliance with the intent of the program. Does this violate the definition of T? If a federal office asked the state department to mail the guidelines to schools, the supplementary intervention by state officials was part of a realization t in at least one state. Unless the plan specified an *absence* of supplementary stimulation of school staffs, the realization is legitimate. The evaluator learned that a mild stimulus from the center was enough to set off forceful state action. But if the state department itself set out to test manipulation by guidelines, augmenting those guidelines by visits implies a serious misunderstanding of evaluation procedures. The investigators are not carrying out their own plans.

Variety among realizations is helpful, as long as they fall within the intended T. The evaluator of the preliminary test for surgeons seeking recertification was supposed to learn about the policy, not about any one test. He would obviously rise more nearly to the level of policy if he can distribute two or three test forms, each to one sample of surgeons.

Another example of benefit from variety can be found in a study of the effect of rewarding pupils with tokens redeemable for prizes. It would make sense to change the payoff rules from classroom to classroom. To fix on one payoff rule would sacrifice reproducibility$_3$, since the replicator would be free to choose another schedule. Reproducibility$_2$ might of course be expected if a payoff rule were mentioned in the plan. The plan could specify several alternatives to get controlled variety. Should the rules be mentioned? The answer depends on the purpose of the evaluation. Teachers given general guidelines adapt rules according to their own judgment. Is that judgment a phenomenon of interest to the policy makers, or is it "noise" in the system? If the former, firm specification of rules would be inappropriate.

A similar point is to be made about all the adventitious aspects of a treatment realization: the teacher who delivers the lessons, the work schedule of the experimental classes, the topics assigned for student essays, and so on. In principle, anything not pinned down as constant by the definition of a sub-T or by an explicit redefinition should, in the realizations, vary over the realistic range. Fisher (1966, p. 102), thinking of field tests of fertilizer and the like, said just that: "Any conclusion, such that it is advantageous to increase the quantity of any ingredient [of a treatment], has a wider inductive basis when inferred from an experiment in which the quantities of other ingredients have been varied than it would have from any amount of experimentation in which these had been kept strictly constant. The exact standardization of experimental conditions, which is often thoughtlessly advocated as a panacea, always carries with it the real disadvantage that a highly standardized experiment supplies direct information only in respect to the narrow range of conditions achieved by standardization."

In a sense, the treatment realization consists of everything that the unit experiences. Activities going on alongside the target treatment are part of the treatment experience. An intervention to reduce violence, for example, meshes with the stationary aspects of the school program: busing, the split of students into vocational and academic tracks, and the like. These so-called treatments in the background are not subject to manipulative control. Documentation of them identifies sub-U that merit separate interpretation.

The same is to be said of treatments previously experienced. One could test a remedial or therapeutic program on clients never before given individual help or on veterans of previous (failed) attempts to give similar help. An intervention to reduce violence will be nearly a reversal of past practice in one school but only a minor alteration in another. When a program is installed, last year's treatment of each unit and possibly of each individual within a unit ought to be identified. A report that properly relates outcomes to this background will be easier to confirm than a report that ignores background. The classic Brownell and Moser (1949) evaluation of "meaningful" teaching of subtraction provides a particularly striking example. Instructional methods were assigned to classes in grade 3, but the investigators astutely inquired about the teaching in grades 1 and 2. They found that the third graders profiting from meaningful teaching were those whose teachers in prior years had frequently explained elementary procedures, thus equipping their students to utilize explanation. (I shall say more about this study in Chapter Nine.)

Documentation of the treatment delivered makes the evaluator aware of instances where plans miscarry, and it also improves interpretation (external inference). If T fails because few surgeons took the preliminary test seriously, the failure is genuine, but the implications are entirely different from those of a full realization that failed. Inadequate delivery is especially embarrassing when equivalent groups were assigned for the sake of comparing treatments. A common reaction is to discard units whose treatment deviated from the plan. But an investigator who does this has "relinquished control of the situation to the subject [or the deliverer of the treatment] and [is] left with a nonexperimental study" (Aronson and Carlsmith, 1968, p. 42). The equivalence of the groups is questionable; and even if they seem equivalent after cases are discarded, the direct inference is not to the original U.

Reproducibility$_2$ of the analysis within either group may be high if the discarding of cases is made explicit. The investigator may have started with the intent to learn what happens when the planned T is truly realized. Units where the realization fell short are irrelevant to him. In the surgery study, the average score on the board examination over *all* candidates answers a legitimate question about the net value of T as realized. However, not all those cases studied the materials provided. If cases who did not make full use of the materials are discarded, the success rate of the remaining cases is a valid estimate for the subset of the original U who (because of unidentified moderating conditions) would have used the materials fully. The U that estimate applies to is ill specified, since this aspect of the realization was uncontrolled. There is no unimpeachable way to pick an equivalent control group whose pass rate can be compared with that of U.

Nonmanipulative Studies. The evaluator often comes on the scene after a program is in operation. He may be asked to evaluate a long-standing institution or activity, or a pilot operation that someone else has set up. He may be asked to evaluate a policy by locating sites where it is in effect—desegregation by busing, for example. In such an endeavor, the evaluator can only select realizations; he does not control treatment. Whoever plans such a study should bear in mind what would be held constant or deliberately varied—or, as a minimum, recorded—if treatment could be manipulated. A few characteristics will be used in selecting realizations, and the rest will be documented as fully as possible.

The evaluator who manipulates treatment is more likely to achieve the realization he wants, and only the manipulator has a chance to control assignment. Even so, the evaluator will not always find installing T in new sites a better plan than locating instances of T already in place. Manipulation adds to cost. Worse, it may require a choice of U, T, or O that does not follow naturally from the statement of the problem. A manipulated study, for example, has to deal with a recent realization. Rarely can one control an intervention beyond its first year, even when one is not under pressure for an early report. If T is to be a lasting program, a first-year realization will be unrepresentative. Mature realizations can be studied within the time frame of an evaluation only if the treatment has been in place in some sites in years prior to the study.

Educational treatments ripen (McLaughlin, 1980). Nevertheless, those who write on educational research and evaluation—if not educators themselves—speak as if a mature program will do no worse and no better than it did when newly hatched. This is not credible. A teacher does not use a curriculum the same way in later years as she did during the first year. The teacher hits on tactics that work, then adds materials of her own to plug gaps. The teacher may decide not to bother with troublesome laboratory setups. She may gain confidence or lose enthusiasm. If a treatment affects the same students for several years, they begin to adapt to it. They learn to take advantage of a certain kind of instruction (as in the Brownell and Moser finding). The desegregated school settles into its own sociometric pattern; the community slowly comes to terms with the change or regroups along new battle lines. Also, as time passes, people move into and out of the treatment site. The investigator loses sight of those who move away (in the case of desegregation, perhaps because of the treatment). And those who move in present a dilemma for analysis, since they have not experienced the same treatment as those present from the start.

Plans for Observing

The investigator can specify the universe O by identifying certain fixed procedures and by defining a distribution for each variable facet. For strict reproducibility$_2$, a plan for sampling of conditions from these facets is required. The theoretical ideal is to list all admissible observers and draw the required number at random, or at random within types of observer. This is also true for occasions, test items or tasks, and other variable conditions of observation. The logic is the same as in sampling of units. Blocking and increasing sample size both improve reproducibility.

In practice, formal sampling of conditions is rare. For example, strict sampling of occasions is uncommon, since testing dates or visits to sites have to be accommodated to the convenience of the units. Again, the roster of admissible observers is hypothetical; one can specify how to recognize a classroom observer acceptable for purposes of a study, but there is no list of all qualified persons. The evaluator can, however, arrange to distribute observers impartially over treatments or types of units and over early and late tests.

Tasks, questionnaire items, and interview probes are likely to be fixed at the time of planning. Although there is nothing sacred about the specifics of particular tasks or questions, one set is chosen; there may be additional sets of test items in a design with two or more waves of testing. Reproducibility$_2$ is improved by fixing tasks, provided that these particular tasks are specified as O and will be used by replicators. When O is defined as a class of tasks, several of the tasks can be used, each with one subset of subjects. Advice to let tasks vary is akin to the advice against making the range of t narrower than the domain identified as T.

Estimating Measurement Error. The evaluator has to be satisfied with a limited sample of tasks, occasions, observers, and so on. If the variability associated with each such facet has been estimated, the design can sample most thoroughly where the variation is greatest.

The error of measurement associated with every score can be estimated in pilot studies. How much should be invested in such a study depends, of course, on the importance of the variable and the knowledge about error available from prior experience. A traditional pilot study tries out the procedure just as the investigator intends to use it in the main study (provided that the pilot study finds no serious flaw). The so-called G study (G for "generalizability"; see Cronbach and others, 1972) is quite different in character. The design for a G study usually should not resemble the measurement plan in the main study. It will ordinarily obtain several observations on each of a comparatively small number of units, scheduling the observations so that inconsistency over situations or tasks, over occasions, over observers, and sometimes over scorers can be estimated. This makes it possible to calculate in advance the error of measurement expected in each of several designs that might be contemplated for the main study.

It is traditional in the fields of psychology and education to consider a measuring procedure good if its reliability coefficient is high. But that coefficient is not the proper standard for outcome measures in evaluation. It tells how consistently a procedure assesses differences among individuals; and individual scores contain larger errors than means of collective units, unless the procedure and conditions of measurement vary importantly from collective to collective. Evaluators are primarily concerned with averages for groups or subgroups of units, and comparatively small samples of behavior can assess these averages adequately. This is welcome because evaluators generally need to examine a large number of variables and cannot afford a large investment in each one. At times an evaluator does require accurate data on individuals, but he should not routinely ask for high reliability coefficients merely because of tradition.

A second reason for deemphasizing the traditional coefficient is that the errors associated with group differences may not be adequately represented by procedures that focus on individual differences. Substantial errors of measurement can arise from a local idiosyncrasy of procedure that a within-group study overlooks. But the generalizability study can be shaped to assess properly the accuracy of scores for groups (Cronbach, 1976).

Error of measurement is ordinarily identified with lack of consistency over trials with instruments that are alike in form and content. In evaluation, however, the important issue is consistency over instruments that differ in their specifics, unless O is given a highly restrictive definition. The methods of Jöreskog and Sörbom (1979) investigate this question, although their analysis, designed for scores at the individual level, has to be adapted to serve the evaluator. Within a school, proficiency on fractions may correlate highly with proficiency on decimals; students who best understand one will best understand the other. But across fourth-grade classes in many schools, the correlation of class averages on the two tests will be reduced by the fact that some schools introduce decimals early and others postpone them.

Sampling Procedure. The amount of observation in a study is adjustable. A common practice is to apply the measuring procedure to every aggregate unit and to every individual within the unit, but costs can be reduced by collecting data on fewer subunits than were treated. In the Violence study, for example, cases drawn from each school constituted the sample. The investigators planned to examine the percentage of students marking each response alternative on specific questionnaire items. The standard error of a before-and-after difference is 5 percent for 200 cases and 3.5 percent for 300 cases. A sample of 200 seems to give reasonable precision, and an additional 100 cases would add only modestly to precision. If a question can be worded in two or three ways, it may be a good idea to split the sample of 200. The composite of the subsamples will give a report less influenced by specific wording and hence a reproducible estimate on O (reproducibility$_3$).

A single occasion—one date in April, say—is ordinarily taken as representative of end-of-year performance. At the time plans were laid, presumably any other date during the month would have been just as acceptable for the posttest. But, to take one example, attitudes in the schools included in the Violence study might shift from week to week, as incidents intensify school spirit or heat up latent antagonisms. If two or three occasions were selected for posttesting in the Violence study, with a fraction of the 200 students in the school being questioned on each date, reproducibility would be enhanced.

In general, it is advisable to consider the sample size for

each facet of each instrument. The planner may conclude that asking everyone the same three questions about one dimension is appropriate, whereas for another dimension it is better to employ three sets of three questions, giving each to a third of the subjects; for yet another dimension, only a forty-item scale will suffice. Variation associated with the occasion (for example) combines with the uncertainty from sampling of students. Reducing either source of variation is beneficial. Control is gained by sampling most heavily those facets that introduce most variability, insofar as costs permit.

Sequential observation can increase reproducibility or lower cost. In a sequential procedure, a small sample of information is first collected. These data direct further testing effort to particular units or particular subquestions. It makes sense to terminate observations in a classroom when three successive visits have produced similar reports, just as it makes sense to schedule additional visits after observers have reported different stories on different days. Again, effort is expended where uncertainty is greatest.

In evaluation extra data can reasonably be collected on a group that did unexpectedly well or badly; in this respect the design is reshaped after the posttest. Where some individuals are assessed more painstakingly than others, great care is of course required in projecting the responses onto the same numerical scale. Recently developed methods of latent-trait scaling are well suited for this purpose (Lord, 1980). With these techniques it becomes possible to tailor the test to the subject. In one such plan, a preliminary "routing test" assesses the student's general level and indicates whether she should receive an easy, hard, or intermediate main test. The number, the difficulty, and even the character of later questions or tests may be determined on the basis of the initial data. This produces a desired level of precision with fewer items.

The "Pygmalion" study (Rosenthal and Jacobson, 1968) hinged on changes in measured IQs. The research question was whether the typical teacher's handling of a child was biased by a favorable report on the child's promise, with the result that the child would develop more rapidly than her control. Members of the teacher's class whose pretest IQs were low were randomly divided between experimentals (favorable report to teacher) and controls (no report); only the experimenter saw the IQ scores. The pretest was so difficult that many children performed at the chance level; their scores were therefore highly unreliable. The errors of measurement, carried over to the index of improvement, obscured the findings, especially since random sampling happened to produce treatment groups with unequal pretest means.

I see three interrelated faults in the design. First, the investigators called for a pretest equivalent to the posttest. The only possible justification for this is that they had fixed on measuring "change," but they would have been wiser to use an easier test at the start of the year. Learning in the first grade takes place so fast that the same test is unlikely to serve both in September and in May. Second, the assignment plan was unnecessarily loose. Had the investigators paired up cases having adjacent ranks on the pretest and assigned randomly within pairs, they would have had a far more reproducible result. Third, they missed the chance to improve the pretest data. Every child whose pretest (or posttest) score was at or near the chance level should have been retested with an easier test form (preferably before cases were assigned to treatments).

Quality Controls. Unless the evaluator keeps a sharp eye on procedures, all manner of things can go wrong with data collection. In some schools too little time is allowed for a test, and scores of the whole group are depressed. In other schools scores do not have the intended meaning because some children fail to comprehend the directions. Interviewers, when encoding remarks, bias the tally toward what they expect or prefer to hear. Teachers asked to keep weekly logs on instructional procedures bury the forms on their desks, then fill in two months' worth of information on the day they have to mail in the forms. The precautions to prevent and detect departures from the intended procedure differ with the measurement technique. Guidebooks on methods of testing, field interviewing, and observing mention many such safeguards. Chapter Two described how quality of data was maintained in the Nutrition study. To improve reproducibility$_2$, any safeguard adopted ought to be included in the description of O.

Operations for Data Reduction

In the targeted study, one would like to think that independent analysts would transform a set of raw observations into essentially the same final conclusions. Reproducibility of the inference process is improved by reducing reliance on judgment, although, as I have already pointed out, judgment cannot be eliminated. In a statistical study, reproducibility$_2$ might be achieved by setting out a single analytic procedure in general terms. This does not provide for reproducibility$_3$, which requires not adherence to specified procedures but agreement among conclusions from procedures selected independently in a reasonable manner. The assumptions that one analyst considers credible may not seem right to another. An analyst who applies just one statistical procedure runs considerable risk that an independent analyst of equal competence will disagree. It is therefore advisable, as Chapter Seven explained, to carry out several credible alternative analyses.

Strengthening data-gathering operations can make a strong model more credible, and it is a safe bet that an analyst will prefer strong over weak models when he has confidence in the stronger assumptions. The fewer adjustments and allowances he needs to make, the less chance that his procedures will veer off from what other analysts do. By way of illustration, recall what was said earlier in this chapter about preventing loss of cases. Once units drop out, the benefits of controlled assignment are attenuated. Since analysts differ in their judgment about how to compensate, the planner who reduces attrition increases internal validity.

The open-endedness of naturalistic studies and unstructured measures means that the character of the data cannot be anticipated. Even so, much can be done to objectify the analysis, especially when analysts can center on questions that run across many cases. It is possible, for example, to instruct computers to score protocols (essay tests, interview responses) with respect to grammar, use of words having a negative emotional tone, and so on. In naturalistic observation no one expects investigators working from the same guidelines to report precisely the same incidents about a case. But if the evidence is not reproducible, perhaps the information conveyed will be. A reasonable check on this might be to have readers mark an objective questionnaire so as to describe a case, some readers working from reports of one set of informants and others from another set. In instances where a question can be answered by readers in both groups, one would want the answers to be similar. The questions of course have to be general, bearing on style and effectiveness and not on concrete incidents. Procedures of this character have been developed for research on personality (Cronbach, 1948; Block, 1960).

Reproducibility of descriptive impressions across observers is more likely to be achieved when the final summary questions are specified during planning and the observers are well briefed (Guba and Lincoln, 1981). The collection of data is shaped by this intended use, yet there is no barrier to the reporting of incidents that only one observer sees. (Nor does the technique preclude a report on a matter omitted from the original set of questions.)

When statisticians speak of *bias,* they refer not to prejudice but to a systematic error in a procedure—an error that causes answers to run consistently higher or lower than they should. By *efficiency* they mean the ability to produce estimates that agree closely with each other. Statisticians prefer to use a procedure that is both unbiased and efficient, but it is often possible to improve efficiency by accepting some bias. Freedom from bias is a virtue, then, but not an absolute virtue. The competing claims of efficiency are made unforgettable in Kendall's (1959) sad tale of Hiawatha, whose arrows were distributed in an unbiased fashion on all sides of the bull's-eye but never hit it.

Evaluators know that the estimate of the treatment effect in *UTOS* is unbiased if the treatment groups were randomly assigned, and many of them also think that freedom from systematic error is an absolute virtue. It is not, however, if the decision to randomize limits the study to a small sample. Small samples lead to erratic results. The evaluator, like the statistician, should weight the competing virtues of reducing systematic errors and reducing variable error. By forgoing assignment and collecting data in sites where the treatment is already in place, the evaluator may obtain more data than he could by persuading sites to agree to install whatever treatment is dictated by random assignment.

Neither set of sites is likely to be representative of the U that the target question referred to. On the one hand, self-selection of this treatment or that introduces a nonequivalence that cannot be adjusted away. On the other hand, to regard those who accept randomization as representative of U requires a redefinition of U. The original U becomes a U^*; to think about it, the evaluator has to make assumptions about interactions between the treatments and the site characteristics. Again, credible reasoning is called for.

If, on substantive grounds, an evaluator judges that the units naturally gravitating into a treatment differ greatly in their response from those that would be assigned from U— and if he also thinks that those willing to accept assignment differ little from the true target population—he has made the case for controlled assignment. If, however, he is not persuaded that sizable misrepresentation of U arises from self-selection of treatment, and if it is practicable to make the study without assignment considerably larger, it is probably wise to choose the design without assignment. When the randomized study is small, any one such study may give a result farther from the average of all such studies than the large uncontrolled study will. Randomizing a handful of sites equalizes only in that it prevents an investigator from corrupting the comparison by prejudicial assignments.

Narrowing the Target

The preceding sections of the chapter have concentrated on the study of a target *UTO* already identified. The emphasis has been on specification, on documentation, and on deployment of effort. Side remarks on alternative specifications have touched on choice of *UTO;* that topic now moves into the foreground.

Artificial Restriction as Scientific Strategy. Desire for reproducibility motivates investigators to choose homogeneous, restricted *UTO*. A scientist trying to confirm an idea translates it into definite questions. He entertains a variety of researchable questions; and, other things being equal, he prefers the one over which he has firmer control. The minimum ideal of reproducibility is to specify the question so definitely that the investigator gets the same answer every time (within the limits of sampling error). Once that is reasonably well achieved, he communicates enough to claim reproducibility$_2$. When the question is specified operationally and analyzed with a credible model, internal validity is high. However, a *UTO* with these properties is likely to be comparatively remote from the *UTO of interest to anyone but a specialist. The strategy that relies on narrow specification has its strength and its weakness.

Psychological research programs, starting with the laboratory work of Wilhelm Wundt and Edward Titchener, typically standardized procedures and narrowed questions on the preconception that causes of behavior operate singly and could be isolated (Gillis and Schneider, 1966). White (1977, p. 81) comments:

> Learning theory was deliberately organized to facilitate proof, the experience of one man exactly confirmable by the experience of another. The experimental study of learning has rested upon special procedures so arranged to facilitate replication, communication of procedure and findings, and systematic variation of factors. Only be-

cause we seek exact social cooperation among scientists would we ever ask a child to engage in half-hour bouts of solitary learning, with experience doled out to him in little parcels called trials, with simple little discrete events supposedly connected to simple little discrete action patterns. There is, of course, a large trade-off involved in the enhancement of the principle of proof. We trade off against complexity of reflection and analysis of experience; we want to maintain an orderly public discussion, and an orderly public discussion is greatly facilitated if we confine the discussion to what is publicly visible. So we enforce "parsimony" and we trade off against plausibility. In order to create our proof system, we are forced to create situations for children that are very unlike the natural situations in which they ordinarily learn, situations that we will have to interpret if our research is to be anything more than an empty game, if it is to have implications for the natural phenomena of human behavior.

Now, proof is of the very essence in scientific work, and, on the face of it, as we maximize proof, we maximize the scientific quality of psychological work. The proof–plausibility trade-off in psychological work is very painful to those within and without the field and has been so ever since its beginning. Wundt, as has been noted, doubted that all psychology could ever be gotten into the laboratory, and there is today a significant modern movement that joins him in arguing that we must conjoin to laboratory work studies in anthropology—as modern proponents put it, work that is ethologically, ecologically, or naturalistically valid. They want more plausibility in the situations in which we observe behavior.

Standardization of treatment realizations obviously limits the reach of a study; the thoughtful but ambivalent discussion by Aronson and Carlsmith (1968, pp. 46–49) is to be noted. Cole, Hood, and McDermott (1979) go further, contending that experimenters who restrict attention to highly specified situations mistakenly see virtue in "ecological invalidity." If the laboratory approaches used to examine memory and thinking "preclude the operation of principles essential to the organization of behavior in nonlaboratory experiments, theories and data derived from the laboratory cannot be used as a basis for predictions about the behavior of individuals once they leave the laboratory" (p. 2).

Putting the finding from a standardized study into words invites overinterpretation. Even if the investigator provides a description that allows reproducibility$_2$, his audience loses track of key elements and thinks that a more general question has been answered. Within experimental research on learning, unthinking overinterpretation of research on an operationally narrow U may be blamed for a major scientific controversy. A generation ago, Fiske (1978) reminds us, psychologists studying learning were split into camps. The Hull-Spence theory disagreed with Tolman's purposive behaviorism on many points. In particular, Tolman and his associates reported that rats in a maze learned not only the path to the reward but many other things about the maze. The rat's "latent learning" about the maze was evidenced, they said, in later runs where relocation of the goal box called for a modified response. Controversy flourished because Spence and his associates could not accept the principle of latent learning, and they could not reproduce the Tolman results when running rats in accord with Tolman's design.

The controversy faded as psychologists became less preoccupied with these two theoretical systems; but the facts about latent learning were clarified only two decades later, when Florida investigators (Jones and Fennell, 1965) attributed the discordant results to differences between Berkeley rats and Iowa City rats. They tested rats from the same stock as Tolman's Berkeley rat colony alongside descendants of the Iowa City Colony. Each colony had come from an inbred strain, inbreeding being a control that makes U more homogeneous and so increases reproducibility over samples. Jones

and Fennell found particularly slow maze learning in the
Berkeley rats, who had a special style of adapting to the situation. In Fiske's words, "When the starting box was opened,
they would take their time about coming out, sniff about,
amble along exploring their surroundings, and eventually
move to the goal" (1978, p. 62). Iowa City rats headed for the
goal as directly and promptly as they could. Doing no exploration, they could not have learned much about the environment.

The attempted replications at Iowa had not studied the
Berkeley *U*. It was not that Tolman failed to describe his *U*;
Iowa investigators could have obtained rats from the Berkeley colony. Each group was reasoning about a broad domain
on the basis of evidence from a narrow one. The Berkeley
conclusion with validity for a one-species *U* was "Latent learning occurs in rats." This conclusion was carelessly trans-
formed into "Latent learning occurs in all rats," and Spence's
group refuted that.

If too narrow a *UTO* can delay understanding in pure
science, it can have even more serious consequences in evaluation. Science captures a small bit of ground and moves out
circumspectly. By contrast, if the policy-shaping community
is going to take an evaluation seriously, it will surely do so before any replication or study on a **UTO* comes in. Social
issues are discussed in language that reaches beyond the observations. Nevertheless, reproducibility$_2$ is a virtue, and evaluation planners do have the option of making *U*, *T*, or *O*
more homogeneous. Reducing variance within a domain reduces variance from study to study.

Restricting U. The experimenter in the animal laboratory chooses healthy animals from a single strain. He takes
pains to familiarize them with their environment and with
such handling as the experiment will require. That is to say,
he prepares them to be as much alike as possible, so that their
differences will not add "noise" to the data. The evaluator has
almost no chance similarly to prepare the persons or institutions he observes, except by the usual gestures to enlist cooperation.

The evaluator does have the option of restricting U to a comparatively homogeneous class of individuals or sites. Cost was the first consideration in deciding to carry out the Nutrition study (see Chapter Two) in a single country. The decision to study remote villages was based on practical considerations; it would have been hard to keep track of subjects and their experiences in larger communities. To reduce adventitious variance, the planners restricted the study to villages that were similar in several respects. The diversity of Guatemalan villages in general would, they thought, blur the controlled experimental comparison; the restricted domain left less variance uncontrolled.

Educational investigators may try an innovation on students who have been carefully screened. For example, if a program is intended to improve the reading ability of children who speak Spanish better than English, the evaluator may specify narrow criteria for admission to the experimental group, instead of collecting data on whatever children school districts would send into the program if left to their own devices. But the investigator would then fail to learn about a salient fault of bilingual education in practice— namely, the tendency to prescribe it for children whose Spanish is poor. Recruiting "suitable" volunteer teachers likewise reduces variance. If these teachers take the program specifications more seriously than a representative group would, realizations of the treatment become uniform.

Restricting T. Laboratory investigators standardize treatment as fully as possible. Chemicals are purified, temperature is regulated, dishes are sterilized, and uniform methods of handling animals are prescribed. The reaction under observation is isolated from the world—in a test tube, perhaps, or a soundproof room. Every psychology student has seen a drawing of Pavlov's dog standing patiently in a harness that minimized variation of postural cues and held the dog ready for the crucial stimulus. The more background variation is reduced, the more likely it is that another investigator will be able to duplicate a finding. For the same reason, visual displays, timing of reinforcements, and other details of manipulated treatments are specified. These devices narrow the definition of T; they are usually chosen to intensify the effect of a treatment so that it will show at its strongest. To the extent that standardization can control variables other than the few on which interpretation is to center, interpretation becomes less equivocal.

Restricting O. To promote reproducibility, natural scientists develop standard techniques for measurement of weight, voltage, density, and so on. Automatic devices are used to reduce observer error. For example, the beam balance translates an imbalance of one milligram into an unmistakable displacement of a pointer. Motions of Drosophilia are monitored with the aid of a light beam and a photocell; the summary over any desired time period, accumulated electronically and entered onto a data tape, is free from human error. Again, investigations of drug effects are carried to the point of a "triple blind." Doses of drugs and placebos are identified by code number. Neither the patient, the physician treating the patient, nor the observer knows which patient received the drug. In an educational study that uses essay tests, the counterpart procedure is to mix papers before scoring; pretests are distinguished from posttests, and papers of one treatment group from those of another, only by a code. This procedure also guarantees that the operation is uncorrelated with age, race, and other characteristics of U.

The evaluator, however, will find it difficult if not impossible to blind observers. A classroom observer, for example, almost surely knows which treatment the unit being observed was assigned to receive, because the treatment is being carried out before his eyes. An interviewer can scarcely fail to learn which subjects are receiving benefit payments and which are controls.

Social scientists are nevertheless able to standardize procedures in many ways. To reduce variance, observers are trained to attend to the same aspects of behavior and to encode borderline instances in the same way. Also, to reduce variability within the class of O, evaluators analyze test or questionnaire items statistically during pilot studies, and those items that correlate only weakly with the others are discarded. This practice makes for greater agreement among alternative test forms. However, these steps do little for reproducibility$_3$ because a specification that appeals to one investigator may appear unsuitable to another. Choice of O will remain an act of judgment unless social scientists concur on the best indicators for each generalized label they use (alienation, knowledge of arithmetic, or whatever). Such a development is not in prospect.

The subtlety desirable in defining O is illustrated by a problem encountered in the Violence study. Statements of students about the school atmosphere were to be a dependent variable, since one aim of the intervention was to reduce tension and fear. The plan called for sampling 200 students at random. Average questionnaire scores for separate sex-by-race groups were calculated. Because a school composite was wanted, the group scores were combined, with weights proportional to the makeup of the whole student body. But since the makeup of the student body changes somewhat from year to year, the weighted score could change even if there were no attitude change in any of the subgroups. Therefore, it was decided to keep weights the same from Year 1 to Year 2. The artificially weighted composite in Year 2 had questionable meaning in a school where the makeup of the student body changed, but so would the naturally weighted composite.

From Internal to External Inference

We have seen, then, that reproducibility suffers from two kinds of variation. First, variation arises when the initial study and the replication employ different procedures. This occurs because loose plans left too much room for discretion or inadvertent variation or because the replicator does not know what procedures were employed in the first study. (This, in turn, would mean that the first investigator did not make procedures explicit or did not communicate them.) Second, variation arises when the phenomenon under study is heterogeneous, and results from independent realizations would therefore be likely to differ even if data-gathering procedures were identical. However, reproducibility can be achieved in a heterogeneous domain, provided that sampling is careful and the sample large. If U or T or O is heterogeneous, one would want a diverse sample from it. A large sample of units is not enough if the treatment realizations do not spread over the specified domain.

Semantic legerdemain can wave away the requirement of a large sample. But a small sample (for UTO or a sub-UTO) gives an indefinite result, perhaps best described by a broad confidence interval. Although each replication will arrive at a different sample statistic, the broad intervals from the replication will overlap and so give similar impressions. (One can generate little enthusiasm when the statement having internal validity is "The study leaves us highly uncertain on this point.")

Under special circumstances, an operational policy can and will be imposed uniformly; among social policies, payment procedures are the chief example. Most policies, however, can be applied adaptively or selectively. Heterogeneity then becomes highly important to observe, but concern shifts to external validity. If three fourths of the units given T_1 respond favorably to their t and one fourth respond badly, the obvious question is "Why?" Suppose that T_2 costs the same and its success rate is only .5. The plan T_1, then, is superior on average. But imposing it uniformly would be questionable if features of u or t that were associated with failure can be discovered. Let us move on to aspects of design that facilitate inference beyond the prespecified UTO and sub-UTO.

TARP as Example. This chapter has called attention to the many ways in which targeted studies can be strengthened, and the next chapter takes up ways to strengthen external inference. At this juncture we look at the Transitional Aid Research Project (TARP), as described by Rossi, Berk, and Lenihan (1980). TARP appears to represent realistic, reproducible social experimentation at its best, yet it exemplifies particularly well the general point that measurement of the treatment effect is rarely the main function of a field trial. To assess the effect of its target T, TARP was explicitly designed to achieve internal validity; in the end, however, its main contribution was the case it made for a T^* that had not been observed.

A large fraction of released prisoners commit new crimes and return to jail. Modest financial support would, it was hoped, help the released criminals resist the temptation to commit crimes and encourage them to seek work. With this in view, the experimenters arranged to provide approximately $70 per week to experimental subjects from the time they left prison until they found employment; their histories were followed for one year after release.

A pilot experiment in Baltimore had had encouraging results, but it was inconclusive as a guide to policy: The sample was small, the cases selected were prisoners considered likely to return to crime, and the investigators had intensive contacts with the subjects—contacts that would not be present in an operational program. The TARP experiment, which was to be large enough to achieve reasonably precise estimates of effect, set out to study a cross-sectional group of prisoners and simulate genuine operational conditions. (Despite the judgment of federal officials that the Baltimore experiment was insufficient basis for a policy recommendation, the California legislature acted to make benefits available to released prisoners. According to Rossi, Berk, and Lenihan, this action was traceable to the Baltimore findings.)

Among states with a sufficiently large flow of prisoners leaving jail, twenty expressed interest in the TARP study. In the end, Texas and Georgia were selected as sites. Some states rejected the plan to assign subjects randomly, and others did not have satisfactory computerized follow-up systems. Use of two states rather than one significantly broadened the target and thus encouraged generalization.

Three experimental formulas were tried. As these worked out in one state, Group 1 received $70 a week for up to twenty-six weeks, the payment being reduced if the week's earnings exceeded $8. (In effect, the first $70 of earnings was offset by an equal decrease in benefits.) Group 2 was on the same formula with thirteen weeks of eligibility. Group 3 also was paid for up to thirteen weeks, but its payments were reduced by only $1 for each $4 of earnings. This group was included on the supposition that the heavier penalty imposed on Group 2 would be a disincentive to seeking a job. Group 4 received limited payments for work-related expenses, such as tools, and was also offered help with job placement; it received no weekly allowance. Group 5 was left entirely alone by TARP except for four interviews; a $15 payment was made for each of these. Finally, Group 6 was examined only on the basis of the routine records of the system. The state employment service administered the funds and also made an effort to find jobs for the experimental subjects.

A roster of prisoners coming up for release was available, and certain cases were removed (particularly those whose homes would be too remote for follow-up interviews). The file was then classified with regard to sex, age, parole or discharge, urban or rural residence, and sometimes other information. Within each cell of the design, cases were assigned mechanically to treatment groups. The intent—which was realized—was to achieve 200 subjects in each of the first five groups and 1,000 in the sixth group. After attrition, final sample sizes for some outcome variables were around 80 percent of the number assigned to treatment.

The treatments were not fully delivered, but realistic rather than ideal delivery had been a significant part of the plan for T. Subjects had to come in to request each payment, and many did not request payments that they could have had. Interviews showed that many experimental subjects did not understand what payments they were eligible for. In particular, Group 3 did not understand the generous provision of its 25 percent "tax rate."

The gross summative findings were mostly unfavorable to the experimental T as delivered. Experimental groups did not show a crime rate different from that of controls, but they did have fewer weeks of employment, which implies that payments acted as a work disincentive. (But there was no difference between Group 2 and Group 3—groups that were set up to provide a targeted test of the disincentive hypothesis. A conservative analyst, following Fairweather's maxims, would have to read the data as implying that the 25 percent penalty is no better than the 100 percent penalty, the less costly treatment.) Another finding was favorable: Over the whole year, Groups 2 and 3 earned as much money as the control groups, even though they worked fewer weeks. These figures, together with the figures on weeks of employment, strongly imply that the experimental subjects were finding better jobs than were the control subjects. (A direct measure of wage rates was not available and would have been difficult to collect, since subjects held part-time jobs and shifted jobs frequently.)

This is the place to mention, without going into detail, the heroic methods of data analysis used to get beneath the surface of the summative comparison. Rossi's group went far beyond analysis of covariance to fit systems of structural equations to the data. The analyses also made extensive use of the econometric adjustments described in Chapter Six, to take into account not only attrition but such facts as the inevitable negative correlation between weeks of employment and number of weeks spent in jail.

In many of these analyses, the evaluators proceeded much as the INCAP investigators did, setting aside the original treatment categories and using as independent variable a continuous (less controlled) measure; that is, the total number of TARP dollars received. This was strongly correlated with group membership, but it was also affected by employment and by return to jail. The regression equations are offered as a description of *utos*, in the past tense, and not as generalizations to be translated directly into policy. Two illustrative statements from the report of Rossi, Berk, and Lenihan (1980) are: "Every additional week of employment appeared to reduce the number of property arrests by nearly .03 over the course of twelve months" (p. 238) and "Every $100 [from TARP] reduces the number of property arrests by about .02" (p. 239). These are to be understood as summary statistics with a dozen variables held constant. The effect on arrests, for example, is estimated as the difference for persons who are alike in age, financial resources, weeks of employment, and weeks in jail, among other "predictors," but unlike with respect to payments received.

The main points emerging from these correlational analyses can be stated simply: The person who is employed is less likely to commit crimes; the person who receives TARP payments is less likely to seek a job diligently; among those whose employment status is the same, the person receiving more money from TARP is less likely to commit crimes. This last hypothesis was developed after the experiment; the report elaborates it to consider additional precursor and intermediate variables. Perhaps the study could have been sharpened if such a substantive scenario had been laid out in advance. Even without that, by thinking of dozens of variables to cover in the interviews and in the search of records, the investigators had put themselves in an excellent position to explain why the TARP intervention failed. The sentences quoted in the preceding paragraph, which are part of the test of this hypothesis, are entirely consistent with the notion that the work-disincentive effect of TARP and the crime-reducing effect balanced out in the overall arrest rate.

The investigators emphasize the indication that experimental subjects, who could afford a longer period for seeking satisfactory work, tended to locate better-paying jobs. To capture this benefit without the work disincentive, they recommend a T^* in which payments are not reduced when the person takes a job. Some form of "severance pay" over several months after release would, they think, be easier to defend than a program linked to the system for unemployment benefits. Although the investigators advance this scheme with conviction, they call for thorough trials to develop an optimal plan (and not merely to test, summatively, some one plan).

In the pilot trial in Baltimore, 30 percent of those given no financial aid were arrested on theft charges, compared to 22 percent of the experimentals. No work disincentive was detected. Rossi's group suggests that this occurred because of the care taken, in the intimate Baltimore study, to make certain that recipients understood the rules. (Also, the "tax rate" under Baltimore rules was less severe than in TARP.) The pilot experiment presumably was sound, but not a good basis for extrapolation.

Setting up a formal comparative study under realistic field conditions seems to have been a wise design decision for TARP. The effect to be detected would be rather weak, according to the Baltimore experience, and it proved to be weak in Georgia and Texas. Baseline figures could not substitute for a no-treatment control because of the link between crime and fluctuating employment rates. Random assignment was ethical, and the meticulous stratification produced a high degree of equivalence (prior to attrition). Looking back, however, I wonder whether setting up three control groups was a wise investment. The analysis used the control cases but did not develop information from the contrast among Groups 4, 5, and 6. The function of the control groups would have been more important if a strong treatment effect had appeared. Although they guarded against the contention that the interviewing or the job placement services rather than the payments produced the effect, I am not persuaded that separating such rival hypotheses justified three control groups.

The central aspects of the treatment and research plan have reproducibility$_2$ (not reproducibility$_3$, because one investigator's reasonable payment rules are unlikely to have the same effect as those of the next investigator). The job placement aspect of the treatment probably was not reproducible; it is not clear what the state employment services were asked to do for members of the six groups, and the project collected virtually no information regarding the actual placement efforts.

The most notable feature of the study, however, is the investigators' diligence in collecting information beyond that needed to make the target comparison of arrest rates. This enabled them to finish with positive suggestions rather than with rejection of the proposal to help released prisoners. The supplementary data could have had great additional value if there had been contradictory findings in Texas and Georgia. The investigators considered discrepant results likely in view of differences between the two administrative systems and the two labor markets. In fact, results from Texas and Georgia were consistent in all important respects, but the data could have suggested a plausible explanation for a treatment-by-state interaction if one had turned up. The investigators also explored some differential effects arising from sex, race, and family dynamics.

It would be wrong to suggest that the TARP study is immune to criticism. That would contradict my basic proposition that for any one study many alternative designs and analyses are reasonable. It would downplay a number of uncertainties of which Rossi, Berk, and Lenihan (1980) are openly aware. The severely objective, quantitative style of the evaluation neglected the obvious opportunity for narrative reports of what TARP payments meant to individual prisoners. Limitations there are, but the TARP study shows policy-oriented experimentation at its best.

9

✍ *Planning to Provide Relevant Answers*

After any evaluation members of the policy-shaping community will make judgments about action alternatives that depart from those in the original program, or they will try to adapt the program to new conditions. An evaluation should thus be planned with an eye to the consumers' need to reach such judgments. Investigative tactics that support thinking about *UTOS are the subject of this chapter; these tactics are to some degree incompatible with the previously described controls that tend to narrow *UTO*.

No investigation can answer all questions. The variety of U^*, T^*, and O^* that will concern the different sectors of the audience is endless, and future settings can be only dimly foreseen. The planner seeking relevance aims at a target that becomes visible only after he has fired off his best shot. The task is so demanding as to make the aspiration seem almost foolish, but there is room for optimism. The task is not radically different from that of suppliers of business information, who try to provide executives and investors with facts applicable in fast-changing circumstances, or from the task of educators supplying facts and concepts for their students' future use.

The logic of external inference was described in Chapter Five. The interpreter locates cases within *utoS* that are similar to **UTOS*, compromising on similarity to take advantage of more cases. Several subsets may be examined, each of which deviates from **UTOS* in its own way. A subset may consist of a single unit, or, at the other extreme, the whole of *utoS* may be the starting point. Perhaps the inference is more often based on the whole, if only because using statistics already compiled is easier than digging into the data to construct a better match. Differences between the subset and **UTOS* are identified. Accepted beliefs or presumptions indicate which differences can be disregarded, and they are used to make allowance for the remaining, relevant differences.

This description does less than justice to the complexities and ambiguities of the process. Social scientists lack the tightly articulated Model II's that would generate firm statements about **UTOS*. Many lines of reasoning about the differences between *utoS* and **UTOS* are pursued simultaneously. Conclusions about a social program are not derived directly and exlusively from evaluations of that program. Other sources of social knowledge—folklore, history, anecdotes, research on tangential topics—flow into the interpretation (Weiss, 1977; Lindblom and Cohen, 1979).

What can planners of evaluations do to make external inferences more credible? The reasonable approach is to try to foresee some of the questions likely to be current when results of the evaluation begin to come in and for some time thereafter. The investigator's conversations during early phases of planning and his own knowledge enable him to form an impression of the treatment alternatives likely to be entertained in the future, of the units to be served, and of the outcomes someone will care about. The planner who takes these not as givens but as capable of further shaping will begin to see directions in which later discussions may turn. He then has the opportunity to center an inquiry on a *UTO* that comes comparatively close to a **UTO* that he expects to be under discussion. Also, he will realize what information, if collected, would make it easier to extend the results to various other **UTOS*.

The devices used to support extrapolation can be identified with one or more of the following functions: (1) reducing the differences that must be allowed for, (2) supporting the inference with supplementary information, and (3) communicating the argument. The third of these entries may seem out of place, but the validity of the evaluation comes down to the validity of the ideas that the community takes from it. Comprehension and acceptance of an inference by critical audiences are important indications that the evaluation has succeeded. Although subsequent social actions will put some extrapolations to the test of experience, the influence of a study depends on its credibility when it is released and critical challenge begins. Sound findings on one or another vexing social problem no doubt lie entombed today in the file drawer of some mute inglorious Mendel. However excellently those conclusions fit reality, they will not influence thought until they come to light and are judged credible. Basic science can honor and capitalize on posthumous reports, but a program evaluation not found credible and pertinent in its own time has failed.

I simplify discussion by speaking as if just one external inference from just one *utoS* is contemplated. The logic applies to additional inferences from the single study and to the planning of companion studies. For example, I say that bringing *UTO* close to **UTO* strengthens the argument. This statement applies when there are several **UTO;* matching up several *UTO* or sub-*UTO*, one to each **UTO*, obviously maximizes closeness, though only limited matching is possible. Neither this nor any other tactic should be carried to its extreme. All such devices are to be blended into a workable plan.

Shortening the Extrapolation

The original design can increase the likelihood that the completed study will give plausible answers to questions of a potential user. The user will want to infer—to forecast—what would be found if a fresh study were targeted on the *UTOS that concerns her. The inference becomes more secure when a part or all of the original utoS is close to her *UTOS. To select the sub-uto that gives the most satisfactory match, she needs information about features of the utoS. This enables her to judge the closeness of the match and to recognize differences to allow for. The evaluator provides for these needs by bringing a UTO close to one or more anticipated *UTO, collecting data on highly diversified uto, and recording copious information about the u, t, o, and S. The evaluator of course can do nothing about the setting but describe it, although he might decide not to carry out a study if the present times are so abnormal that a serious mismatch to the later S* is likely.

Sometimes the policy maker's *UTO is almost exactly like UTO. Even so, some external inference is required. Change from S to S* is inevitable, and minor shifts in the population and treatment will creep in. Looking at those differences and deciding what allowance to make for them constitute a process of external inference (even when it is decided that no allowance is needed!).

The surgery study discussed in the preceding chapter can serve as an example of this process. There is no reason to anticipate major change from year to year in the preliminary test or the board examination. The population of surgeons coming up for recertification is highly stable with respect to such variables as kind and recentness of training and experience. In the trial year, the preliminary test was available to only a representative fraction of the eligibles. Although the situation would of course change if the test became available to everyone, one could reasonably presume that that change would matter little. The passage of time, however, would alter what it is safe to presume. In deciding whether to produce self-help materials in each subsequent year, the surgeons' officers would have to look for changes and reason afresh about their influence. Moreover, assessing a major change would require considerable imagination. If, for example, the board shifted its examination over to videotaped presentations of cases, the old type of preliminary test would have to be reconsidered. The officers would be helped in their reasoning if the evaluator could tell them how the older printed items shaped the surgeons' efforts at self-education.

For the individual surgeon who is deciding how seriously to work on the preparatory materials, the $U*$ is herself. She wants information about the sub-U close to *her* qualifications, not about the global U. The original study might well ask each surgeon to estimate how familiar she is with current knowledge about each of twenty subfields. Cross-tabulation, against these responses, of success rate in the experimental and control groups would give the next surgeon an excellent means of judging how much the preliminary test would benefit her. Even when extrapolation is at a minimum, then, supplementary data "explain" the main finding and thus make it more useful.

Selecting a UTO *Relevant to Users.* Satisfying users' needs begins with selecting pertinent questions for investigation (Chapter Seven). The divergent phase of evaluation planning turns up far more questions than can be studied directly and systematically; the principles of leverage and reduction of uncertainty guide the convergence toward areas where *$*UTO$* can be expected to concentrate. The planner's effort to imagine processes that will contribute to or reduce the effectiveness of the program anticipates similar reasoning that will go on after a report on outcomes is finished. Interested parties will then suggest reasons why the program will not work everywhere or with everyone and will suggest that whatever outcomes were disappointing will be better if T is amended in a certain way. The more directly some part of the evaluation bears on such hypotheses, the more it dispels uncertainty.

Choosing a natural, ecologically representative U can reduce extrapolation in a study. Harvard Project Physics

(HPP), for example, went to the trouble of drawing a nation-wide sample of teachers willing to switch to the HPP course, because the developers saw that population as the natural market for their findings. In a similar spirit, an evaluator charged with investigating the effectiveness of driver education within a state could reasonably draw a probability sample of schools in that state and collect data in those that say they offer driver training. But distributions present at the start of the evaluation are not eternal and will not be representative of the natural population of another time. The Brunswikian view of design tends to regard the ecology surrounding humans as stable; in fact, however, ecological distributions and correlations of variables do change. To observe a representative cross section of the population and lump all the data together is shortsighted. The driver-training average would refer to the mix of realizations in a certain year. But the schools that offer each kind of program are likely to change; $*UT$ will drift away from UT. Representativeness is transient.

Diversifying the ut. Numerous $*UT$ will be considered, especially if decisions are to be decentralized. Each locality—sometimes each client—constitutes a new $U*$. Also, to repeat what was just said, the composite $*UT$ of interest to a central decision maker may change. In the driver-training example, it would be sensible to classify schools according to the nature and intensity of the training, then to sample and analyze within strata. The evaluator might do well to sample more thoroughly those strata that he thinks will predominate in the future. In a given state at a given time, the evaluator might anticipate that schools at a certain budgetary level will drop driver training and that in schools at another level the number of hours on the road will be cut in half. Thus, he will begin to envision the $*UT$ population and design the sample on that basis. Similar thinking is appropriate, of course, if advocates of the program want to promote it in a stratum where few units now accept it. That stratum then is a $U*$ about which debates are to be expected and for which comparatively extensive evidence is pertinent. Reweighting can simulate costs and outcomes in any arbitrary mix of realizations (though such counterfactual extensions incorporate dubious assumptions).

Given the multiplicity of *UT, advice to make the *ut* similar to *UT implies extending the range and variety of the cases observed and linking that variety to variation in outcomes. (Diversifying *o* is important also; I come to observing operations later in the chapter.) It may be advisable to mount studies of distinct kinds in separate *UT*, possibly under different investigators. These can spread out into a variety of sites, can look into variants of a particular *T*, or can study particular processes intensively. Each study or substudy should be planned to come within hailing distance of the concern of some anticipated audience.

Making *U*, *T*, and *O* heterogeneous is nearly the opposite of the scientific tradition of standardization discussed in Chapter Eight. As with most differences between basic science and evaluation, this shift in strategy reflects the fact that evaluation cannot make haste slowly. If it takes scientists a generation to disentangle the genetic secrets of *D. melanogaster*, so be it. Broadening the research to include other species before attaining insight on the first might introduce unhelpful complications. Practical social action, in contrast, must recognize diversity at an early date. Striking an average over diverse phenomena is almost never enough; the task is to understand the diversity.

A central decision maker wants an average for *UTO* as a whole if she plans to decree that all units in her charge, or none, will adopt the practice. (She, like the surgeons' officials, must decide that circumstances *S* have not changed enough to matter.) The local user looks upon the average result as a crude prediction. She can more securely accept the prediction as a guide if she thinks that she will realize a treatment similar to the typical *t* in the original study and that the local installation and clientele will be much like the norm in *U*. To expect the observed outcome of *T* to recur in a *U** that is not typical of *U* amounts to a blanket denial that any characteristic of units affects outcome. With units varying in innumerable ways, to deny interaction is to claim validity for myriad null hypotheses in a single breath.

An evaluator who accepts the likelihood of interaction can frontally test no more than a few interaction hypotheses. Not many variables can be represented formally in a design, so a properly curious investigator commits himself to data snooping. That means no more than taking a hard look at the units where T had greater or less success than would have been expected, and trying to figure out why.

Correlating outcomes with antecedent variables is a common and helpful procedure. (For example, did surgeons in independent practice benefit more from the preliminary test than surgeons in group practice?) A qualitative, narrative study of how the treatment process was facilitated or impeded in particular cases often has somewhat greater heuristic value than a summary that combines all cases in a category. Narrative accounts of events will touch on a great many variables, including some whose importance could not have been anticipated. Retrospective accounts have the obvious advantage that they can center on unusually successful or unsuccessful sites. Reserving modest resources for tracing such histories during the last phase of fieldwork can be a good investment.

Documentation. Descriptive information will be collected on some scale from the outset of fieldwork. The better the description of units, events, and settings, the more adequate can be the judgments required in extrapolation. For example, the user should be able to compare the intended and actual treatment of each unit with the variant she thinks of installing. Not much of the information can be published. Some reports will work the descriptive information into a connected, highly interpreted story. In other evaluations documentation will simply add to the file of coded data the memoranda made by site visitors and interviewers.

Canadians considering the adoption of HPP would be aware that their classes might not match the original U. Knowledge of the preparation or initial abilities of the American students and the teaching methods to which they were accustomed would help Canadians judge how much their situation is like the original one. Documentation thus helps in choosing a sub-*UTOS* on which to base an external inference. If American instruction as a whole is unlike typical Canadian instruction, the Canadians would learn more from whatever subset of the American classes is reasonably like classes in Canada (or like those in Manitoba).

Extreme-Groups Designs. Sampling plans and manipulations can check particular interaction hypotheses efficiently when the *u* and the *t* vary widely in specified respects. Interactions of a variable are more readily detected when cases at the extremes are weighted heavily in the sample (Cronbach and Snow, 1981). It is impossible to apply such a sampling plan systematically to several variables; the number of cells to be filled becomes large, and many cells call for comparatively rare types of units. It is more feasible to load the sample with units or conditions in which success of the proposed treatment is thought to be especially likely and others in which failure is anticipated. This produces an exploratory type of extreme-groups design rather than concentration on a few prespecified interactions.

Almost a commonplace in recent writings on design is the recommendation that a program idea be tested under ideal conditions (prior to or alongside trials under ordinary conditions). Time permitting, this probably would precede a more representative field trial. If prior tryout is not feasible, the superrealization embedded in a larger field test helps in external inference. When results under typical conditions are less than satisfactory, hothouse conditions may keep hope alive; that is, if results are satisfactory when cases are carefully selected and delivery is superior, the treatment concept can be salvaged. The differences between the hothouse results and the typical results will indicate how far activities must move toward the ideal before they will turn a profit.

The opposite tactic, of degrading a treatment or observing it under adverse conditions, can contribute in a similar way. If the treatment does no worse in the inhospitable setting than the baseline treatment, this finding strongly supports the innovation, while a definite negative outcome in one instance signals that T should not be applied everywhere. Interpolating between the perverse sample and the normal sample indicates a boundary within which acceptable results can be expected. Perverse design will not be used often, because it is unethical to expose human subjects to a treatment expected to work out badly. Much of its potential message can be gleaned from the scattered failures that occur without deliberate arrangement. Nonetheless, if adverse conditions exist in some sites where the program might be (or has been) installed, a special effort to observe in these conditions deserves consideration.

HPP might have found a perverse sample instructive. The project set out to carry a "two cultures" message into a market that one culture had dominated. Many physics teachers identify themselves with the scientific-technical culture; one might wonder whether these teachers would find satisfaction in teaching HPP and trying to attain the desired humanistic outcomes. The least intrusive step in design would be a questionnaire to teachers, prior to the study, on their attitude toward themes of the humanities. Data analysis could give special attention to units where teacher attitude was ill matched to the course. A mildly perverse design would oversample scientistic teachers to more clearly test the limits of HPP.

Explanatory Support for Inferences

Inferences about *UTOS* are almost never confined to direct quantitative extrapolations. Quantitative summaries of results in *utoS* serve mostly as a point of departure for more qualitative reasoning. For example, when Rossi, Berk, and Lenihan (1980) calculated that the arrest rate dropped by .02 for each $100 in TARP payments (on the average, other things being equal, and accepting a strong linear model), they intend to suggest something to policy makers. The legislator contemplating a TARP-like plan can better judge what larger

and smaller budgets would buy than she could if left to unedu-
cated guesses. But the analysts do not hint that ex-convicts
will, in general, give up crime if paid $5,000 per year. Their
calculations sum up a bit of past history under a particular
administrative formula. Any major change in the scale or
conditions of payment would throw off a quantitative forecast.

Crossbreaks to Beat the Odds. If diverse *ut* produce consistent data, a simple generalization becomes plausible. If the
success rate of a therapy is similar in many clinics, there is
every reason to think that the background of clients and the
inevitable variations in mode of delivery matter little. Physical
treatments are far more likely to show such stability than are
social interventions. Even with a physical intervention, however, one always tries to beat the odds. The patient told that a
surgical operation succeeds with 80 percent of those suf-
fering from her disorder recognizes that the failures are
probably not attributable purely to bad luck. She will ask
about characteristics frequent in the failing subgroup, looking for a hint that the odds for her are better or worse than
four to one. Crossbreaks provide a basis for understanding
variation.

Profitable attention to a crossbreak is illustrated by the
evaluation of a plan for serving mental patients (Sainsbury,
1975). In one community (Chichester), psychiatrists saw patients in outpatient clinics. Comparison results were obtained
in another community (Salisbury), where patients of the same
kind were moved into a residential mental hospital for treatment. Patients seemed on average to be helped more by the
outpatient arrangement, and their families generally were
positive about it. But a negative side effect was noted. In trying to determine, after two years of treatment, whether the
burden on families of psychiatric patients had been relieved,
Sainsbury and his staff found that relief was more common in
the community where patients were hospitalized. The investigators went on to the crossbreak in Table 7. Apparently, if
the patient presented a moderate burden, a family was disadvantaged by keeping the patient at home.

Table 7. Comparison of Two Systems of Care for Mental Patients

	Chichester (experimental)		Salisbury (control)	
	Total Families	Families Relieved	Total Families	Families Relieved
All families with any burden at referral	163	99 (60%)	99	80 (82%)
Some burden at referral	114	67 (59%)	64	56 (86%)
Severe burden at referral	49	32 (66%)	35	24 (68%)
Families with no burden	108	—	40	—

Note: The percentages are from Sainsbury (1975, pp. 107, 114). I have reconstituted the numbers; rounding errors produce some inconsistencies.

With one site per treatment, Sainsbury had no way to test a generalization over communities; yet he was interested in a *policy*—that is, in generalizing over future sites. He took seriously the relation observed, because he learned that Chichester families received less support from social workers than Salisbury families did. The following interpretation was offered: The psychiatrist (the main contact with the family in Chichester) was sensitive to family needs if the burden was severe and was then likely to make sure that social workers gave support. Where the stress was less obvious, however, families tended to be neglected. From this came a policy recommendation T^*: The innovative plan would have merit if it were changed so that family needs were *systematically* appraised and provided for.

No one believes that a probability not yet explained is beyond explanation. Many characteristics of an institution might reasonably be thought to influence the probable success of a social program that is under consideration. It makes sense to sort out cases that resemble this U^* and report their success rate. Many cells can be defined that resemble U^* in one way or another, and these crossbreaks will generate somewhat scattered estimates for U^*. Moreover, the errors of extrapolation described in Chapter Six enter when cases tabulated in a cell are selected on any basis except the designated classifying variable. Decision makers are then left uncertain about the rate of success to be anticipated locally.

It has been argued that judgments made on an "actuarial" basis—strictly in line with recorded probabilities—are sounder than judgments based on qualitative considerations. This proposition is easy to defend when the actuarial data are based on a good sample and the judgment is being made about further samples from the same population. But, even stated in that conservative manner, the proposition begs the question. Before an analyst can decide that *UTOS is similar enough to the source of the data for the original probabilities to apply, an impressionistic judgment comparing U^*, T^*, O^*, and S^* to the original is required. That judgment is based not on data in the table but on whatever understanding experience has built up.

Qualitative Backup for Quantitative Comparisons. Some of the debates regarding evaluation have encouraged the mistaken impression that objective, quantitative, focused methods are incompatible with humanistic, qualitative, wideband inquiry. In fact, the two should be working hand in hand.

The unsophisticated student of statistics may think that "error variance" is a residual, junk-heap category unworthy of explication; the experienced investigator knows better. After the F ratios are neatly tabulated, he settles down to figure out what the error variance means. A fully quantitative study of a prespecified hypothesis leaves plenty of room for roving curiosity. Who could be a better exemplar of this than Fisher?

He had a fine criterion, yield of wheat in bushels per acre. He found that after he controlled variety and fertilizer, there was considerable variation from year to year. This variation had a slow up-and-down cycle over a seventy-year period. Now Fisher set himself on the trail of the residual variation. First he studied wheat records from other sec-

tions to see if they had the trend; they did not. He
considered and ruled out rainfalls as an explanation. Then he started reading the records of the
plots and found weeds a possible factor. He considered the nature of each species of weed and found
that the response of specific weed varieties to rain-
fall and cultivation accounted for much of the cycle.
But the large trends were not explained until he
showed that the upsurge of weeds after 1875 coincided with a school attendance act which removed
cheap labor from the fields, and that another cycle
coincided with the retirement of a superintendent
who made weed removal his personal concern.
Here we see a statistician accounting to his satisfaction for every systematic variation in his response
variables, even if he has to consider the idiosyncra-
sies of weed species and supervisors to do it [Ed-
wards and Cronbach, 1952, p. 58; based on Fisher,
1920].

The Brownell and Moser (1949) study, discussed in
Chapter Eight, was a remarkably large formal experiment,
yet its usefulness came from the transparent good sense of
the qualitative explanation its narrative data permitted. The
basic summative finding was indefinite: The treatment labeled "meaningful" succeeded with some classes and not with
others. The history behind the cases permitted a more
pointed summation. The method generally succeeded in
classes where arithmetical processes had been explained
throughout the preceding years. That fact enabled one subgroup of educators to decide that their third graders were
indeed suited to the experimental treatment, but the same
fact offered a pessimistic message to the rest.

To stop there would be to misuse the knowledge
gained. What should be done locally where first and second
grades have been taught by rote? A strong hint emerges that
instruction in grades 1 and 2 should be modified—a hint
greatly strengthened by other psychological research. For the
children now entering grade 3 with two years of rote learning

behind them, their match to the sub-U where rote methods worked best is not the point to stress. The study implies that children require time to acquire the skill of attending to explanations in arithmetic. That skill pays off, so now is the time to start teaching it (though devising the T^* that will serve these previously miseducated children remains as unfinished business). This reasoning from the evaluation goes far beyond a consideration of the average in U or a matching sub-U.

The Brownell and Moser story was believable because teachers could readily understand why some classes profited from the experimental instruction and others did not. That explanation emerged when the investigators went behind the framework of the design and talked to enough people to locate a source of the difference in readiness.

Developing a Full-Bodied Account. Experience used in interpreting a summative finding comes partly from supplementary sources. Some of these sources may speak of the program itself, but observation of other programs, tangentially related social research and theory, and commonsense views (community experience) all may carry weight. A study gains authority insofar as it is translated into a story that fits with other experience. When a hearer says, "That explanation makes sense," she means not that it is internally logical but that it is consistent with her concepts of human and institutional behavior.

Narrative information from the sites observed plays a major role in making an interpretation persuasive, because it can convert statistics into a down-to-earth story. Without that, a formal study can make few connections with the layperson's established belief system; a summative finding that controverts prior beliefs will be hard to accept unless the narrative reveals just why events took a surprising turn. Campbell (1975a) endorses the complaint of humanistic critics that typical formal inferences suffer from "overdependence upon a few quantitative abstractions to the neglect of contradictory and supplementary qualitative evidence. Science depends on qualitative, commonsense knowing. . . . Science in the end contradicts some items of common sense, but it only does so by trusting the great bulk of the rest" (p. 8).

After elaborating on this theme, Campbell comes to the question of evaluation: "If we apply such an epistemology to evaluation research, it immediately legitimizes the 'narrative history' portion of most reports and suggests that this activity be given formal recognition in the planning and execution of the study. Evaluation studies are uninterpretable without this, and most would be better interpreted with more" (p. 9). After-the-fact explanation perhaps does not tell the whole story, and sometimes a reconstructed explanation is totally wrong. But when the intermediate factors mentioned in the explanation can be documented and the connections are consistent with general experience and theory, the community rightly trusts the account. Those who must act cannot live by the principle of recalcitrant skepticism.

The effort at the time of planning to anticipate the process of program administration, service delivery, and client response as recommended in Chapter Seven is a first step toward developing explanatory power. When observations confirm, amplify, or radically alter the intitial preconceptions, they make reasonably evident how most of the end results, expected and unexpected, came about. The task of explaining is essentially one of setting forth the scenario once again, starting at the point where the program became available to institutions and clients and tracing subsequent changes in both of them. This account based on hindsight may differ from that of the planners only in its specificity, or it may of necessity be a wholly fresh construction.

In either event, the explanation is a historical account of what led to what, and this brings us to the generalization that *evaluation is historical research*. It differs from most work of historians because the evaluator can collect information with his own eyes and instruments and may be able to arrange events that would otherwise not occur. Quantification is not a distinctive feature of evaluation; nowadays many historians rely on quantitative archives and carry out regression analyses very similar to those found, for example, in TARP.

When it comes to explanation, the evaluator is, like the historian, a storyteller.

The story that he tells gains plausibility when he examines the chain of events link by link, because short-reach inferences are easy to appreciate and accept. Scriven (1959) points out that historical explanations depend for their force on what he calls "truisms"; that is, on commonplace, noncontroversial explanations of specific human actions. Statements appealing to common understanding are abundant in evaluation reports. Evaluators recount tales such as these:

- "The reading activities in the schools funded by the experiment did not differ from those in control schools, because the district superintendent found other funds to help the control schools."
- "Among the televised lessons in this series, the children watched most steadily when a human actor was in view."
- "In study groups of mixed ability, the ablest students were frequently asked for help and had occasion to formulate the subject matter in simple words. Little communication of this kind took place in groups consisting wholly of able students."

Facts like these explain score differences or their absence by appealing to familiar, everyday mechanisms. Some evaluators neither come on the scene personally nor elicit textured accounts from persons who saw the program at first hand. Their interpretations of score differences thus remain comparatively abstract and speculative and carry less conviction than a historical account would. In offering a connected "self-evident" story, the interpreter undoubtedly takes risks. His account, however, contributes to thinking by the very fact that it gives the would-be critic something to sink her teeth into.

Multiple Indicators for Constructs. The policy-shaping community necessarily discusses benefits in generalized terms. The community is interested in literacy or employability, not in the specific measuring operation that the evaluator chose. Specific characteristics make any indicator a less than perfect reflection of the broad variable. The planner of course tries to choose a valid measure for the variable; the difficulty is that the generalized term encompasses quite a variety of variables and that on the surface many indicators may seem valid.

Take the case where an evaluator of compensatory education is asked to assess proficiency in speaking. Three examples illustrate the range of procedures that could be defended. Glucksberg, Krauss, and Weisberg (1966) devised a procedure that is almost wholly standardized. A barrier separates the child who is to communicate from the child who is to listen. On the table before each child is a set of blocks bearing painted shapes; the sets are identical. The communicator is to describe each block so accurately that the receiver will pick out the matching block in her set. Contrast this with the radically unstandardized procedure described by Labov (1970). Two or more urban boys are gathered in the tenement room where one of them lives. The observer sits on the floor with them, dumps out a heap of potato chips, starts a conversation, and lets it flow. This brings out the fluent and complex language that disadvantaged boys rarely or never use in school. In still another procedure, Strandberg and Griffith (according to Cazden, 1972) obtained two distinct indicators by asking young children to talk about snapshots they had taken. Some of the snapshots were made at school, the photographic targets being selected for the child by a teacher; others were made at home and showed objects and scenes selected by the child. These latter subjects, representative of what the child would ordinarily talk about, elicited more extensive and more advanced speech than the former. Groups of children can be expected to rank differently on these various procedures; if the evaluator adopts just one of them, his report on compensatory education will be tilted by the specifics of that procedure.

The Brownell and Moser (1949) work illustrates the same point. Subtraction is subtraction, one might say. Anticipating, however, that critics might find fault with any one measure, Brownell and Moser collected data on more than

one kind of performance. The first test called simply for subtracting 56 from 72 and the like; this echoed the lessons. The
second test was on subtraction of three-digit numbers (264
from 361, for example); the teaching had not covered three-
digit numbers.

The two measures gave different pictures. All groups
did well on the familiar task. The groups taught in a meaningful way averaged slightly above the rote groups. However,
the rote-taught groups handled three-digit numbers poorly,
and they evidently did not understand what they were doing.
The classes to whom one technique of subtraction was explained did poorly; that method was hard to explain, and apparently the teaching had little meaning for the children.
Classes given explanations of an alternative technique were
more often able to handle three-digit numbers; they alone
knew what they were doing. Mastery of subtraction, then, is
not captured by a single kind of test, and generalizations
about meaningful teaching are hollow. Educators at the time
had been arguing for and against attempts to explain procedures to children. The result described here, together with
the information on the relevance of children's past instruction, indicates that meaningfulness lies in the child's response, not in the teacher's effort.

The evaluator should often apply two, three, or more
measures for an important outcome. This is the multimethod
approach proposed by Campbell and Fiske (1959). Such
triangulation enables one to defend the broad label applied
to the data if the several measures tell a consistent story, or to
warn that the label is too broad. Triangulation is proper also
to check out generalized statements about treatment variables, as was illustrated in the preceding paragraph with regard to "meaningfulness." A treatment description at an abstract level is questionable unless the technique has been tried
in several versions and contexts. Analysis that looks for consistency does much to reduce uncertainty about the attempted generalization. Consistency over a limited number
of variations is not conclusive support, of course; a different
context may someday produce a contradictory finding.

Split-sample designs help to overcome the practical

limits to application of multiple indicators. It will be recalled from Chapter Two, for example, that in the evaluation of the Physics study some class members answered one questionnaire and some another. Similarly, one might give a comparatively inexpensive printed test to the majority of students in a class, while pulling out a random few from each class for a test on apparatus. Another plan is to build variety into any one instrument and analyze the parts separately.

The same principle of checking out consistency applies even to instruments that supposedly measure just one thing. The analyst can dig into the character of errors and the response processes that led to them. At one time I was responsible for analyzing an evaluation of a high school program. One facet of the evaluation was to administer an attitude test periodically, since the teachers hoped that the program was making the students more "liberal." They were gratified to discover that the mean Liberalism score increased as students progressed from grade 10 to grade 12. My reanalysis showed that the striking change was not reversal of opinions but, rather, decline in "uncertain" responses. I looked first at students who in grade 10 endorsed liberal statements more than conservative statements. As they advanced to grade 12, they became more liberal, shifting from "uncertain" to "agree" on liberal statements and from "uncertain" to "disagree" on conservative ones. The grade 10 conservatives—the ones that the school most wanted to liberalize—also shifted away from "uncertain," coming to agree with *conservative* statements and to disagree with liberal statements. This unwanted trend was masked in the mean score because the student body was more liberal than conservative at the outset; consequently, shifts in the liberal direction outnumbered shifts toward conservatism.

Capitalizing on Side Studies. The evaluation strengthens inference by making the most of the experience that the evaluation itself offered. Beyond that, drawing on data collected by others strengthens interpretation. Thus, an economist forecasting the effect that an action by the Federal Reserve Board will have three years hence strengthens his case by showing how well his analytic machinery accounts, in retrospect, for data of previous years.

Thinking through an extrapolation in advance may make it possible to envision evidence that would sustain the external inference. Limited though the theory of social and psychological processes is, it may indicate variables on which a prediction would be contingent. Where certain facts are relevant, reasoning cannot proceed unless the facts are provided or an assumption is made. By way of example, consider a procedure for training recruits to fix a certain radar malfunction. It is asked whether the training will produce lasting knowledge, usable when the malfunction occurs in the field a year later. Theory of memory indicates, on the one hand, that retention tends to be good when knowledge is strongly structured; seeing the connections between elements, a person can reconstruct the whole line of thought when traces begin to face. On the other hand, recall for strings of sentences learned by rote or for strings of loosely connected acts is poor. The evaluator, then, will be well advised to find out not only whether the trainees are proficient at the end of the training but whether they see the relationship among the elements of the task, the reason for the order of the steps, and so on. These test questions are not in their own right important to the trainers, but they have leverage because psychological theory can base a significant statement on them.

An industrial psychologist sets out to evaluate a new selection test for computer programmers. If he has validated the test against success in only three installations, for example, extrapolation to programming jobs generally is open to challenge. Applicant pools vary, and so do job requirements. The psychologist strengthens his case by pointing to earlier research on a different aptitude test for programmers whose validity coefficients in thirty-three employment situations proved to be remarkably consistent (Schmidt, Gast-Rosenberg, and Hunter, 1980). (The consistency was apparent only after Schmidt and his associates made subtle adjustments—for variation in range of talent, among other things.) The industrial psychologist relied on knowledge someone else had already consolidated and made public. In the absence of the Schmidt, Gast-Rosenberg, and Hunter report, it would be sensible for the evaluator of the new test to consolidate the pertinent literature, preferably before collecting his own data. This kind of effort is especially important because inconsistency across older studies, if found, would cast doubt on the possiblity of generalization. The new test would then have to be validated specifically for one computer installation after another. An evaluation on a modest scale could not identify categories of sites where the test works well, and a search for a broadly useful conclusion would be doomed to frustration.

Having referred favorably to the report on computer programmers, I should express my reservations about the strategy of *metaanalysis* that it exemplifies. Systematic techniques have been developed for synthesizing quantitative evaluations of treatments designated similarly (as informal education, say, or psychotherapy). The estimated magnitudes of the treatment effects in the several experiments or quasi-experiments are weighted into a generalized estimate. This approach has both merits and limitations (Pillemer and Light, 1980). The test for programmers was fixed in nature, the methods of validating it were essentially standard across studies, and the reanalysis did not take the primary investigators' statistics at face value. All this enabled Schmidt and his colleagues to show metaanalysis at its best. Metaanalysis, however, can degenerate into scientism when the several studies do not aim at a single well-defined target.

Moreover, purely quantitative approaches with prespecified variables are limited in value at best. The primary investigator works at a distance from events. The metaevaluator is much further removed. His field of view is restricted to the treatment contrast around which the study was designed. When the experimental and control treatments are heterogeneous, as in HPP, the treatment effect refers to an essentially nondescript variable. The effect size in TARP referred to a reproducible contrast, but the strength of that work was that the primary investigators set the measure of effect aside so as to interpret something more important. I would also warn metaanalysts against using the original statistical summaries of an evaluation. I have on many occasions tried to unravel reports by going back to the original data. Rather often the effect sizes originally calculated (or statistics having the same function) seemed wrong to me. At issue were such matters as handling of outliers, recognition of ceiling effects or other kinds of nonlinearity, and the ordering of variables in a step-wise regression. Whether I was right or wrong in these instances, it is evident that analysts differ in their judgments. A metaanalysis can be of little value unless every primary data set is analyzed by the same rules.

Planning for Communication

The evaluator comes to know and understand a great deal about a program. The usefulness of his evaluation, however, depends on the degree to which members of the policy-shaping community become aware of his findings, accept them, and derive suitable implications for action from them. Community thinking may be modified by the evaluative report or by a rejoinder long before the best-qualified interpreters have had time to reflect on the findings, reanalyze them, exchange views, and tell laypersons what in the report is credible and what is doubtful.

The reporting task of the evaluator differs from the scientist's. The scientist reports to a select audience that shares his language and style of thought and is obligated to study the original report before taking issue with it. Most disagreements are voiced within limited circles. The interested persons can keep track of the whole controversy and, as a community, can in time decide whether the challenges carry weight. The evaluator, however, is trying to reach numerous and scattered audiences, most of which receive secondary and watered-down accounts of his report. An evaluator who believes that his report has been misinterpreted finds it difficult or impossible to place a clarification before all those who heard the misstatement. (Sometimes he profits from failed

communication, though; the evaluator may capture a headline and plant in the public mind an overstatement that balanced criticism never manages to uproot.)

Filtering of Information. Information is invariably lost in
moving from field observation to report. Some observations
are never relayed by the observer, others are lost in the encoding and statistical summary, and still others are lost because report space is limited. Once the report is written, there
are further filters. Information is squeezed out or distorted
by the sponsor, by the media, or by public discussion. A wrap-
up account highlights selected findings and leaves others
buried. For example, public discussion of Head Start was
preempted by a dispute as to whether it raised IQs. Its demonstrated contributions to health, nutrition, and community
relations seemingly did not count. Early procedures of the
New Jersey income maintenance study were challenged by
the General Accounting Office; as a result, some con-
gressmen were prepared to doubt the conclusions of the finished inquiry and turned to other sources for their information.

Some evaluators may prefer to leave "communication"
to professional communicators. Communicating to nonspe-
cialists about politically sensitive matters is difficult. Partisans
tear sentences from context and color the interpretation.
They strip the conclusion down to bare-bones endorsement
or condemnation, casting aside phrases intended to hedge
the conclusion. Statements about program shortcomings reverberate longer than statements about what is going well.
But the evaluator cannot escape these realities. For if he re-
fuses to run the risks involved in communicating, the journalist who relays his message is far more likely to fuel partisan
fires.

I have detailed elsewhere (Cronbach, 1975b) how the
New York Times reported an experiment carried out in two
sites, noting a positive treatment effect in California and the
opposite effect in Ohio. The positive result supported the hypothesis that telling teachers about children's mental test
scores biased teachers' handling of the children—the so-

called Pygmalion effect. That challenge to conventional educational practice was made the subject of a front-page story. Only the abnormally diligent reader would have found, buried in the fifteenth paragraph on an inside page, the understated remark that the California result was "not clearly corroborated" in Ohio!

Selective Communication. If the evaluator unburdens himself only in a final technical report or in a book-length narrative, his insights will perhaps be forever lost to the proper audience. Social issues and programs compete for the limited attention of an audience. A social evaluation rarely gets a full reading, and readers are unlikely to attend equally to all that is said. Overwhelming readers with detail invites hit-and-miss interpretation of miscellaneous fragments.

Although a massive report makes a poor vehicle for communication, an evaluation ought to be backed up by a proper technical account, as a matter of scientific ethics and as a bid for credibility. A recommendation is vulnerable to partisan attack if the evidence and reasoning are not well displayed. At the same time, any report for distribution must be highly selective. It ought to boil down or omit analyses and data sets that seem unlikely to influence actions or social thought. Anticipating the limits of audience attention, the evaluator might be tempted to confine data collection and analysis to questions broad and salient enough to receive attention. In doing so, however, the evaluation would misapply the principle of leverage.

In a report for general consumption, it may be sufficient to say something like this: "The first treatment apparently had greater appeal than the second, but no important difference was seen in the kinds of clients each attracts." Numerous crossbreaks would have had to be examined to justify that statement, but the tabulations themselves remain in a file drawer. Similarly, the evaluators may learn a great deal by tabulating responses to each item on a posttest of attitude or ability. For the report, however, it is best to display only a few items to illustrate any pattern of treatment differences, along with a few to represent those with no difference.

It will not do to flood the reader with too many facts. Most of the audience cares little about the research procedures used in an evaluation, including the controls that foster reproducibility of the most direct conclusions. When the evaluator attempts to communicate about specifications and operations, almost no one listens. Reproducibility is not the stuff of headlines.

As an example, the controls of the INCAP study implied substantial reproducibility$_2$ for a conclusion of this form: "Making *atole* available through a community health center to all residents produced better performance on Tests X, Y, and Z, at ages three to six, among children whose mothers came in regularly during pregnancy, than making *fresco* available did, in four Guatemalan communities having characteristics A, B, C, and D." But policy makers considering food supplementation as a vehicle for national development would not bear the fine points in mind. They would remember something like this: "Providing more calories to pregnant mothers in rural Guatemala made their children brighter." Specialists, naturally, would retain more of the original conclusion. A nutrition specialist, for example, would note that vitamins and minerals may have been necessary to produce the effect (even though these were supplied to both groups). A social psychologist would note the availability of the food to all residents as a circumstance that made the center appealing and lively; he would wonder whether the success of the program might have hinged on this. If so, restricting food to pregnant mothers (where supplementation seemed to matter most) could weaken acceptance of the treatment or its effect. These specialists, warning against overgeneralization, would be raising questions about external validity—that is, about propositions implicit in the loose conclusion that the audience shaped for itself.

Insofar as the evaluator anticipates a **UTOS* that will be under consideration as a deliberate alternative to *UTO* or as a consequence of looser specification and control, he can offer a judgment on it. He can suggest modifications of the original *T* that seem especially likely to serve a new target population, or he can suggest what subset of that group the original T seems to benefit. Merely to raise a question may be important. Thus, it is useful to warn decision makers that in a large-scale operation it will be harder to maintain standards of service than in the modest *uto* of the study.

Direct Communications. The evaluator should be encouraged to speak directly and informally to parties who are or should be interested in the program. The role of the evaluator resembles in many ways that of the journalist—at least, of the journalist who puts the aim of public enlightenment ahead of the aim of selling newspapers. Such a journalist investigates matters of public interest, judges what observations merit public attention, and tries to attract attention to them. Members of an evaluation team have many opportunities to exchange views within the team and with informants. They therefore are in a good position to carry out the reporting, as well as the investigative, function.

The suggestion that evaluators report to a general audience in attention-catching ways may be objectionable, however, perhaps especially to those who commission evaluations. Sponsors often want to control the release of evaluative information. This control is easy to justify when the evaluator is a technical assistant to a manager. She has the right and duty to decide what information might disrupt the organization if released. There is no issue in this case: The evaluator's audience is the manager. But even if the program does not operate in a context of command, the sponsor may nonetheless want control and may specify that reports are to be submitted for prior review. An official is understandably reluctant to commission work whose releases she cannot control, and evaluators are understandably suspicious of constraints.

That tension can be reduced once the political system comes to comprehend the function of evaluation. The public interest will be served best by institutional arrangements that free evaluators to speak directly to all those who have a stake in the decisions. *Toward Reform* gave greater space to this topic and summed it up this way:

> Managers have many reasons for wishing to maintain control over evaluative information; the

evaluator can respect all such reasons that fall within the sphere of management. The crucial ethical problem appears to be freedom to communicate during and after the study, subject to legitimate concerns for privacy, national security, and faithfulness to contractual commitments [p. 6; see also pp. 210–212].

Collecting Lively Material. At least some members of the evaluation team should be adept at informal communication. A large study of a controversial program probably needs a journalistic consultant or a staff specialist, just as it needs an expert in statistics. Stake (1975), in particular, advocates designing evaluative reports for a broad community and employing unconventional forms of communication. The aim is to give the audience a feeling for the program and for the experience of participants; a colorless abstraction would, in Stake's view, be more open to misunderstanding. Press releases and speeches are a step beyond the blockbuster report. But down-to-earth representation of program events—skits, logs, scrapbooks—would do a better job of storytelling, Stake suggests.

The U.S. Department of Housing and Urban Development, wishing to assess the extent of bias among real estate brokers, arranged for black couples and white couples (matched on ostensible financial resources) to make similar requests for property to inspect (Wienk and others, 1979). A television crew covertly filmed some of the contrasting responses—the properties exhibited to the couples, for example, and the courtesy shown them. Those film clips, stored up for release to television when the conclusions were ready, brought the attention that the agency wanted. The success was a success of planning.

The evaluator who wants to produce vivid reports should begin early to amass material that will add color and realism to what might otherwise be a bald and possibly unconvincing narrative. This calls for some redirection of resources and some modification of field techniques. It is profitable, I have found, for observers to file narrative accounts of revealing incidents seen in classrooms, including representative or colorful remarks from program participants. While these memoranda need not be polished, they should provide context and continuity and should be factual rather than interpretative. Members of the evaluation team, skimming the file from time to time, may notice variables and kinds of events that later observations should be alert to. When actually assembling a written or oral report, they find in the file anecdotes consistent with the conclusions reached by more formal methods. (If not, the conclusions are suspect!) The anecdotes add wonderfully to the interest and belief that the report will command. The anecdotes do not warrant the conclusions; on the contrary, the evaluator reached the conclusion and then selected anecdotes to bring it to life. A selected anecdote can also perform the opposite function, dramatizing the warning that the conclusion does not apply universally.

Multiple Perspectives. The evaluator may obtain alternative judgments based on the data, as well as predictions consistent with different sets of beliefs. Just as it is now recommended that partisans be consulted in locating questions to be investigated, so it is advisable to ask them to interpret the data and thereby help the report writers see the information through others' eyes. Both the Raizen and Rossi report (1981) and *Toward Reform* (1980) suggested institutional devices to facilitate review from the perspectives of stakeholders and of substantive and methodological experts. The goal would not be to arrive at a single verdict but to air disagreements, defuse those based on misconceptions, and acknowledge the warranted uncertainties that remain and the values that each course of action fits with.

Raizen and Rossi (1981, p. 85), in advising the U.S. Department of Education, suggested an annual conference to discuss all the department's major evaluations. An evaluation would be reviewed year after year, from the time of initial design, through initial reporting of results, down to the reporting of statistical reanalyses and criticism by outsiders. The participants would include educators, persons knowledgeable about the interests of minorities and other distinguishable sets of consumers, and technical experts. The hope was that evaluations would be made sounder and would speak more directly to the uncertainties of constituencies, as well as that the repeated public exposure would increase use of the knowledge.

Toward Reform, with the same ends in view, suggested the formation of "social problem study groups." These groups would center on efforts to improve the supply of scientists and engineers, for example, or on programs to benefit young children. A social problem study group would consider all the programs pertinent to its topic, regardless of their sponsorship, along with needs recognized as unmet. Evaluations would be used alongside nonevaluative research to arrive at clearer concepts in the problem area. This plan recognizes that many organized activities—not all of them governmental—affect the same citizens and also that the appropriate mix of reviewers varies from problem to problem.

Such proposals reflect the current recognition that evaluations are simply part of the continuing accumulation of social knowledge. An evaluation feeds social thought as it is planned, as it brings in data, as it comes to a close, and, one may hope, for several years thereafter. The observations and concepts it accumulates will bear on persistent social agendas, whatever the fate of the program it studies. For example, Harvard Project Physics demonstrated the wide variation in classroom climates and began to trace how climate contributes to the yield of a certain kind of instruction. The concept of climates and the techniques for measuring them came to be seen as potentially important in any effort to improve instruction (Walberg, 1977). An evaluation can thus become a source of far-reaching questions.

Institutional arrangements for continuous and multi-partisan discussion of evaluations are likely to be scattered and to cover only a fraction of evaluations. In the absence of such arrangements, the planner of a single evaluation should be able to devise ways to obtain some of the advantages of multiple review and cross talk. The present routines of evaluation, however, work against such efforts. Work is scheduled so tightly that the staff members are kept rushing from due date to due date, and casual exchange of impressions and puzzlements within the staff or with outsiders comes to be a luxury. The tradition is to guard observations and emerging opinions as secrets until the matured report is approved for release. Although project advisory committees ostensibly provide occasions for reviewing what the project is learning, meetings are usually sporadic, brief, and (at least in my experience) crowded with talk about technique and logistics rather than with exchanges centered on substantive interpretations. A serious effort to capitalize on perspectives in the relevant communities will not occur unless some staff members are allocated time for that responsibility.

Best able to interact in this way, I think, are comparatively senior members of the evaluation staff who have acquainted themselves with the impressions that other members of the staff have formed. I suspect that most will be gained from conversations with small groups, not from public hearings. Sitting down with the members or staff of a legislative committee, the evaluator might mention a preliminary finding—say, that a program under trial is being used by one type of client and not by others. An exchange of views on the possible meanings of this finding and on the political potency of strong evidence on the point should assist the evaluation. Such conversations also help the thinking of policy makers to move with the evidence. The evaluator who joins a meeting of program staff in one site can probe in this manner: "I wonder if your group has experienced a difficulty that we have been told about in other sites; we hear that . . ."

These suggestions reinforce once more the view that planning an evaluation is not a logical exercise to be carried out in a back room and completed before fieldwork begins. Nor should the fieldwork come to an end before reporting starts. As *Toward Reform* argued at length, the evaluator begins to educate his clientele as soon as he begins to interact with its members to identify the U, T, and O of interest. The conversation stimulates fresh thought, especially when the evaluator asks for reactions to what an earlier informant said. Merely by displaying the variety of issues, the conversations wean the audience from the idea that a field study can answer such an oversimplified question as "Does compensatory education work?"

As facts come in, they feed into the planning process directly and also through the reactions they elicit from those with whom the evaluator talks. The evaluator comes to recognize gaps in the evidence and conflicting interpretations. Sometimes he can resolve these by adding a supplementary investigation. At the least, uncertainties have been identified that should be laid fairly before the audience.

10

🏂 Evaluation:

The Art of
the Possible

Advice on evaluation design cannot be packed into
a few maxims that would enable the evaluator to make ideal
use of resources, although maxims of a kind could be ex-
tracted from earlier chapters. Two will suffice to lead off this
recapitulation:

- Evaluation is an art.
- There is no single best plan for an evaluation, not even
  for an inquiry into a particular program, at a particular
  time, with a particular budget.

Substantive beliefs, responsibilities to a sponsor, political sympathies, personal preferences among research techniques, styles of personal interaction, and many other variables cause one evaluator to emphasize in an inquiry what the
next evaluator, equally competent and sincere, would not.
Design choices depend on judgments about the facts likely to

emerge and the weight they may carry in an ever changing political world. Although forecasts are bound to be inaccurate, each of many forecasts can generate a productive evaluation. Budgets will always force omission of some good choices of directions for inquiry and evaluative activities. By being thoughtful about priorities, however, the evaluator can hope to settle on one of the better overall plans. He and the sponsor should then be content even if no final answers result from the study. To reduce uncertainties can have great social value.

Grander aspirations were urged on the evaluation profession during the 1970s. Egregiously unattainable ideals were illustrated in a checklist prepared by the General Accounting Office (GAO) to steer the evaluation planning of federal agencies (Comptroller General, 1978). It advocated striving for conclusions that are certain—that is, immune to criticism because of the stringency of the design (see *Toward Reform,* pp. 215–218). The document was distributed as a draft for comment; and, thanks to the comments offered, the GAO decided not to publish the checklist. Other manuals have urged the evaluator to accept the burden of proving the worth of an innovation. In addition, the philosophy that some aspects of social issues can and should be removed from politics and resolved by some authority had, for a time, more advocates than detractors.

Professionals now are close to agreement on issues about which they contended hotly a few years back. Present differences are in emphasis rather than in practices recommended. For example, some writers urge the evaluator to apply his own best judgment to the facts and recommend a social action. Others want the evaluator to act as eyes and ears for a pluralistic community, keeping his social values out of what he says. Everyone, however, seems to agree that the community *is* pluralistic and that the evaluator should acquaint himself with what subcommunities believe and care about. A constituency may not think to ask about certain side effects that would, if present, concern them very much. Therefore, the evaluator who favors leaving judgment to the community is prepared to bring to their attention whatever *he* considers important. At the other extreme, the evaluator who favors telling society what action to take knows that he cannot persuade unless his argument is attuned to audience beliefs and value systems. Even those who say that the evaluator should take his charge from the sponsor would, in the divergent phase of planning, examine how the policy-shaping community perceives the topic under investigation. A few pages back, I mentioned proposals to open the process of interpreting findings to outsiders—that is, to citizens. The fact that two heterogeneous committees brought forth much the same proposal suggests that we see here another example of consensus in the making.

The current literature, I think, is in accord with this chapter. My summary might almost be pieced together by quoting Cook, Gilbert, Mosteller, and authors of *Social Experimentation* (Campbell, Riecken, and Glennan and perhaps others), though I have pushed *against* statements of these very writers in earlier chapters. These authors were probably never at odds with the methodology that this book sets forth; but, in describing design, they presented just one aspect of it, in silhouette. This book tries to light up design from all sides. My associates and I made a start in that direction in *Toward Reform*. Such chapters of that work as "Allocating Research Resources" and "The Shape of the Field Study" provide a statement wholly consistent, I think, with this summary section. As I have minimized repetition from *Toward Reform*, I invite readers to turn there for examples and analyses that augment what this book says.

Aspects of Experimentation

The current arguments for strong design list features of an evaluation that make striving for internally valid comparison especially advisable, alongside features that make strong design unprofitable or inappropriate. Almost no one now singles out one design as universally best for studying program effectiveness.

Proponents of social experiments bundle together many tactics of design: intervention, standardization of treatment, setting up a no-treatment control, pitting alternative program plans against each other, and establishing equivalent groups for purposes of comparison. Even though these techniques fit together, it is often sensible to adopt some of them without the others. For example, it is natural for evaluators to think that manipulating treatments is part of comparative, randomized experiment. Consumers Union, however, evaluates brands of tomato juice already on the market; what is manipulated in its comparative double-blind tests is the assignment of samples to tasters. Social research might, in principle, arrange for controlled assignment into treatments already in place.

The outmoded recommendation that the program evaluator prefer true experiments is hopelessly ambiguous. Which aspects of experimentation are wanted? What questions should a particular experiment address? Since any one evaluation takes up many questions, the whole of the inquiry will not be experimental in form, and only a few of the potentially relevant experiments will be mounted. To sum up the reasoning from earlier chapters, I shall take up each of the tactics separately. Whenever I speak of the advantages of a technique, the reader must bear in mind three qualifying addenda: "where ethical," "where consistent with the remainder of the design," and "to the extent practicable." These caveats, though obvious, are too important to be left unsaid.

Manipulation of Treatments. Consider, first, deliberate installation of a treatment for research purposes. The plan may try to standardize a treatment in all main particulars, but adaptable or nondirective treatments can equally well be set up (as in Harvard Project Physics and the Violence study). Naturalistic or qualitative methods are not incompatible with manipulated treatment. For a naturalist who is trying out methods of covering scars from strip mining, it would be appropriate to observe the recuperating ecology. To keep a naturalistic account of the social dynamics in a school system that is trying out a voucher plan would be equally appropriate (Cohen and Farrar, 1977).

Manipulation has distinct advantages and, of course, some disadvantages. The chief advantage is that deliberate intervention can produce specimens that would otherwise be unavailable or would occur too infrequently. In an exploratory search for a program worthy of development, a wide variety of treatment plans can be installed in different sites. Manipulation helps to target a confirmatory inquiry because the investigator can fix the experimental variable. (When the intent is not realized uniformly, that is a finding, not a fault.) The chief drawback of manipulation is that the evaluator or sponsoring agency may be unable to install a treatment truly relevant to policy. A pilot-scale operation may not face the difficulties of community-wide or nationwide operation. The psychology of staff and clients in a short-run trial may differ from that of participants in an established program. Sometimes treatments already in place are closer to the treatment for which evaluation is wanted than a fresh installation would be.

Targeted Research. Next, consider targeting. Under what circumstances does it make sense to concentrate evaluation resources and examine just one or a few specified treatments? Targeted research concentrates resources to confirm the answer to a supposedly dominant question.

Finding a question of paramount importance is a major intellectual achievement. An investigator doing basic research in the natural sciences spends most of his time and effort accumulating varied experience and reflecting on it. Many cultures of a microorganism are started, observed, and washed down the drain before the investigator knows what his main question is and what conditions to set up for the definitive study. Inquiries about social programs do not ripen this way. The decade-long series of income maintenance studies is perhaps unique. In most problem areas, the program proposals change from one year to the next. Rarely does a particular line of action appear so promising that evaluators are encouraged to drill deeper and deeper in the same spot.

This book has reviewed many experiments in which contrasts were specified and systematic assignment was used to eliminate bias. Considered together, the contributions were not those that textbooks tell us to expect from experiments. Nearly all the studies were well done, and most received favorable attention in their time. I chose them as illustrations of what can be expected from strong designs, but no single comment I shall make applies with equal force to all the examples. For specific comments below, I identify chief exemplars by letters, as follows: (a) the Nutrition study (INCAP), (b) the Physics study, (c) teaching of subtraction, (d) teacher expectancy ("Pygmalion"), (e) the Violence study, (f) the income maintenance experiment, (g) financial aid to released prisoners (TARP), and (h) the bail bond experiment.

Some of the studies had formative uses and suggested modified treatment plans (a, c); others had "conceptual" uses, bringing to consciousness previously underrated influences (b, c, f). A few remained strictly summative (d, h), but a measure of effect size for the planned contrast was rarely their main contribution. Attention turned to comparisons and relationships that were not controlled.

Movement away from the ostensible target took many forms. Self-selection (including selection of treatment variant and selective dropout), along with chance error, frustrated the intent to hold constant everything but the planned contrast (a, b, d, g). The statistical analysis replaced the experimental/control contrast with a continuous "independent" variable, one in which the manipulation was augmented or diluted by self-dosage (a, g). When manipulated features were overlooked in the treatment description, readers misperceived what the experiment was about (h). The nature of the control treatment varied over sites; this was lost from view in one study (b). Effects associated with the treatment contrast varied over subgroups; some of these variations were identified as systematic (a, c).

In many investigations the effect depended on factors associated with the site—with the local labor market or the school curriculum, for instance (c, f). Each site was then a distinct unit, and the number of sites was rarely large enough for statistical power. One of the experiments, repeated in two sites, showed a definite positive effect in one and a definite negative effect in the other. Selective reporting conveyed the impression of a positive result (d). In another experiment the planned contrast showed "no effect." Instead of taking that for an answer, the investigator defended a treatment modification likely to stimulate the desired responses without the interfering responses that the experimental treatment had generated (g).

It appears that field experiments are valuable not because they settle pointed summative questions but because, like other acute observations, they turn up thought-provoking relationships. When fully interpreted, the illustrative studies functioned in accord with Popper's (1959) recommendation: "[The] main task of social science . . . is to trace the unintended repercussions of intentional human actions" (p. 281; italics removed). Its "practical role is the modest one of helping us to understand even the more remote consequences of possible actions; in other words, to choose our actions more wisely" (p. 283).

In the illustrative experiments, after-the-fact interpretations carried weight as much because they made qualitative good sense as because of the formal properties of the data (c, g). In the experiment with conflicting results (d), however, it was possible to make good sense of selected data that fitted a certain prejudice. That reminds us of familiar warnings against credulity—warnings that justify an effort toward scientific control. Since this bit of credulity was fed by a randomized experiment with objective measurement, we are also warned that unbiased design is no panacea for evaluations. The political world is not often in the market for the whole truth.

There is no reason to take a position for or against targeting of evaluations. Targeting is a matter of degree. Planners surely would not encourage an evaluation staff to observe program operations with no questions in mind and with no preliminary ideas about measurement or documentation. Nor would they instruct staff members to report what predefined procedures disclosed about prespecified questions but to say nothing about other facts and impressions they pick up. The planning process advocated in Chapter Seven spreads resources so that some questions are studied rather thoroughly, others are checked on systematically but less extensively, and still others are left to incidental observation. Raising priorities for some questions at the expense of others will remain as an option down to the very end of the fieldwork if resources are not committed prematurely.

Some concentrating of resources is advisable. One wants in particular to reduce uncertainty about the politically salient matters that will count most in making policy. But concentrating resources too heavily is inadvisable. A given situation is going to be too unstable and too little understood for anyone to know what will count most two years hence. Targeting does not preclude exploration, although it of course narrows the variety of observations. How much to narrow the investigation by the devices described in Chapter Eight is not a matter for a general recommendation. If I have preached too zealously on the virtues of studying diverse plans and realizations, that is because the previous literature has given undue prominence to confirmatory validation of prespecified, narrow hypotheses.

Control Groups. A design that looks into a single treatment takes general experience as a frame of reference for judging how satisfactory the program is. Many writers of a few years back seemed to be saying, "To appraise a program, only an experimental comparison with an untreated control group is adequate." But it is an error to speak of an all-or-nothing choice. Adjusting the size of a control group up or down, according to its cost and interest, gives that control whatever emphasis is compatible with competing claims on resources. Moreover, to prescribe that there be *a* control group is oversimple because many distinct control groups can be defined for any one program. Baseline or control treatments have specific characteristics. When the main treatment is followed by a welcome result, a number of explanations are possible. A control treatment is capable of indicating whether particular counterinterpretations are tenable. Such an investment properly has a claim on resources if those counterinterpretations are plausible and bear on policy.

A word on internal validity in Campbell's sense is appropriate here, although I shall not summarize most of Chapters Four and Five. In Campbell's rationale an experimental manipulation either made a difference or it did not. However, while an observed difference does imply causality if the design was sufficiently strong, even the strongest design supports only plausible reasoning and not proof. Moreover, the evaluator's hearers want to know, to the extent possible, *what* made the difference. That turns attention to external validity. Many controls said to strengthen internal validity actually bear on external validity instead, serving to weaken (or confirm) a specific substantive explanation. Whether a control group can guard against the most important counterinterpretation of a finding depends on the program under study and the current beliefs regarding it.

The burden of proof falls, I would say, on anyone proposing to invest substantial evaluation resources in a no-treatment group or a pseudotreatment group. The control group does check on effects of the economic cycle and similar ambient events during the trial period. Yet in the bail bond study, the control group was unnecessary, if not a source of misinterpretation. In the INCAP and TARP studies, it served mostly to increase the range of data; that is, it strengthened the correlational analysis of a partly manipulated variable.

The null treatment is almost never a blank dose. When a social intervention is being tested, the no-treatment group is experiencing a nondescript and changing mixture of social services of the same general kind. The most precise estimate of a treatment effect becomes a transient result, rendered obsolete by a change in the treatment plan or in the mix of nonexperimental services and in patronage of them. The norms that a control group provides may or may not add sufficiently to available knowledge about maturation (concurrent with an educational program) or spontaneous recovery (concurrent with medical treatment) to be worth its cost.

Any plausible counterhypothesis that could becloud in-

terpretation deserves the planner's attention, but sometimes
supplementary data can be used to check it out at modest
cost. A particularly good example is the British breathalyser
study mentioned in Chapter Seven. The mandatory test for
drivers suspected of drinking to excess was introduced nationwide in England, thus leaving no comparison group save
prior history. Ross (1973) obtained comparative evidence
from time series—on sales by pubs and on traffic accidents
and arrests—to estimate the immediate impact of the breathalyser and to show that it became less effective after a few
months of use. (More recent events showed the treatment effect to be evanescent; see *Toward Reform,* p. 294.) In the
breathalyser study, the option of a control group was not
available. The evaluation planner who does have the choice
may judge that he can defend a frame of reference without a
formal control group.

   Comparing Alternative Treatments. A second kind of comparison has a much more persuasive claim on resources.
Comparing two approaches purporting to resolve the same
problem is likely to be of great interest when opinion about
them is divided. The analyst retains the same opportunity to
study either competitor in its own terms that he would have if
it were the sole treatment investigated. Doubling the number
of units studied for the sake of comparison, however, cuts
into the resources available for more intensive or longer-last-
ing study of one treatment (and for inquiries into other questions). A comparative investigation can be big or little. It can
be part of a pilot study. It can be a comprehensive appraisal
of a supposedly finished plan, or it can check on a small but
important element of a plan. It can provide the outer shell of
a design, or it can be an adjunct to developmental work on a
single main treatment (Tharp and Gallimore, 1979). Trials of
variants have obvious utility; how much formal comparison
adds to a study can be weighed only in the specific instance.

   Control of Assignment. Equivalent treatment groups simplify presentation of a comparison, but any plan that assigns
cases randomly to treatments has the same freedom from
bias. Reasons of cost or presumed benefit often justify creating nonequivalent treatment groups by means of uneven

sampling fractions. Defensible adjustments estimate what equivalent groups would have shown. The assumptions become debatable, however, if the two sets of cases do not spread over the same range.

Strong control over assignment is most advantageous when four severe conditions are met:

1. The treatments have been refined to the point where further major revision is unlikely to be necessary. If formal testing comes before either treatment has stabilized, it remains easy to argue that the ranking of treatments would be reversed if faults in the losing treatment— faults uncovered during the trial—were corrected.
2. There is a defined population to which the winning treatment is to be applied. The set of units being assigned is systematically representative—in background characteristics and in collective form—of that population. Otherwise, the effect observed may be irrelevant. Volunteers willing to accept random assignment may be unlike the target population. Vaccinating scattered persons for a contagious disease does not test a community-wide vaccination effort.
3. The survivors who actually provide data for the comparison are not systematically different from the units on whom data are lacking. Selective dropout damages comparability.
4. It is appropriate to judge both treatments on the same outcome measures. When treatment groups receive different lessons or services of different kinds, comprehensive comparison of outcomes is next to impossible. Comparison limited to some common denominator cheats both treatments of credit earned.

The baseball commentator Joe Garagiola was once heard to say, "Good pitching always beats good hitting, and vice versa." Perhaps the best advice to evaluators runs along similar lines: Comparability of groups adds more to validity than does representativeness, and vice versa.

Near the end of Chapter Six, I summed up a number

of distressing logical difficulties in interpreting comparisons. The many critical articles on adjusting for nonequivalence have, astonishingly, been too mild in their criticisms. Taken together, the difficulties have forced technical specialists to become suspicious of all formal extrapolations in program evaluation (and perhaps in social science generally; see Cronbach, 1982). Random assignment reduces some uncertainty, but estimates of outcomes in a population not strictly sampled remain suspect. Representative sampling of those who naturally enter a treatment provides a way to escape the difficulties of extrapolation, but that approach ordinarily makes treatment groups noncomparable. Moreover, the natural mix can change, pressing policy makers back to the hazards of extrapolation. I draw two main implications from the discouraging news. First, I echo the old, if much ignored, advice to analyze data in several ways, with alternative sets of assumptions. Second, I recommend the tracing of processes that intervene between the manipulation and the measurement of main dependent variables as a way to give body to interpretations.

Gaining Credibility

Reproducibility. Chapter Eight was devoted to devices that would enable the next investigator to confirm what the first reports. Some of the controls have the effect of narrowing the inquiry; nothing more need be said about trade-offs between breadth of inquiry and firmness of answers. It is worth repeating, however, that reproducibility is not exclusively an ideal of the quantitative method (Denzin, 1971). A narrative, naturalistic study has a greater or lesser degree of reproducibility. The example of Hearnshaw's biography of Burt (Chapter Four) shows how qualitative studies can claim reproducibility.

Many of the devices for furthering reproducibility serve to make clear what the original investigator did. These controls are welcome because no one can make proper inferences from a factual report without knowing just what the

facts are. Although evaluation studies are unlikely to be replicated, replicability is still important. Uncertainty is reduced
insofar as the report of the design persuades a critic that the
finding would reappear if replication were attempted (relevant aspects of the world remaining stable). It is the facts
about *utoS*—about the sample and the sites within it—for
which reproducibility is critical; reproducibility of internal *inferences* may or may not matter greatly to the evaluator's audiences.

Diversity. Policy makers will attempt to judge which sites
can make profitable use of a treatment, will consider recruiting clients from a group unlike the original group, and will
worry about outcomes that the original study did not assess
directly. Moreover, they will consider treatments that depart
from what was field tested. The evaluation is one of the bases
on which judgments about new departures are reached, and
Chapter Nine reviewed tactics that allow the evaluation to
contribute more in divergent discussions.

The typical schematic description of a design suggests
that evaluation consists of before-and-after measurement on
an unanalyzed unitary treatment. But the final average for a
treatment group aggregates the end states in a great number
of case histories (of sites and of individuals within sites). The
gross outcome is meaningful only if the treatments and the
conditions are essentially fixed. Otherwise, to learn what the
field trial had to teach, the evaluator must drop back to a
finer analysis of events and treatment groups, both of which
should be disaggregated.

The planner of the evaluation is advised to try to anticipate both the events that will impinge on treated units and
the successive changes that will be seen in the units when all
goes well. He is also advised to anticipate what may go wrong
and how both anticipated and unanticipated deviations can
be detected. All this suggests what information, if collected, is
likely to have explanatory value and to bear on plans for future programs. When the facts are in, the evaluator should be
able to spell out what went on in program sites and to do this
not abstractly but by telling a story about the moves of the

players or about the twists of fate on which events turned—a story that commonsensical listeners will readily comprehend. Obtaining diverse data at many points along the time scale (and capitalizing on diversity in the analysis) is the principal means to this end.

Realization of a social program comes about through many successive actions in many places. Local control is so powerful in most systems that deliver services, and guidelines leave so many gaps for judgment or habit to fill in, that diversity is to be expected. Sites will differ in patterning of outcomes as well as in degree of success. Clients will receive different amounts and kinds of service, even in a controlled experiment. And those who seem to have been treated similarly by agencies will respond differently.

Qualitative Approaches. Structured data on intermediate variables and naturalistic recording of events as they unfold are both valuable. To profit from structured methods, the investigator needs good hunches about what intermediate variables are pertinent. Less structured methods have the advantage when program events and client responses are hard to foresee, as is perhaps always the case in evaluation. Of course, the benefits from interviews and qualitative observation are offset by well-known difficulties: cost, inconsistency among observers and interviewers, and the indigestibility of masses of transcript or field memoranda. Integrating naturalistic techniques with the remainder of the plan means holding them to a cost-effective scale, hence reserving them for what they can do best.

To ask whether a study should be quantitative and structured or qualitative and naturalistic is misguided; and the advice to set up the two kinds of inquiry independently, side by side, is too rigid to be a general policy. Observers and interviewers should not spend the same amount of time in the field during each month of the trial, should not cover all sites uniformly, and should not pursue the same questions on every visit. As with measurement efforts, procedures that lead to qualitative reports should be distributed in accord with the uncertainties salient at a given time. These reports should be stimulated by quantitative findings, and they should suggest points that a structured inquiry can pin down.

Learning About Design

No one learns to plan and conduct evaluations from a book. The way to learn is to try and try again, part of the time under circumstances where a more experienced practitioner can comment on the plans and suggestions that emerge from early data. Not many would-be evaluators have that opportunity. Some learn the business from the bottom up by signing on with a contract research operation; in a large firm, however, junior members are not likely to participate in much of the planning or to gain experience with a variety of styles. Some learn the business by taking principal responsibility for evaluation in a school system or other agency; they gain a wondrous range of experience but rarely have seasoned colleagues at hand to advise them. Even so, discouragement is not in order. On the one hand, no one ever learns all there is to know about evaluating; each experience teaches some new lesson. And, on the other hand, the intelligent beginner can make a welcome contribution. Handed an evaluation task for which no one in the organization is particularly well qualified, the novice finds it easy to produce data that stimulate thought and open up possibilities. The evaluator is in many cases the only person free to roam nearly everywhere and talk to nearly everyone, and so he can form a picture of the situation available to no one else. Using that opportunity tactfully requires maturity rather than expertise. Experience and specialized knowledge are bound to help—not in eliminating difficulties but in supplying more and more tactics for getting around them.

In an attempt to provide on-campus training in evaluation for advanced graduate students, I operated a course at Stanford for more than a dozen years (on occasion, in association with Decker Walker, Jill Maling-Keepes, or Marcia Linn). Others are unlikely to conduct a course in just this manner, but a brief description of it may be suggestive both to teachers of evaluation and to neophytes. The course lasted one quarter and accommodated fifteen students (more when there were two instructors). The class discussed specimen evaluations and writings on evaluation; much of this book grew out of a syllabus for those sessions. The students—most of whom had worked in school systems, service agencies, or government bureaus—reported on experiences they had had. But everyone's main effort went into individual student projects.

Each student was expected to invent an evaluation task and work out a plan in five installments. Each installment was reviewed (within twenty-four hours when possible), and the instructor challenged something on nearly every page. Challenges took the form of suggesting a technical device, of raising an objection that someone disappointed in the evaluation findings would raise, or perhaps of requesting additional specification. The student was expected to respond to each such note—if only with a checkmark to say "Comment noted" or "Suggestion accepted." (But the student who was too acquiescent soon learned the unwisdom of that tactic.) Some installments went through three cycles of review; to keep the cumulative record intact, students were forbidden to retype the papers, and changes of pen color were used as a way of dating comments. Each page, then, bore vivid testimony to the theme of this book; namely, that myriad choices enter into a full evaluation plan and that the planner should be conscious of such choices and the reasons for each of them. The exchanges also evidenced that many decisions were a matter of personal choice, not of right or wrong.

A budget range for project proposals was set, the amount being fixed at what I judged one evaluator with modest experience could personally supervise. The amount included no costs of program operation. The standard budget (which changed from year to year with inflation) could be negotiated upward or downward. It typically provided for some professional staff or consultation, as well as for the evaluator's salary and direct costs of data collection and analysis. The budget was to cover about fifteen months (again, subject to negotiation); this usually allowed for a period of planning and instrument development, a run-through of the course of instruction or some months of service to clients (and sometimes for two or more trials on a staggered schedule), post-testing, and analysis. One further restriction was that the program had to obtain much of its budget from a sponsor interested in propagating the program in additional sites. This saved the evaluator from subservience to local program managers and defined at least part of his target audience.

The variety of the projects saved the instructors from boredom and provided an endless source of stimulating dilemmas for class discussion. In one term the mix might include these evaluations: a broadcast series to teach adults about personal finance, a program to teach up-country villagers in a Third World country about modern agriculture and community management, an American corporation's plan to prepare Japanese managers of its branches, a career-planning service associated with a methadone clinic, and a science museum for children—all this alongside more ordinary projects in the common school subjects, bilingual education, and compensatory education.

Although the programs were not spelled out in any detail, their character had to be defined and some concrete illustrations of activities given. Were the broadcasts on money matters to be all talk? Dramatic skits? At a level requiring a hand calculator for full benefit? Interpersonal connections had likewise to be defined; for example, would the evaluator provide feedback week by week to the producers of the broadcasts? The initial sketch took up such questions as these: Did the sponsor expect more summative or more formative information? Who would play a role in decisions subsequent to the evaluation? Would decision making be centralized or a matter for local option? What are the significant political tensions and organizational rivalries? This plot development helped everyone move away from artificial simplicities and, to a degree that surprised the students and often the instructors, had an important bearing on procedures in the evaluation. (How does an evaluator commis-

sioned by a ministry collect information on instruction in outlying villages? The roads from the capital are impassible
during the season when farmers have time for class meetings,
and the local elders are alert to any intrusion from the
capital.)

The time line became as much an armature of the plan
as the number of sites to be studied and the formal comparison (if any). Projects that initially were thought of as assessments of activities newly installed for tryout changed to tests
on a second-generation version once it was realized that a
brand-new program would be too much in flux to justify the
evaluation budget. An initial plan to hire an experienced
teacher as year-round observer collapsed in the final competi-
tion for budget, being replaced by a plan to engage an ex-
teacher for a certain number of carefully spaced days. Wherever possible, pilot tests of plans for measuring and observing
were built in. This often amounted to reserving one or two
classes or a subsample of community informants to be guinea
pigs, questioned or observed a month ahead of the schedule
for the other units. If questions had to be revised, data from
the pilot version could not be mingled with the rest; but this
was perhaps a small price to pay for raising the quality of the
main data.

With respect to the makeup of the staff, the projected
schedule of the program under study, the number of units to
be studied, the plans for selecting or assigning these units, the
number of waves of measurement or observation, and the
timing of other evaluation activities, a rough sketch was made
as soon as the content of the project was agreed on. The answers were revised week after week as it was recognized that
important topics were being neglected, that the plan called
for far more simultaneous activities than the staff could cope
with, and, above all, that the budget would not buy everything that the evaluator wanted. In the course of these revi-
sions, students came to appreciate the wisdom of letting early
data indicate which sites and variables required close attention and which could be treated superficially. There was no
way to simulate the experience of true sequential design, with

revision of plans on the basis of data, but plans did shift from the style of "what will be done" to "what will be decided late in March."

Page allotments for installments were set to produce about fifty pages overall. On many matters, such as interview questions, the student was to give a few specimens, not a full plan. (The specimens permitted a little coaching on technique, a little admonition on invasion of privacy, and the like.) Naturally, many projects ran over length, many fell behind schedule, and many were retrieved from disastrous sprawl only by last-minute amputation of one or more lines of effort. The last two pages were to be a self-critique: How good is the plan? How easy is it to evaluate in this field? The students' comments made it clear that the exercise rarely left them satisfied with their plans but that they had become highly conscious of complications they had not known to be part of the evaluator's life.

The important features of the exercise, I think, were its concreteness, its modest scale (which made it possible to fill in a comparatively complete plan), and its dialectical interaction. Although the dialogue burdened student and instructor, it made possible an astonishingly rapid growth in sophistication, especially in students' awareness of the alternatives that they would have to give up in order to pursue the lines of inquiry that they had settled on. I made too many comments, some of them too blunt or too sharp. The same activity spread over two quarters could have gone more smoothly, but it would have been difficult to maintain the same interest in a fantasy over the longer period.

I offer this account not because I expect readers to imitate an activity devised for unique circumstances at one university at one particular time. I have been telling a parable. Need I draw the moral? Developing an evaluation is an exercise of the dramatic imagination.

↳ References

Ahlgren, A., and Walberg, H. J. "Changing Attitudes Toward Science Among Adolescents." *Nature*, 1973, *245*, 187–190.

American Institutes for Research. *Evaluation of the Impact of ESEA Title VII Spanish/English Bilingual Education Program.* Palo Alto, Calif.: American Institutes for Research, 1977.

Anderson, S., and others. *Statistical Methods for Comparative Studies.* New York: Wiley, 1980.

Ares, C. E., Rankin, A., and Sturz, H. "The Manhattan Bail Project: An Interim Report on the Use of Pre-Trial Parole." *New York University Law Review*, 1963, *38*, 67–95.

Aronson, E., and Carlsmith, J. M. "Experimentation in Social Psychology." In G. Lindzey and E. Aronson (Eds.), *Handbook of Social Psychology.* Vol. 2. Reading, Mass.: Addison-Wesley, 1968.

Bakan, D. *On Method: Toward a Reconstruction of Psychological Investigation.* San Francisco: Jossey-Bass, 1967.

Baker, F. B. "Experimental Design Considerations Associated with Large-Scale Research Projects." In J. C. Stanley (Ed.), *Improving Experimental Design and Statistical Analysis.* Chicago: Rand McNally, 1967.

Barnow, B. S., and Cain, G. G. "A Reanalysis of the Effect of Head Start on Cognitive Development: Methodology and Empirical Findings." *Journal of Human Resources,* 1977, *12,* 177–197.

Barnow, B. S., Cain, G. G., and Goldberger, A. S. "Issues in the Analysis of Selection Bias." In E. W. Stromsdorfer and G. Farkas (Eds.), *Evaluation Studies Review Annual.* Vol. 5. Beverly Hills, Calif.: Sage, 1980.

Berk, R. A., and Rossi, P. H. "Doing Good or Worse: Evaluation Research Politically Re-Examined." *Social Problems,* 1976, *23,* 337–349.

Bernstein, I. N., and Freeman, H. E. *Academic and Entrepreneurial Research.* New York: Russell Sage Foundation, 1975.

Berryman, S. E., and Glennan, T. K., Jr. "An Improved Strategy for Evaluating Federal Programs in Education." In J. Pincus (Ed.), *Educational Evaluation in the Public Policy Setting.* (Report R-2502-RC.) Santa Monica, Calif.: Rand Corporation, 1980.

Block, J. *The Q-Sort Method in Personality Assessment and Psychiatric Research.* Springfield, Ill.: Thomas, 1960.

Boruch, R. F. "Coupling Randomized Experiments and Approximations to Experiments in Social Program Evaluation." *Sociological Methods and Research,* 1975, *4,* 31–53.

Boruch, R. F., and Cecil, J. S. *Assuring the Confidentiality of Social Research Data.* Philadelphia: University of Pennsylvania Press, 1979.

Boruch, R. F., and Cordray, D. S. "An Appraisal of Educational Program Evaluations: Federal, State, and Local Agencies." Unpublished report (ED 192466), Northwestern University, Evanston, Ill., 1980.

Boruch, R. F., and Gomez, H. "Measuring Impact: Power in Social Program Evaluation." In L. -E. Datta and R. Perloff (Eds.), *Improving Evaluations.* Beverly Hills, Calif.: Sage, 1979.

Boruch, R. F., Wortman, P. M., Cordray, D. S., and associates. *Reanalyzing Program Evaluation.* San Francisco: Jossey-Bass, 1981.

Bracht, G. H., and Glass, G. V. "The External Validity of Experiments." *American Education Research Journal,* 1968, *5,* 437–474.

Branscomb, L. M. "Science in the White House: A New Start." *Science,* 1977, *196,* 848–852.

Brownell, W. A., and Moser, H. E. "Meaningful Versus Mechanical Learning: A Study in Grade III Subtraction." *Duke University Research Studies in Education,* No. 8, 1949.

Brunswik, E. *Perception and the Representative Design of Experiments.* Berkeley: University of California Press, 1956.

Bryk, A. S. "Analyzing Data from Premeasure/Postmeasure Designs." In S. Anderson and others, *Statistical Methods for Comparative Studies.* New York: Wiley, 1980.

Bryk, A. S., Strenio, J. F., and Weisberg, H. "A Method for Estimating Effects When Individuals Are Growing." *Journal of Educational Statistics,* 1980, *5,* 5–34.

Campbell, D. T. "Factors Relevant to the Validity of Experiments in Social Settings." *Psychological Bulletin,* 1957, *54,* 297–312.

Campbell, D. T. "Methodological Suggestions from a Comparative Psychology of Knowledge Processes." *Inquiry,* 1959, *2,* 152–182.

Campbell, D. T. "Prospective: Artifact and Control." In R. Rosenthal and R. L. Rosnow (Eds.), *Artifact in Behavioral Research.* New York: Academic Press, 1969a.

Campbell, D. T. "Reforms as Experiments." *American Psychologist,* 1969b, *24,* 409–429.

Campbell, D. T. "Qualitative Knowing in Action Research." Occasional Paper, Stanford Evaluation Consortium, Stanford University, 1974.

Campbell, D. T. "Assessing the Impact of Planned Social Change." In G. M. Lyons (Ed.), *Social Research and Public Policies.* Hanover, N. H.: Public Affairs Center, Dartmouth College, 1975a.

Campbell, D. T. "Conflicts Between Biological and Social Evolution and Between Psychology and Moral Tradition." *American Psychologist,* 1975b, *30,* 1103–1126.

Campbell, D. T. "Degrees of Freedom and the Case Study." *Comparative Political Studies,* 1975c, *2,* 178–193.

Campbell, D. T. "The Social Scientist as Methodological Servant of the Experimenting Society." In S. S. Nagel (Ed.), *Policy Studies in the Social Sciences.* Lexington, Mass.: Lexington Books, 1975d.

Campbell, D. T., and Erlebacher, A. E. "How Regression Artifacts in Quasi-Experimental Evaluations Can Mistakenly Make Compensatory Education Look Harmful." In J. Hellmuth (Ed.), *The Disadvantaged Child.* Vol. 3. New York: Brunner/Mazel, 1970.

Campbell, D. T., and Fiske, D. W. "Convergent and Discriminant Validation by the Multitrait-Multimethod Matrix." *Psychological Bulletin,* 1959, *56,* 81–105.

Campbell, D. T., and Stanley, J. C. "Experimental and Quasi-Experimental Designs for Research on Teaching." In N. L. Gage (Ed.), *Handbook of Research on Teaching.* Chicago: Rand McNally, 1963.

Cazden, C. B. *Child Language and Education.* New York: Holt, Rinehart and Winston, 1972.

Clemens, S. L. *Life on the Mississippi.* New York: Harper & Row, 1901. (Originally published 1875.)

Cline, M. G., and others. *Education as Experimentation: Evaluation of the Follow Through Planned Variation Model.* (2 vols.) Cambridge, Mass.: Abt Books, 1974.

Cochran, W. G., and Rubin, D. B. "Controlling Bias in Observational Studies: A Review." *Sankhya-A,* 1973, *35,* 417–446.

Cohen, D. K., and Farrar, E. "Power to the Parents?—The Story of Education Vouchers." *The Public Interest,* 1977, No. 48, pp. 72–97.

Cohen, D. K., and Weiss, J. A. "Social Science and Social Policy: Schools and Race." *Educational Forum,* 1977, *41,* 393–413.

Cohen, J. *Statistical Power Analysis for the Behavioral Sciences.* (2nd ed.) New York: Academic Press, 1977.

Cole, M., Hood, L., and McDermott, R. *Ecological Niche-Pick-*

ing: Ecological Invalidity as an Axiom of Experimental Cognitive Psychology. New York: Laboratory of Comparative Human Cognition, Rockefeller University, 1979.

Coleman, J. S. *Policy Research in the Social Sciences.* Morristown, N.J.: General Learning Press, 1972.

Coleman, J. S. "Problems of Conceptualization and Measurement in Studying Policy Impacts." In K. M. Dolbeare (Ed.), *Public Policy Evaluation.* Beverly Hills, Calif.: Sage, 1975.

Coleman, J. S. "Policy, Research, and Political Theory." *University of Chicago Record,* 1980, *14* (2), 78–80.

Coleman, J. S., Hoffer, T., and Kilgore, S. "Public and Private Schools." Draft report, National Opinion Research Center, Chicago, 1981.

Coleman, J. S., and others. *Policy Issues and Research Design.* Chicago: National Opinion Research Center, 1979.

Comptroller General. *Assessing Social Program Impact Evaluations: A Checklist Approach.* Washington, D.C.: General Accounting Office, 1978.

Conner, R. F. "Selecting a Control Group: An Analysis of the Randomization Process in Twelve Social Reform Programs." *Evaluation Quarterly,* 1977, *1*, 195–244.

Cook, T. D. "'Sesame Street' and the Medical and Tailored Models of Summative Evaluation Research." In J. G. Abert and M. Kamrass (Eds.), *Social Experiments and Social Program Evaluation.* Cambridge, Mass.: Ballinger, 1974.

Cook, T. D. "An Evolutionary Perspective on a Dilemma in the Evaluation of Ongoing Social Programs." In M. B. Brewer and B. E. Collins (Eds.), *Scientific Inquiry and the Social Sciences: A Volume in Honor of Donald T. Campbell.* San Francisco: Jossey-Bass, 1981.

Cook, T. D., and Campbell, D. T. "The Design and Conduct of Quasi-Experiments and True Experiments in Field Settings." In M. D. Dunnette (Ed.), *Handbook of Industrial and Organizational Psychology.* Chicago: Rand McNally, 1976.

Cook, T. D., and Campbell, D. T. *Quasi-Experimentation: Design and Analysis Issues for Field Settings.* Chicago: Rand McNally, 1979.

Cook, T. D., and McAnany, E. G. "Recent United States Experiences in Evaluation Research with Implications for Latin America." In R. E. Klein and others (Eds.), *Evaluating the Impact of Nutrition and Health Programs.* New York: Plenum, 1979.

Cook, T. D., and others. *Sesame Street Revisited.* New York: Russell Sage Foundation, 1975.

Cook, T. D., and others. *An Evaluation Model for Assessing the Effects of Peace Corps Programs in Health and Agriculture.* Washington, D.C.: Practical Concepts Incorporated, 1977.

Coombs, C. H., Raiffa, H., and Thrall, R. M. "Some Views on Mathematical Models and Measurement Theory." *Psychological Review,* 1954, *61*, 132–144.

Cornfield, J., and Tukey, J. W. "Average Values of Mean Squares in Factorials." *Annals of Mathematical Statistics,* 1956, *27*, 907–949.

Cronbach, L. J. "A Validation Design for Qualitative Studies of Personality." *Journal of Consulting Psychology,* 1948, *12*, 365–374.

Cronbach, L. J. "Report on a Psychometric Mission to Clinicia." *Psychometrika,* 1954, *19*, 263–270.

Cronbach, L. J. "The Two Disciplines of Scientific Psychology." *American Psychologist,* 1957, *12*, 671–684.

Cronbach, L. J. "Evaluation for Course Improvement." In R. W. Heath (Ed.), *New Curricula.* New York: Harper & Row, 1963.

Cronbach, L. J. "Beyond the Two Disciplines of Scientific Psychology." *American Psychologist,* 1975a, *30*, 116–127.

Cronbach, L. J. "Five Decades of Public Controversy over Mental Testing." *American Psychologist,* 1975b, *30*, 1–13.

Cronbach, L. J. "Research on Classrooms and Schools: Formulation of Questions, Design, and Analysis." Occasional Paper, Stanford Evaluation Consortium, Stanford University, 1976.

Cronbach, L. J. "Designing Educational Evaluations." Occasional Paper, Stanford Evaluation Consortium, Stanford University, 1978.

Cronbach, L. J. "Hearnshaw on Burt." *Science,* 1979, *206*, 1392.

Cronbach, L. J. "Prudent Aspirations for Social Inquiry." In W. Kruskal (Ed.), *The State of the Social Sciences: Fifty Years at Chicago.* Chicago: University of Chicago Press, 1982.

Cronbach, L. J., and Furby, L. "How We Should Measure 'Change'—or Should We?" *Psychological Bulletin,* 1970, *74,* 66–80.

Cronbach, L. J., and Gleser, G. C. *Psychological Tests and Personnel Decisions.* Urbana: University of Illinois Press, 1957.

Cronbach, L. J., and Meehl, P. E. "Construct Validity in Psychological Tests." *Psychological Bulletin,* 1955, *52,* 281–302.

Cronbach, L. J., and Schaeffer, G. A. "Extensions of Personnel Selection Theory to Aspects of Minority Hiring." Report 81–A2, Institute for Educational Finance and Governance, Stanford University, 1981.

Cronbach, L. J., and Snow, R. E. *Aptitudes and Instructional Methods.* (2nd ed.) New York: Irvington, 1981.

Cronbach, L. J., and Webb, N. "Between-Class and Within-Class Effects in a Reported Aptitude × Treatment Interaction: Reanalysis of a Study by G. L. Anderson." *Journal of Educational Psychology,* 1975, *67,* 717–724.

Cronbach, L. J., and others. *The Dependability of Behavioral Measurements.* New York: Wiley, 1972.

Cronbach, L. J., and others. "Analysis of Covariance in Nonrandomized Experiments: Parameters Affecting Bias." Occasional Paper, Stanford Evaluation Consortium, Stanford University, 1977.

Cronbach, L. J., and others. *Toward Reform of Program Evaluation: Aims, Methods, and Institutional Arrangements.* San Francisco: Jossey-Bass, 1980.

Darlington, R. B. "Reduced-Variance Regression." *Psychological Bulletin,* 1978, *85,* 1238–1255.

Deming, W. E. "The Logic of Evaluation." In E. L. Struening and M. Guttentag (Eds.), *Handbook of Evaluation Research.* Vol. I. Beverly Hills, Calif.: Sage, 1975.

Denzin, N. K. "The Logic of Naturalistic Inquiry." *Social Forces,* 1971, *50,* 166–182.

Descartes, R. *Discourse on Method.* (J. Veitch, Trans.) Chicago: Open Court, 1910. (Originally published 1637.)

Donnison, D., and others. *Social Policy and Administration Revisited.* London: Allen & Unwin, 1975.

Edgington, E. S. *Randomization Tests.* New York: Marcel Dekker, 1980.

Edwards, A. L., and Cronbach, L. J. "Experimental Design for Research in Psychotherapy." *Journal of Clinical Psychology,* 1952, *8*, 51–59.

Eisner, E. "Thick Description." In D. Hamilton and others (Eds.), *Beyond the Numbers Game.* Berkeley, Calif.: McCutchan, 1978.

Elashoff, J. D., and Snow, R. E. (Eds.). *Pygmalion Reconsidered.* Worthington, Ohio: C. A. Jones, 1971.

Ennis, R. H. "On Causality." *Educational Researcher,* 1973, 6 (2), 4–11.

Epstein, S. "The Stability of Behavior. II: Implications for Psychological Research." *American Psychologist,* 1980, *35*, 790–806.

Fairweather, G. W. *Methods for Experimental Social Innovation.* New York: Wiley, 1967.

Fairweather, G. W. "Community Psychology for the 1980s and Beyond." *Evaluation and Program Planning,* 1980, *3*, 245–250.

Fairweather, G. W., and Tornatzky, L. G. *Experimental Methods for Social Policy Research.* Elmsford, N.Y.: Pergamon Press, 1977.

Festinger, L., Riecken, H. W., and Schachter, S. *When Prophecy Fails.* New York: Harper & Row, 1956.

Fetterman, D. M. "Blaming the Victim: The Problem of Evaluation Design and Federal Involvement, and Reinforcing World Views in Education." *Human Organization,* 1981, *40*, 67–77.

Feyerabend, P. *Science in a Free Society.* London: N L B, 1978.

Finney, D. J. "The Statistician and the Planning of Field Experiments." *Journal of the Royal Statistical Society,* 1956, *119*, 1–27.

Fisher, R. A. "Studies of Crop Variation. I: An Examination of the Yield of Dressed Grain from Broadbalk." *Journal of Agricultural Science,* 1920, *11*, pt. 2, 107–135.

Fisher, R. A. *The Design of Experiments.* (8th ed.) Edinburgh: Oliver and Boyd, 1966.

Fiske, D. W. *Strategies for Personality Research: The Observation Versus Interpretation of Behavior.* San Francisco: Jossey-Bass, 1978.

Freeman, H. E. "Conceptual Approaches to Assessing Impacts of Large-Scale Intervention Programs." *Proceedings, American Statistical Association* (Social Statistics Section), 1964, pp. 192–198.

Freeman, H. E., and others. "Relations Between Nutrition and Cognition in Rural Guatemala." *American Journal of Public Health,* 1977, *67,* 233–239.

Freeman, H. E., and others. "Nutrition and Cognitive Development Among Rural Guatemalan Children." *American Journal of Public Health,* 1980, *70,* 1277–1285.

Gadenne, V. *Die Gültigkeit psychologischer Untersuchungen* [*The Validity of Psychological Investigations*]. Stuttgart: Kohlhammer, 1976.

Gergen, K. J. "Social Psychology as History." *Journal of Personality and Social Psychology,* 1973, *26,* 309–320.

Gergen, K. J. "The Emerging Crisis in Life-Span Developmental Theory." In P. B. Baltes and O. G. Brim, Jr. (Eds.), *Life-Span Development and Behavior.* Vol. 3. New York: Academic Press, 1980.

Gilbert, J. P., Light, R. J., and Mosteller, F. "Assessing Social Innovations: An Empirical Base for Policy." In C. A. Bennett and A. A. Lumsdaine (Eds.), *Evaluation and Experiment.* New York: Academic Press, 1975.

Gilbert, J. P., and Mosteller, F. "The Urgent Need for Experimentation." In F. Mosteller and D. P. Moynihan (Eds.), *On Equality of Educational Opportunity.* New York: Random House, 1972.

Gilbert, J. P., Mosteller, F., and Tukey, J. "Steady Social Progress Requires Quantitative Evaluation to Be Searching." In C. C. Abt (Ed.), *The Evaluation of Social Programs.* Beverly Hills, Calif.: Sage, 1976.

Gillis, J., and Schneider, C. "The Historical Preconditions of

Representative Design." In K. Hammond (Ed.), *The Psychology of Egon Brunswik.* New York: Holt, Rinehart and Winston, 1966.

Glucksberg, S., Krauss, R. M., and Weisberg, R. "Referential Communication in Nursery School Children: Method and Some Preliminary Findings." *Journal of Experimental Child Psychology,* 1966, *3,* 333–342.

Goldberger, A. S. "Abnormal Selection Bias." Unpublished memorandum, Social Systems Research Institute, University of Wisconsin, Madison, 1980 (with addendum, June 1981).

Green, P. "The Obligations of American Social Scientists." *Annals of the American Academy of Political and Social Science,* 1971, *394,* 13–27.

Greenbaum, W., Garet, M. S., and Solomon, E. R. *Measuring Educational Achievement: A Study of the National Assessment.* New York: McGraw-Hill, 1977.

Guba, E. G., and Lincoln, Y. S. *Effective Evaluation: Improving the Usefulness of Evaluation Results Through Responsive and Naturalistic Approaches.* San Francisco: Jossey-Bass, 1981.

Hamilton, D., and others (Eds.). *Beyond the Numbers Game.* Berkeley, Calif.: McCutchan, 1978.

Hausman, J. A., and Wise, D. A. "The Evaluation of Results from Truncated Samples: The New Jersey Income Maintenance Experiment." *Annals of Economic and Social Measurement,* 1976, *5,* 421–445.

Hearnshaw, L. S. *Cyril Burt, Psychologist.* Ithaca, N.Y.: Cornell University Press, 1979.

Heckman, J. J. "Sample Selection Bias as a Specification Error." *Econometrica,* 1979, *47,* 153–161.

Hollister, R. G. "Comments." In R. E. Klein and others (Eds.), *Evaluating the Impact of Nutrition and Health Programs.* New York: Plenum, 1979.

House, E. R. *Evaluating with Validity.* Beverly Hills, Calif.: Sage, 1980.

House, E. R., and Mathison, S. "Review of *Toward Reform of Program Evaluation.*" *Evaluation News,* 1981, *2,* 314–320.

House, E. R., and others. "No Simple Answer: Critique of the 'Follow Through' Evaluation." *Harvard Educational Review,* 1978, *48*, 128–160.

Huitema, B. E. *The Analysis of Covariance and Alternatives.* New York: Wiley, 1980.

Hunt, J. McV. *Intelligence and Experience.* New York: Ronald Press, 1961.

Irle, M. "Is Aircraft Noise Harming People?" In M. Deutsch and H. A. Hornstein (Eds.), *Applying Social Psychology.* Hillsdale, N.J.: Erlbaum, 1975.

Jensen, A. R. "How Much Can We Boost IQ and Academic Achievement?" *Harvard Educational Review,* 1969, *39*, 1–123.

Jones, M. B., and Fennell, R. S., III. "Runway Performance in Two Strains of Rats." *Quarterly Journal of the Florida Academy of Sciences,* 1965, *28*, 289–296.

Jöreskog, K. G., and Sörbom, D. *Advances in Factor Analysis and Structural Equation Models.* Cambridge, Mass.: Abt Books, 1979.

Jouvenel, B. de. *The Art of Conjecture.* New York: Basic Books, 1967.

Kaplan, A. "Noncausal Explanation." In D. Lerner (Ed.), *Cause and Effect.* New York: Free Press, 1965.

Kaufman, H. *Are Government Organizations Immortal?* Washington, D.C.: Brookings Institution, 1976.

Keeney, R. L., and Raiffa, H. *Decisions with Multiple Objectives: Preferences and Value Trade-Offs.* New York: Wiley, 1976.

Kendall, M. G. "Hiawatha Designs an Experiment." *American Statistician,* 1959, *13* (5), 23–24.

Kish, L. "Representation, Randomization, and Control." In H. M. Blalock and others (Eds.), *Quantitative Methodology.* New York: Academic Press, 1975.

Klein, R. E. "Malnutrition and Human Behavior: A Backward Glance at an Ongoing Longitudinal Study." In D. A. Levitsky (Ed.), *Malnutrition, Environment, and Behavior.* Ithaca, N.Y.: Cornell University Press, 1979.

Klein, R. E., and others. "Effects of Maternal Nutrition on Fetal Growth and Infant Development." *PAHO Bulletin,* 1976, *10*, 301–316.

Klein, R. E., and others. "Malnutrition and Mental Development in Rural Guatemala." In N. Warren (Ed.), *Advances in Cross-Cultural Psychology.* New York: Academic Press, 1977.

Kruglanski, A. W. "Context, Meaning, and the Validity of Results in Psychological Research." *British Journal of Psychology,* 1975, *66,* 373–382.

Kruglanski, A. W., and Kroy, M. "Outcome Validity in Experimental Research: A Reconceptualization." *Representative Research in Social Psychology,* 1976, *7,* 166–176.

Kruskal, W., and Mosteller, F. "Representative Sampling." *International Statistical Review,* 1979, *47,* 13–24, 111–128.

Labov, W. "The Logic of Non-Standard English." In F. Williams (Ed.), *Language and Poverty.* Chicago: Markham, 1970.

Lakatos, I., and Musgrave, A. (Eds.). *Criticism and the Growth of Knowledge.* Cambridge, England: Cambridge University Press, 1970.

Lana, R. E. "Pretest Sensitization." In R. Rosenthal and R. L. Rosnow (Eds.), *Artifact in Behavioral Research.* New York: Academic Press, 1969.

Lawley, D. N. "A Note on Karl Pearson's Selection Formulae." *Proceedings of the Royal Society of Edinburgh,* 1943, sec. A (Mathematics and Physics), *62* (I), 28–30.

Lee, B. G. "Mission Operations Strategy for Viking." *Science,* 1976, *194,* 59–62.

Light, R. J., and Smith, P. V. "Choosing a Future: Strategies for Designing and Evaluating New Programs." *Harvard Educational Review,* 1970, *40,* 1–28.

Lindblom, C. E., and Cohen, D. K. *Usable Knowledge,* New Haven, Conn.: Yale University Press, 1979.

Lindquist, E. F. *Design and Analysis of Experiments in Psychology and Education.* Boston: Houghton Mifflin, 1953.

Lord, F. M. "A Paradox in the Interpretation of Group Comparisons." *Psychological Bulletin,* 1967, *68,* 304–305.

Lord, F. M. *Applications of Item Response Theory to Practical Testing Problems.* Hillsdale, N.J.: Erlbaum, 1980.

Lord, F. M., and Novick, M. R. *Statistical Theories of Mental Test Scores.* Reading, Mass.: Addison-Wesley, 1968.

Lykken, D. T. "Statistical Significance in Psychological Research." *Psychological Bulletin,* 1968, *70,* 151–159.

McCain, L. J., and McCleary, R. "The Statistical Analysis of the Simple Interrupted Time-Series Quasi-Experiment." In T. D. Cook and D. T. Campbell (Eds.), *Quasi-Experimentation: Design and Analysis Issue for Field Settings.* Chicago: Rand McNally, 1979.

McCord, J. "A Thirty-Year Follow-Up of Treatment Effects." *American Psychologist,* 1978, *33,* 284–291.

MacDonald, B. "Evaluation and the Control of Education." In D. Tawney (Ed.), *Curriculum Evaluation Today: Trends and Implications.* London: Macmillan, 1976.

MacKenzie, B. D. *Behaviorism and the Limits of Scientific Method.* Atlantic Highlands, N. J.: Humanities Press, 1977.

Mackie, J. L. "Causes and Conditions." *American Philosophical Quarterly,* 1965, *2,* 245–264.

Mackie, J. L. *The Cement of the Universe: A Study of Causation.* Oxford, England: Clarendon Press, 1974.

McLaughlin, M. W. "Evaluation and Alchemy." In J. Pincus (Ed.), *Educational Evaluation in the Public Policy Setting.* (Report R-2502-RC.) Santa Monica, Calif.: Rand Corporation, 1980.

Manis, M. "Comment on Gergen's 'Social Psychology as History.'" *Personality and Social Psychology Bulletin,* 1975, *1,* 450–455.

Meehl, P. E. "Nuisance Variables and the *Ex Post Facto* Design." In M. Radner and S. Winokur (Eds.), *Minnesota Studies in the Philosophy of Science.* Vol. 4. Minneapolis: University of Minnesota Press, 1970.

Meehl, P. E. "High School Yearbooks: A Reply to Schwartz." *Journal of Abnormal Psychology,* 1971, *77,* 143–148.

Meehl, P. E. "Specific Etiology and Other Forms of Strong Influence: Some Quantitative Meanings." *Journal of Medicine and Philosophy,* 1977, *2,* 33–53.

Mill, J. S. *A System of Logic.* (8th ed.) London: Longmans, Green, 1872.

Mosteller, F., and Tukey, J. W. *Data Analysis and Regression.* Reading, Mass.: Addison-Wesley, 1977.

Moynihan, D. P. *The Negro Family: The Case for National Action.* Washington, D.C.: U.S. Department of Labor, 1965.

Moynihan, D. P. *Maximum Feasible Misunderstanding.* New York: Free Press, 1969.

Nesselroade, J. R., and Baltes, P. B. (Eds.). *Longitudinal Research in the Study of Behavior and Development.* New York: Academic Press, 1979.

Olson, R. J. "A Least Squares Correction for Selectivity Bias." *Econometrica,* 1980, *48*, 1815–1820.

Padover, S. K. (Ed.). *A Jefferson Profile as Revealed in His Letters.* New York: John Day, 1956.

Parlett, M., and Hamilton, D. "Evaluation and Illumination: A New Approach to the Study of Innovatory Programmes." In D. Hamilton and others (Eds.), *Beyond the Numbers Game.* Berkeley, Calif.: McCutchan, 1978.

Pearson, K. "On the Influence of Natural Selection on the Variability and Correlation of Organs." *Philosophical Transactions of the Royal Society,* 1903, sec. A, *200,* 1–66.

Perelman, C., and Olbrechts-Tyteca, L. *The New Rhetoric: A Treatise on Argumentation.* Notre Dame, Ind.: University of Notre Dame Press, 1969.

Pillemer, D. B., and Light, R. J. "Synthesizing Outcomes: How to Use Research Evidence from Many Studies." *Harvard Educational Review,* 1980, *50*, 176–195.

Popper, K. R. "Prediction and Prophecy in the Social Sciences." In P. Gardiner (Ed.), *Theories of History.* New York: Free Press, 1959.

Powers, E., and Witmer, H. *An Experiment in the Prevention of Delinquency.* New York: Columbia University Press, 1951.

Raizen, S., and Rossi, P. H. *Program Evaluation in Education: When? How? To What Ends?* Washington, D.C.: National Academy Press, 1981.

Reichardt, C. S. "The Statistical Analysis of Data from Nonequivalent Group Designs." In T. D. Cook and D. T. Campbell (Eds.), *Quasi-Experimentation: Design and Analysis Issues for Field Settings.* Chicago: Rand McNally, 1979.

Reichardt, C. S., and Cook, T. D. "Beyond Qualitative Versus Quantitative Methods." In T. D. Cook and C. S. Reichardt (Eds.), *Qualitative and Quantitative Methods in Evaluation Research.* Beverly Hills, Calif.: Sage, 1979.

Rein, M. *Social Science and Public Policy.* New York: Penguin Books, 1976.

Riecken, H. W. "Social Experimentation." In C. C. Abt (Ed.), *The Evaluation of Social Programs.* Beverly Hills, Calif.: Sage, 1976.

Riecken, H. W. "Practice and Problems of Evaluation: A Conference Synthesis." In R. E. Klein and others (Eds.), *Evaluating the Impact of Nutrition and Health Programs.* New York: Plenum, 1979.

Riecken, H. W., and Boruch, R. F. (Eds.), *Social Experimentation,* New York: Academic Press, 1974.

Rivlin, A. M. *Systematic Thinking for Social Action.* Washington, D.C.: Brookings Institution, 1971.

Rivlin, A. M. "Allocating Resources for Policy Research: How Can Experiments Be More Useful?" *American Economic Review,* 1974, *64*, 346–354.

Roberts, K. H., and Burstein, L. (Eds.). *New Directions for Methodology of Social and Behavioral Science: Issues in Aggregation,* no. 6. San Francisco: Jossey-Bass, 1980.

Rosenthal, R., and Jacobson, L. *Pygmalion in the Classroom.* New York: Holt, Rinehart and Winston, 1968.

Ross, H. L. "Law, Science, and Accidents: The British Road Safety Act of 1967." *Journal of Legal Studies,* 1973, *2*, 1–75.

Rossi, P. H. "Issues in the Evaluation of Human Services Delivery." *Evaluation Quarterly,* 1978, *2*, 573–599.

Rossi, P. H., Berk, R. A., and Lenihan, K. J. *Money, Work, and Crime.* New York: Academic Press, 1980.

Rossi, P. H., Freeman, H. E., and Wright, S. R. *Evaluation: A Systematic Approach.* Beverly Hills, Calif.: Sage, 1979.

Rossi, P. H., and Lyall, K. C. *Reforming Public Welfare: A Critique of the Negative Income Tax Experiment.* New York: Russell Sage Foundation, 1976.

Rothkopf, E. "The Sound of One Hand Plowing." *Contemporary Psychology,* 1978, *23*, 707–708.

Rubin, D. B. "Assignment to Treatment Group on the Basis

of a Covariate." *Journal of Educational Statistics,* 1977, *2*, 1–26.

Runkel, P. J., and McGrath, J. E. *Research on Human Behavior: A Systematic Guide to Method.* New York: Holt, Rinehart and Winston, 1972.

Sainsbury, P. "Comprehensive Approach to Evaluation and Community Research." In J. Zusman and C. Wurster (Eds.), *Program Evaluation: Alcohol, Drug Abuse, and Mental Health Service Programs.* Lexington, Mass.: Lexington Books, 1975.

Saxe, L., and Fine, M. "Expanding Our View of Control Groups in Evaluations." In L. -E. Datta and R. Perloff, (Eds.), *Improving Evaluations.* Beverly Hills, Calif.: Sage, 1979.

Schmidt, F. L., Gast-Rosenberg, I., and Hunter, J. "Validity Generalization Results for Computer Programmers." *Journal of Applied Psychology,* 1980, *65*, 643–661.

Schultze, C. *The Politics and Economics of Public Spending.* Washington, D.C.: Brookings Institution, 1968.

Scriven, M. "Truisms as the Grounds for Historical Explanation." In P. Gardiner (Ed.), *Theories of History.* New York: Free Press, 1959.

Scriven, M. "The Methodology of Evaluation." In R. E. Stake and others (Eds.), *Perspectives on Curriculum Evaluation.* AERA Monograph Series on Curriculum Evaluation, No. 1. Chicago: Rand McNally, 1967.

Scriven, M. "Prose and Cons About Goal-Free Evaluation." *Evaluation Comment,* 1972, *3*, 1–4.

Shannon, C. E., and Weaver, W. *The Mathematical Theory of Communication.* Urbana: University of Illinois Press, 1949.

Simon, H. A. *The New Science of Management Decision.* New York: Harper & Row, 1960.

Smith, M. D., Schagrin, M. L., and Poorman, E. L. "The Multimedia System of Harvard Project Physics." *School Science and Mathematics,* 1968, *68*, 95–102.

Snow, R. E. "Representative and Quasi-Representative Designs for Research on Teaching." *Review of Educational Research,* 1974, *44*, 625–626.

Social Action Research Center. *The School Crime Intervention*

Component of the Teacher Corps Youth Advocacy Program Evaluation. San Rafael, Calif.: Social Action Research Center, 1979a.

Social Action Research Center. *The School Team Approach: Phase I Evaluation.* San Rafael, Calif.: Social Action Research Center, 1979b.

Social Action Research Center. *Schools Initiative Evaluation: Technical Report.* San Rafael, Calif.: Social Action Research Center, 1980.

Spiker, C. C. "Behaviorism, Cognitive Psychology, and the Active Organism." In N. Datan and H. W. Reese (Eds.), *Life-Span Developmental Psychology: Dialectical Perspectives on Experimental Research.* New York: Academic Press, 1977.

Stake, R. E. (Ed.). *Evaluating the Arts in Education: A Responsive Approach.* Columbus, Ohio: Merrill, 1975.

Stake, R. E. "Responsive Evaluation." In D. Hamilton and others (Eds.), *Beyond the Numbers Game.* Berkeley, Calif.: McCutchan, 1978.

Stanley, J. C. "Controlled Field Experiments as a Model for Evaluation." In P. H. Rossi and W. Williams (Eds.), *Evaluating Social Programs.* New York: Seminar Press, 1972.

Stebbins, L. B., and others. *Education as Experimentation: A Planned Variation Model.* Vol. 4–A. Cambridge, Mass.: Abt Books, 1977.

Stenhouse, L. "Some Limitations of the Use of Objectives." In D. Hamilton and others (Eds.), *Beyond the Numbers Game.* Berkeley, Calif.: McCutchan, 1978.

Sturz, H. "Experiments in the Criminal Justice System." *Legal Aid Briefcase,* February 1967, pp. 1–5.

Taylor, A. J. P. *English History, 1914–1945.* Oxford, England: Oxford University Press, 1965.

Tharp, R. G., and Gallimore, R. "The Ecology of Program Research and Evaluation: A Model of Evaluation Succession." In L. B. Sechrest and others (Eds.), *Evaluation Studies Review Annual.* Vol. 4. (Beverly Hills, Calif.: Sage, 1979).

Thompson, M. *Evaluation for Decisions in Social Programs.* Lexington, Mass.: Lexington Books, 1975.

Timpane, P. M. "Educational Experimentation in National Social Policy." *Harvard Educational Review,* 1970, *40,* 547–566.

Toward Reform. See Cronbach and others, 1980.

Travers, J., and Light, R. L. *Learning from Experience: Evaluating Early Childhood Demonstration Programs.* Washington, D. C.: National Academy Press, 1982.

Tukey, J. W. "Conclusions vs. Decisions." *Technometrics,* 1960, *2,* 423–433.

Tukey, J. W. *Exploratory Data Analysis.* Reading, Mass.: Addison-Wesley, 1977a.

Tukey, J. W. "Some Thoughts on Clinical Trials, Especially Problems of Mutiplicity." *Science,* 1977b, *198,* 679–684.

Tyler, R. W. *Basic Principles of Curriculum and Instruction.* Chicago: University of Chicago Press, 1950.

Walberg, H. J. "A Model for Research on Instruction." *School Review,* 1970, *78,* 185–200.

Walberg, H. J. "Psychology of Learning Environments." In L. S. Shulman (Ed.), *Review of Research in Education.* Vol. 4. Itasca, Ill.: Peacock, 1977.

Weiss, C. H. *Evaluation Research.* Englewood Cliffs, N.J.: Prentice-Hall, 1972.

Weiss, C. H. (Ed.). *Using Social Research in Public Policy Making.* Lexington, Mass.: Lexington Books, 1977.

Weiss, C. H., and Bucuvalas, M. J. "The Challenge of Social Research to Decision Making." In C. H. Weiss (Ed.), *Using Social Research in Public Policy Making.* Lexington, Mass.; Lexington Books, 1977.

Welch, W. W. "A Review of the Research and Development of Harvard Project Physics." Columbus, Ohio: ERIC Information Analysis Center for Science Education, 1971.

Welch, W. W., and Bridgham, R. G. "Physics Achievement Gains as a Function of Teaching Duration." *School Science and Mathematics,* 1968, *68,* 449–454.

Welch, W. W., and Walberg, H. J. "A National Experiment in Curriculum Evaluation." *American Educational Research Journal,* 1972, *9,* 373–383.

Welch, W., Walberg, H. J., and Watson, F. G. "Curriculum

Evaluation: Strategy, Implementation and Results." Unpublished manuscript, Harvard Graduate School of Education, Cambridge, Mass., 1970.

Whinery, L. H., and others. *Predictive Sentencing: An Empirical Evaluation*. Lexington, Mass.: Heath, 1976.

White, S. H. "Social Proof Structures: The Dialectic of Method and Theory in the Work of Psychology." In N. Datan and H. W. Reese (Eds.), *Life-Span Developmental Psychology: Dialectical Perspectives on Experimental Research*. New York: Academic Press, 1977.

Wholey, J. S. *Zero-Base Budgeting and Program Evaluation*. Lexington, Mass.: Lexington Books, 1978.

Wholey, J. S. *Evaluation: Promise and Performance*. Washington, D.C.: Urban Institute, 1979.

Wholey, J. S., and others. *Federal Evaluation Policy*. Washington, D.C.: Urban Institute, 1970.

Wienk, R. E., and others. *Measuring Racial Discrimination in American Housing Markets: The Housing Practices Survey*. Washington, D.C.: U.S. Department of Housing and Urban Development, 1979.

Wilensky, H. *Organizational Intelligence: Knowledge and Policy in Government and Industry*. New York: Basic Books, 1967.

Wiles, P. "Crisis Prediction." *Annals of the American Academy of Political and Social Science*, 1971, *393*, 32–39.

Winch, R. F., and Campbell, D. T. "Proof? No. Evidence? Yes. The Significance of Tests of Significance." *American Sociologist*, 1969, *4*, 140–143.

Witmer, H. L. "Analysis of Methodology," In D. G. French and associates, *An Approach to Measuring Results in Social work*. New York: Columbia University Press, 1952.

Wortman, P. M. "Differential Attrition: Another Hazard of Follow-Up Research." *American Psychologist*, 1978, *33*, 1145–1146.

Yarbrough, C., and others. "Response of Indicators of Nutritional Status to Nutritional Interventions in Populations and Individuals." In S. J. Bosch and J. Arias (Eds.), *Evaluation of Child Health Services*. Washington, D.C.: U.S. Government Printing Office, 1978.

🕊 Name Index

✍ Subject Index

A

Aggregation analysis, 186–187
Aldeas, 49–58. *See also* Nutrition
  study
Area bombing example, 151, 172
Atole, 49–51, 53–54, 56, 130. *See*
  also Nutrition study
Audience of evaluation: and evaluator's teaching role, 8–12; and
  outcomes of evaluation, 317–
  319

B

Bail bond experiment, 326; true
  history of, 144–149
Bandwidth, 36–37, 241
Bayesian analysis, 178–181

Behavioral objectives, 222–224
Belief system: model as, 174–175;
  prior probabilities and, 179. *See*
  also World view
Beyond the Numbers Game (Hamilton
  and others), 25–28
"Beyond Qualitative Versus Quantitative Methods," (Reichardt
  and Cook), 26
Bias: from incomplete covariate,
  191–199; from operational covariates, 195; and Pearson-Lawley model and its derivatives,
  191–193; in selection, 234; statistical, 273
Bilingual education evaluation, 16–
  17, 168
Black box input-output analysis,
  223–224